SHOOTER

Also by Donald A. Davis

Lightning Strike
The Last Man on the Moon (with Gene Cernan)
Dark Waters (with Lee Vyborny)

SHOOTER

*The Autobiography of the
Top-Ranked Marine Sniper*

Gunnery Sgt. Jack Coughlin, USMC, and
Capt. Casey Kuhlman, USMCR
with Donald A. Davis

ST. MARTIN'S PRESS
NEW YORK

www.stmartins.com

Library of Congress Cataloging-in-Publication Data

Coughlin, Jack.
    Shooter : the autobiography of the top-ranked Marine sniper / Jack Coughlin and Casey Kuhlman with Donald A. Davis.
        p. cm.
    ISBN 0-312-33685-3 (hc)
    ISBN 0-312-33686-1 (pbk)
    EAN 978-0-312-33686-8
    1. Coughlin, Jack. 2. Snipers—United States—Biography. 3. United States. Marine Corps—Non-commissioned officers—Biography. 4. Iraq War, 2003—Personal narratives, American. 5. Sniping (Military science) I. Kuhlman, Casey. II. Davis, Donald A. III. Title.

DS79.76.C68 2005
956.7044'3373'092—dc22
[B]

                                     2004063286

10 9 8 7 6 5 4

To our families and to the Corps

CONTENTS

ACKNOWLEDGMENTS

This book contains the personal stories of two individuals, but it took magnificent efforts from many people to complete. We owe great debts to them all.

First, we would like to thank our agent, Jim Hornfischer, who believed in the project, and in us, from the minute we sent him the proposal. Without his sage advice, steady hand, and extraordinary knowledge of the book world, this project would never have been created. He is our agent for a career. Thank you.

Our writer, Don Davis, molded our original manuscript into a wonderful story. More than that, Don gave us graduate degrees in both writing and in the business of writing. Thanks to you and Robin for your professionalism and way with words.

There are many people at St. Martin's Press to thank. John Murphy also believed in the book from the beginning and maneuvered it through some tough publishing wickets. Our editor, Charlie Spicer, was magnificent in offering cogent editorial insights and showed us the proper path when things got tough. Joe Cleemann, Joe Rinaldi, Henry Kaufman, India Cooper, Keith Hayes, and many others all worked hard to turn our dreams into reality.

Our brothers in the United States Marine Corps deserve special salutes. To list all of their names would require an encyclopedia, but let it be said that the authors had the honor to stand on the shoulders of giants. We admire you all.

As our former commander, Colonel Bryan McCoy, taught us, you can never achieve great things without believing in what you are trying to accomplish. Darkside Six made believers out of us. Special thanks also go to Sergeant Major Dave Howell, Major Matt Baker, and Major Martin "Crawdad" Wetterauer. And thanks to our small team of warriors who stayed with us as we roamed around Iraq and kept our asses alive—Daniel Tracy, Jerry Marsh, Luis Castillo, Dustin Campbell, Clint Newbern, and the Panda Bear, Orlando Fuentes. We are eternally indebted to all of you. Rest in peace, Mark Evnin.

To the men of the Bull, you can walk with the pride of knowing that you carried on the Raider legacy. To our peers, our mentors, and those that followed us in the most magical organization we have ever experienced, the Marine Corps, thank you for teaching us, for being our brothers, and for fighting alongside us. And to the scouts and snipers, you are special.

Most of all, we want to express our love and gratitude to our families and close friends, and we end this with personal notes of dedication to them.

On the Coughlin side—Cassie and Ashley, you know that you are the lights of my life, and Daddy loves you. Mom, you can rest now. I'm done. I love you. To my sisters Karen, Susan, Kathy, and Marybeth, you are the best. Darrell and Willie, thanks. Tina and Neil, there in my time of need as always, I love you both. To Boom Boom, the Sox did it, only a year too late for you. I love you, bro. Dad, I love and miss you every day, and I try to be as good a father as you were to me.

On the Kuhlman side—I send this book to my parents, who supported me while I transformed from a kid to a Marine and back again, and to my brother, Brian: the writer, the therapist, the student. To Joe, Dave, and Jared, my fan club and, more important, my friends.

And to the Corps, and all the Marines who are still serving—keep the faith, and Semper Fi!

—Jack Coughlin and Casey Kuhlman

SHOOTER

1

Touch of an Angel

At another time, on another battlefield, my radio call sign had been "Gabriel," because the archangel and I have a lot in common. Legend says Gabriel's trumpet will sound the last judgment. I do the same sort of thing with my rifle.

In 1993, I was the sergeant in charge of a Marine sniper section with Task Force Somalia, and on the evening of January 6, General Jack Klimp barked, "Gabriel, the 10th Mountain CP [command post] says they are under attack. Grab a couple of your boys and go check it out." I took a three-vehicle convoy bristling with machine guns through the north gate of the Mogadishu stadium, turned right for about thirty yards, then hung a sharp left on the 21 October Road, the main drag through the tattered capital of the famine-gripped country. Resting between my knees was a M82A1A Special Application Scoped Rifle (SASR), a .50 caliber beast of a weapon that weighs more than twenty-eight pounds and fires an armor-piercing incendiary tracer bullet that can punch a big hole through a sheet of steel, and an even bigger hole through flimsy flesh.

Dusk had not yet settled over the city, so the temperature still simmered in the nineties, and children who resembled the walking dead begged for food as we passed. Some three hundred thousand people had already starved to death in Somalia, and many more would die as long as the feuding warlords chose to violently expand their fiefdoms rather than feed and protect their people. When I saw flies crawl on the face of a dead child, it was easy to hate the vicious fighters who were causing such slaughter.

We called the ragtag militia "Skinnies" and "Sammies." It is natural for a Marine to denigrate the enemy, because it helps dehumanize them. The Germans were "Krauts" in the big wars, the North Koreans and Chinese were "gooks" in Korea, and in Vietnam the enemy was "Charlie." We had to call them something and didn't want to think of them as real people, for that might make us hesitate for a fatal moment. The old saying "Know your enemy" does not apply in such cases, for some things are better left unknown.

I had alerted my boys to be ready for a fight because once out of the stadium we never knew if someone would shoot at us. There were always snaps of random gunfire sparking around Mogadishu, but the entire route to the command post of the Army's 10th Mountain Division, about a hundred yards off the 21 October, was quiet. The gates of the walled compound swung open as we approached, and we were welcomed by a colonel who apparently had been expecting the whole damned Marine Corps to come charging over the hill. Instead, they got me and about ten other guys.

The 10th Mountain, a strong division with thousands of combat troops, was spread out all over and beyond Mogadishu and had left only a few security troops to protect their headquarters, in the heart of a city that seethed with unrest. Nevertheless, other than some chipped plaster on the outside walls, I saw no sign that any dangerous firefight had taken place.

The colonel didn't know he was dealing with a Marine sergeant, since we never wore rank insignia in combat situations, so he treated me as an equal. He escorted me up to the third floor of the command post building, and I put up a hand to shield my eyes from the glaring sunlight. Only six hundred yards away were three long warehouses that our intelligence sources said were packed to the rafters with weapons of the warlords. As long as the guns stayed inside, there was no problem, but if the militiamen decided to come out and play, they would be more than this group of cooks, bakers, and candlestick makers could handle.

A lot of people were hurrying around those warehouses, busy movement with nothing getting done, for they were not taking things in and out. Every so often, they would steal a glance over at us. Although there had been no more than the occasional harassing shot so far, I believed that these guys were doing more than just passing through the area and that the situation had the potential to worsen. I told the colonel I'd be right back, and my Marines and I sped back to the stadium, racing to beat the approaching darkness.

General Klimp, the commander of the Marines in Task Force Mogadishu, had been receiving similar reports from other intelligence sources, and by the time I got back to the stadium headquarters, his staff was already laying plans for how to deal with the situation brewing around the warehouses.

Ever since arriving at the stadium on the last day of 1992, American forces had been out patrolling the dangerous streets and taking guns away from thugs. The orders were to let them surrender, but dealing with these maniacs one by one was a slow business. Klimp figured that if they were converging on the warehouses, we could bag a bunch at one time, so he gave orders to surround the buildings, not let anyone in or out, and blare a Psy Ops message over loud-speakers throughout the night telling the militias not to fight and to surrender at dawn. With any luck, they would disobey.

Klimp then told me to establish an overwatch position, and I once more hustled my boys back through the streets and back into the 10th Mountain compound. By the time night fell, I was on the roof with three other snipers, a couple of guys with M-60 machine guns, and a forward air controller, known as the FAC, to coordinate heli-copter gunship backup when the ground troops moved in at dawn.

I found a spot between an air-conditioner duct and the three-foot-high parapet that surrounded the roof and squeezed into a tight sit-ting position, my boots and butt making a solid three-point stance, elbows on knees and eye to the 10-power Unertl telescope on the big SASR rifle, which rested on a pad across the parapet. I had a mar-velous field of view, and the powerful scope brought everything into such sharp relief that I felt I could reach out and physically touch the men moving around the warehouses. Measuring with our laser range finders, we jotted out green range cards to show the exact dis-tance between us and every building, window, and pile of junk be-hind which an enemy might hide.

As night finally came about 7:30 P.M., a snipers' nest manned by some of the best marksmen in the Marines had been created above a potential battlefield. I checked my weapon one more time—one big .50 caliber round in the chamber and five more in my clip— then slipped on my night vision goggles. If something happened, I had no intention of letting it devolve into a fair fight.

Few things in nature are as punishing as an African storm that tries to convert the parched land into a swamp in only a few hours. The scalding heat of the day vanishes in an instant, it is difficult even to breathe because so much water is falling, and the rain chills the bones and rapidly lowers the body temperature. Just such a storm swept in from the Indian Ocean about an hour after nightfall. Our carefully prepared snipers' "hide" began to feel more like an icy swimming pool, and we took turns going inside to get a cup of hot coffee and stay dry for a few minutes. One of my boys tore the canvas top from a Humvee and ripped it into crude shelters, but there was no real escape from the pounding rain. We were miserable.

Worse, the sheets of rain degraded our night vision goggles and left us blind to what was going on around the warehouses, although we could hear people shouting and motors turning over. The Skinnies were making mischief.

Dawn, the demanded time for surrender, approached. Our missile-carrying Cobra helicopters were inbound, guided by the FAC, who was working the radios beside me. We had not slept at all, and as the rain tapered off, we threw aside the canvas covers and stood to our guns, while our goggles showed blurred images of an incredible scene. A bunch of gunmen were in positions of cover, and the Skinnies had rolled out a couple of T-52 tanks and a big radar-guided antiaircraft weapon, a ZSU-23/4, which had four 23 mm cannons and is known as a "Zeus." If the choppers arrived on schedule, that thing could blow them out of the sky. "Abort! Abort!" the FAC screamed into his radio handset.

We had wanted a fight, and it looked like we would get one, but we still gave them a final chance to surrender. As the loudspeakers shouted the warning, I heard General Klimp speaking calmly into my headset. "Gabriel, can you take out that Zeus without hurting anybody else?"

"Yes," I replied, forgetting to add "sir." I was curt because I was busy, firmly locked into a rigid sitting-Indian position with my body square behind the rifle, and with my scope sighted on the ammunition feed tray of the ZSU. If ordered, I would disable the big gun. The Cobras had come to a halt and were hovering just behind our building, their rotor blades thudding like a mad drummer. The Zeus gunner heard them, too, and began cranking his weapon up to aim directly over our rooftop position in order to catch the arriving choppers when they popped into view.

As usual, just before combat, life slowed down for me. It is as if a viewer is fast-forwarding a movie and then suddenly clicks to slow motion. My eyesight sharpens; I can hear the slightest sound but can tune it out if it is not important. Even my sense of smell is heightened. I believe that a really good sniper not only has muscle memory developed by years of constant practice but also has some special unknown gene in his body chemistry, because I was operating more on instinct than on training.

I looked carefully past the feed tray and examined the magnified image of the gunner seated between the two pairs of mounted cannons. He wore a dirty T-shirt and some kind of cutoff trousers, with flip-flop sandals on his feet. I had a good line.

"Take the shot," said the general, and I fired, taking the big kick of the recoil as my rifle thundered. The heavy round punched through the metal feed tray, then slammed into the gunner like a bowling ball going a hundred miles an hour. The last I saw of him, he was flipping upside down over the back of the seat, thin legs splayed in the air, and barefoot because he was blown right out of his sandals.

My shot started the battle and brought an answering blast from another Zeus. Its big rounds chewed at the concrete, green tracers laced the dawn sky, and we dove beneath the parapet for cover. That was only a momentary reaction. My spotter shouted, "You gotta engage or he'll tear this building apart! Stop him, Jack!" Chunks of cement exploded around us as the quadruple cannon rattled nonstop. I had rolled over like a turtle, still in the cross-legged position, and my spotter grabbed my collar with his left hand to help yank me up straight again.

Fighting had erupted all around the perimeter of the warehouses, and the din was incredible, but all we were concerned with was that Zeus. I came over the parapet again with that green shit flying all around and shells smashing the building. I opened up at the very center mass of the Zeus, killing this gunner, too, and my armor-piercing bullets tore the weapon apart.

The tanks were next, and my boys took down every Skinny who tried to climb aboard them. In case anyone was already inside, I reloaded and put three bullets into the hulls where a gunner would be, then three more into the driver's positions. Our two machine gunners poured fire into the militiamen and around the perimeter; our grunts took care of anyone they saw with a gun. Then I began searching for, and finding, what are called "targets of opportunity."

The Marine Cobra helicopters rose up and joined the fight, coming in right over our heads and unleashing a deafening typhoon of missiles, cannon, and snarling machine gun fire on the warehouses. Their rotor blasts threatened to tear us off the building, and their spent brass showered down on us, steaming hot. Then a couple of Marine tanks lumbered into the area and added even more firepower. The cease-fire command came only about four minutes after I had made the first shot, and the absolutely devastated area fell silent. Flames ate at the warehouses, and columns of smoke blackened the morning sky.

Then, off to the right, another Skinny with an RPK light machine gun jumped into a window and opened up on the grunts below. My spotter looked quickly at the range card we had sketched earlier, saw that the window was exactly 623 yards away, and called the shot. "Target One—Alpha 623!" he called, and three snipers put the guy just a little above the crosshairs of their scopes to allow for a bit of an arc at that distance. We all fired at the same instant, and the guy was torn apart when our three rounds simultaneously exploded into his chest, shoulder, and stomach. The grunts rushed in to clear those buildings, and another cease-fire was ordered.

I pushed in a fresh five-round clip and scanned the area carefully. A tall, strangely well-groomed man was on the balcony of a nearby building, waving to militiamen gathered below. I locked onto him but, under the rules of engagement, did not fire, since he was not a direct threat and the men below were only milling about. A "technical," a truck with a machine gun mounted on the back, drove up, and gunmen congregated around it. I didn't know whether this guy was a warlord, but he sure seemed to be organizing a counterattack. I reported the situation and was told that if the gate to that compound opened, I was to take him out.

People around the man began pointing and gesturing my way, and when the man on the balcony turned, he saw a big SASR rifle and the large eye of my telescope pointing straight at his nose. He dropped his hands slowly and went inside, leaving the men in the courtyard below as a leaderless mob. This fight was over.

The 10th Mountain compound had a mess tent, and the cooks, bless their hearts, had been busy at their stoves while the fighting raged outside the walls. After the long night in the rain and the ferocious battle, my boys and I were starved, and I loaded a plate with potatoes, eggs, and some awesome links of sausage. We had stood down, but my adrenaline was still pumping and my combat senses were still sharp. The taste buds were wide-awake, and I shoveled in the food. My fellow snipers and I yelled insults at each other, and everything was in vivid color.

The colonel who had welcomed me came into the tent. He was one of those big dudes, a six-foot-something who looked sharp in his creased battle-dress uniform with a pistol on his hip. He swaggered to our table and looked with disdain at the stack of food disappearing into me, a man who had just finished killing a bunch of people. "How can you sit here and eat like this?" he asked.

"I'm fucking hungry," I replied, detecting a problem. A hush settled over the mess tent.

"Well," said the colonel with a rather theatrical sigh, "I guess that's the difference between us."

I stand five-nine and weigh 165, but I never back down from bullies. I rose from the bench and moved into his personal space. "No. The difference between us is that I don't squeal for help when somebody shoots at me."

The colonel huffed, and his eyeballs bulged with surprise. "Who the fuck are you, anyway? What's your rank?" He still had no clue, pulling this chickenshit routine right after we had saved his ass.

I had been through too many fights in too many places on this planet to take any shit from this guy, colonel or no. Hell, he had probably been shuffling papers at his desk a few nights ago when I was out on foot patrol in the rain with the French Foreign Legion. "My name is Gabriel," I said, smirking. My senses were quivering again, my muscles tense. I knew my boys had my back if an Army-Marine brawl erupted. "And my rank is none of your damned business. You got a problem, take it up with General Klimp."

The first sergeant stepped between us before anyone threw a

punch. The colonel left, we finished our meal and returned through quiet streets to the stadium. Instead of chewing me out, General Klimp signed the papers awarding me a Navy–Marine Corps Commendation Medal for my work that day.

The Army colonel had been wrong to believe that snipers, who are specially trained for years not to let emotion get in the way of the job, do not have human responses. We just don't let anyone see them.

It was later that evening when my body, exhausted from the lack of sleep and the exertions of the day, told me it was time to be alone. I found a shadowy storage room deep beneath the stadium, sat on a wooden crate, and allowed myself a private, two-minute nervous breakdown. During combat, I never doubt what I am doing, but it does get to me later, and I shook like a leaf as I sat there and reviewed the carnage I had caused that day.

There had been a lot of shooting out there, but I carried the big gun, and I had put holes in tanks, technicals, armored vehicles, and people. I was credited with eight confirmed kills and probably got more than that, but numbers never matter. I remembered each target vividly, seeing them again just as I had with my scope when I blew away their last moment of life. These regular little sessions with myself are as close as I come to thinking of the enemy as individual human beings who might have families and dreams and identities of their own. Today, they were trying to kill Americans, so I had no choice but to do my job before they could do theirs.

I was not wallowing in some trough of melancholy or depression, for these moments are merely chances to let my brain catch up with what my trigger finger has been doing. After a few minutes, the shaking subsided, and with my self-examination done, I got my shit together and went back to work.

2

The Secret Arts

Time passes slowly in a sniper hide as you lie totally silent, sometimes for days, except for a periodic whispered radio check, and are bedeviled by bugs, hunger, thirst, and weather. While your partner is on watch, your thoughts can drift, and I spent many idle hours thinking about the odd track that brought me to whatever hole in the ground I was occupying at the moment. A rock and baseball had a lot to do with it.

I was born on January 12, 1966, into a 100 percent Irish family. Home was a three-story, six-bedroom colonial house located in a neighborhood of similar homes in a nice area of Waltham, Massachusetts, about twenty miles from downtown Boston. I lived there from the time I came home from the hospital until I left to join the Marines nineteen years later.

I had four sisters, all of whom were older than I, and every time one of them would marry and move out, I would be bumped up to a larger bedroom. Mom had her hands full taking care of us.

One thing that set our house apart was that it would change colors periodically, for my father was a painting contractor. I remember waiting on the glassed-in porch for him to come home (at the time, the house was yellow, with brown trim) and running outside when his green work truck came into the driveway, covered with ladders, filled with buckets and brushes, and smelling of paint and turpentine. His work clothes were a splatter of small rainbows.

My parents were a perfect fit among the other couples who had moved into the changing neighborhood, all of them young blue-collar types who had worked hard in their early years of marriage, had families, and were now taking newer, bolder steps into the world, everyone intent on taking life to the next level. One neighbor bought a heating oil business, and a plumber set up his own shop, but my dad took a different path.

Had he wanted to, he probably could have continued to build his contracting business, but his passion was not business and house painting. He was into books and history. I recall seeing my father in a chair, reading, many times at night, after another noisy dinner in which we all got a say in the conversation. He eventually went back to school and got his degrees, then moved into teaching.

His legacies to me were not vague ideas from academia though. They came from those hard years as a painter when he had postponed his teaching dream to support his family through sweat and toil. I was shown, not told, the workingman's belief in hard labor, never giving up, valuing the family, and meeting your responsibilities. He was my hero.

I was not one of those aw-shucks country boys who learned to shoot before he learned to walk. My father did not even own a gun, and we never went hunting together. In fact, I never fired a rifle before joining the Marine Corps, and I still do not hunt animals. I am not against the sport; I just see no thrill, or challenge, in shooting an animal. Once you hunt men, nothing else can compare.

Growing up in an urban area taught me priceless street survival skills, and I learned how to be aggressive and protect myself at a young age. Some of the sternest lessons came from my sisters, who kept locking me out of the house when they were supposed to be babysitting me, because, they claimed, I was a pest. I used my outside time on sports and became a pretty fair athlete, with quick reflexes honed through hours of climbing trees and chasing balls and hockey pucks. When I looked up during a ball game, I would usually see at least one of my parents watching.

Coming home from school one day, I wandered into a rock fight between older kids, and a sharp stone smashed into my eye socket and knocked me unconscious. I awoke in the hospital, blind in my right eye because so many blood vessels had burst under the impact, and remained there for four days while the doctors decided whether surgery would be necessary. Each time the eye was tested, all I could see was the dark red color of my own blood.

Luckily, they chose not to cut. Instead, they put me on strict regimens that meant going to the eye doctor regularly for many years. As time passed, the eye not only repaired itself, but my vision kept improving until it surpassed normal and reached a level of 20/10. I can see perfectly today, and even better when I'm sighting through the scope of my rifle on a target a thousand yards away. After the severe damage to what would eventually become my "shooting" eye, it was only a quirk of fate that I could even qualify to be a sniper. There had been a good chance that I would be blind instead.

I returned to playing sports, and, like my dad with books, baseball was my own personal passion, the thing for which I lived. While pitching in high school, I conducted a real-world psychology experiment by messing with the minds of my opponents. Although my delivery was accurate, I cultivated the image of being a wild thrower and made a point of hitting a couple of batters in every game. When my best friend stepped up to bat for a rival team, I nailed him with the first pitch. If the batters worried about what I might do, they could not devote their full attention to their own purposes, so the fear that I might bonk them on the head gave me a clear advantage. I would later discover that the same sort of intimidation works on a battlefield.

My dream was to make it to the big show. Like so many dreams, it never materialized.

Pitching won me a full athletic scholarship to a major university, but the possibility of ever playing baseball in the major leagues was shattered during fall practice in my freshman year, when I hurt my pitching shoulder. It was the death of my boyhood dream and left me with an inner void where my purpose and goals in life should have been. I soon grew bored with being a mere student and determined that, unlike my father, academia was not for me. Math and science and English literature didn't interest me. I needed a new path.

So when a friend suggested, "Let's join the Marines," I thought it was a great idea. I had never really considered military service, but maybe the Corps could furnish the teamwork and competitive excitement that had vanished from my life. *Sands of Iwo Jima* and all that. It was time to start a new dream, so we headed down to the recruiting station and told a bemused gunnery sergeant, "We want to go infantry, and we want to go now!" He handed us the papers with a smile. The year was 1985. I was nineteen years old and on my way to Parris Island, South Carolina, for Marine boot camp.

After I'd endured the usual misfortunes that befall every Marine trainee, something interesting happened out on the rifle range, where we learned to use our M-16s. My barracks mates bragged about what good shots they were, how they grew up handling guns and could head-shoot a squirrel at a hundred yards, and I, knowing nothing about weapons, was in awe of their professed abilities. But once we hit the range, I discovered that shooting was easy! I could do it! When I pulled the trigger, I actually could see the vapor trail of the bullet leaving my rifle, and I received the top score in the platoon.

I was hooked on the military world, embraced life in the field, and was ticketed for coveted advanced training that only made me want more of the same. The Marines obliged, and I soon found myself attending Scout/Sniper School.

It takes more than good numbers on a rifle range to get into the school. Shooting, in fact, is only 25 percent of what a sniper does. Candidates are handpicked from among thousands of Marines, and even volunteers are not guaranteed acceptance. Every Marine is supposed to know how to shoot, and any fool can say, "I want to be a sniper," but fools are not who we want.

Most of the candidates flunk out, so only the best make it through a grueling course that requires as much brain as brawn, because there is no such thing as a stupid sniper. The academic demands, from mathematics to botany, were harder than in any college classes I had taken and were only part of sixteen-hour days that also included backbreaking physical exercise. It was exactly what I wanted and needed at that point in my life, and I fit in there much better than I ever had at the university.

I grew steadily more comfortable with my rifle. It was a thrill every time we went to the shooting range, where I never had a bad day. Every time I pulled the trigger, every single time, I knew exactly what would happen, and even when I missed the bull's-eye, I knew why. Nothing in my life, even throwing a ninety-mile-an-hour fastball, had

ever given me such a feeling of being especially talented and confident, which drove me to gain even more knowledge and become
even more accurate. Being a sniper soon became my life's calling.

The scouting component was one of the most interesting courses
I ever attended, better than survival schools, better than university
classes, and even better than airborne training, for it was there that
instructors taught me how to become invisible. I learned how to
track my enemy and how to get up close enough to count the bad
guys, determine how long they had been in the location, what they
were doing, and what they were about to do. Once I had hunted
them down, the job became how to remove or capture them. I
learned to deal with physical discomfort and to accomplish my mission in rain, snow, desert wasteland, and triple canopy jungle where
the vegetation was so thick that it was dark during the middle of the
day. I was taught to get in, get close, kill quickly, and get out, without ever being seen.

As my skills developed, senior Marines who had been in the
Corps longer than I had been alive took me, a young private first
class, beneath their wings and became my private tutors in the secret
arts of killing. There seemed to be nothing that these incredible
guys could not do, and they coached me in how to go by the book
and when to throw away the book and think for myself.

By the time I finished the sniper course, I had an instinctual feel
for my rifle and knew how to precisely lead a target, which way he
likely would turn in a given situation, how to make range estimates,
and how to mathematically determine the effect that wind and
weather have on a shot. Somehow, I didn't need paper and pencil to
solve the calculus, because I could almost sense what the bullet was
going to do.

The tough schools and the rugged fieldwork were followed by

intense exercises and then, finally, dangerous assignments in the real world. At no point did I ever consider that I was slowly turning into a killer, but I was.

The first ten years of my career passed in a blurry whirligig of action as I moved from hot spot to hot spot, never knowing where I would land next, totally focused and energized by the magnitude of the events that unfolded around me in jungles, cities, and sandy wastes from Europe to the Philippines to Panama.

It was if I had stepped right out of college and into a war movie that never ended. Not only was I good at what I did, but I was also single, which meant that I could move out at a moment's notice and had the extra advantage of being relatively expendable. I thought I was perfectly content, running around looking for trouble, and had no desire to get married and settle down.

But shortly after I returned from Somalia and took up new duties at 29 Palms, California, things changed one night at a club in nearby San Bernadino, when I met Kim, a pretty, intelligent blonde from Long Island, New York. She was twenty-four years old and had taken an English degree from the State University of New York at Stony Brook and then joined the Air Force. She had two stripes and I had three, so we both had the enlisted person's unorthodox view of officers and the world. The more we talked, the more we wanted to talk, and she didn't even blink when she learned on that first night that I was a sniper.

Suddenly, something important was shoving my job out of the way. Could I have a real life, just like everybody else? She was based at March Air Force Base outside of San Bernardino, and I was soon driving down there a couple of times a week, then every weekend.

Within only six months, we decided to get married, and we eloped on October 3, 1993. Only afterward did we venture back to Massachusetts and Long Island to meet the families and throw reception parties for our hometown friends.

Back in California, we settled down in San Bernardino for a few months, but Kim quickly became pregnant, so she quit the Air Force and we moved into base housing at 29 Palms. Our first child, Cassandra, was born in July 1994, a talkative little Irish girl with light red hair, and she immediately stole my heart. Soon we bought our own place, a nice house with a swimming pool in 29 Palms, located in a rare neighborhood inhabited by few, if any, other Marine families.

It was as if I were on a voyage of discovery, and I jumped into this new personal life with both feet. My life revolved completely around my family, and even while I was working, I would look forward to going home, so there was never any boy's night out for me. Instead of drinking beer in a bar, the big, bad sniper would lie down on the living room sofa with his baby daughter and watch television until she fell asleep, then tuck her into bed.

Kim got a job on the Marine base in finance, the same sort of thing she had done in the Air Force, and also studied for her teaching credentials. Not long afterward, she managed to convert a substitute job into a full-time teaching position at the high school that simultaneously helped her toward earning a master's degree.

But the sniper was always in the house, too, although we both tried to keep him bottled up in a cupboard and out of sight. I believed that Kim understood how to separate Jack the husband and father from Jack the sniper. I would go away, sometimes for long periods, do what I had to do, and return home. We never, ever, discussed my work. It was not the sort of thing that husbands and wives talk about.

"Hi, honey. How was your day?"

"Oh, I killed some guys. How was your day?"

I was not being secretive by choice, but I was forbidden to discuss my work with anyone who was not directly involved in the job, even my best friends. To do so posed the risk that vital information might reach the ears of people who would think nothing of bringing vengeance down upon the ones I loved. I would not let that happen, so I kept my mouth shut. Such is life in the shadows.

If I awoke suddenly in the middle of the night with a start so violent that it shook the bed, Kim knew not to question why or what was going on in my head. She was careful not to startle me with a sudden touch. Instead, once she was sure that I was awake and knew that I was safe at home, she would gently take my quaking hands in her own and say softly, "I'll just fix your hands."

I continued to be away a lot, more than I wanted. Such a combination of absence and stress does not always make the heart grow fonder, so it was almost inevitable that strains developed between us. We separated for three months in 1997 and actually went so far as to file divorce papers. I knew, however, that it would be best for Cassie to grow up in a house with her mom, so Kim and I got back together.

Not long after that, our second daughter, brown-haired Ashley, was born, and I fell in love all over again with the latest chatterbox in my life. After a hard day in the field, I would go home and play daddy, wading through a crowd of plastic dolls on the floor and watching so many cartoons on television that I developed a genuine hatred for that purple dinosaur, Barney.

Things stabilized between Kim and me, but we knew that we were going to have to be very careful in the future.

3

Thou Shalt Kill

The manual says, "The primary mission of a scout/sniper in combat is to support combat operations by delivering long-range precision fire on selected targets from concealed positions. The scout/sniper also has a secondary mission of gathering information for intelligence purposes."

I consider that definition to be a waste of a sniper's unique skills. It is anchored in the way wars were fought in ancient times and confines us to working in much the same ways as the sharpshooters did along the trench lines of World War I, hiding in the mud and waiting for an enemy soldier to appear. We can all do it.

A few years ago, I was part of a Marine Recon Team raid on an enemy encampment. My spotter and I crept into the area, found the bad guys, established a hide—a camouflaged position deep in a burned-out room on the third story of a building—and hunkered down there for about twenty-four hours, feeding quiet radio reports on every move they made. During the night, the rest of our Recon Team moved up while I covered them from about eight hundred yards away. It was straight out of the book, about supporting a military operation by delivering precision fire from a distance, and would require no fancy shooting on my part.

I locked my scope on a guard who was carrying a light machine gun, and when the attack signal was given and the Recon Team rose like shadows in the new dawn, I fired one shot, knocking the guard backward, down, and dead. Our guys overwhelmed the camp in a savage assault, and I took out another target, then lined up on a third soldier who was carrying a rocket-propelled grenade and trying to flank our team. I brought him down, too. The raid took no more than a couple of minutes, and a dozen enemy soldiers lay dead. From a distance of eight football fields away, I had killed three of them. It was a perfect mission, since we accomplished our assignment and sustained no casualties. But when I emerged from the hide to shake out my cramped muscles, I once again had the gnawing feeling that I could have done much more than just lie there and wait.

In my opinion, the quick pace of war today has rendered the traditional role of the sniper obsolete. In a raid of this sort, the tactic still worked well, but modern battlefields are changing, and long-distance precision shooting means little if tanks and armored personnel carriers filled with infantrymen have already moved the fight five miles beyond you.

Somehow, we needed to be able to move, far and fast, and I dreamed of running a Mobile Sniper Strike Team that could roam the battlefront and take the fight to the enemy. Scraps such as the one in Somalia only validated my belief that important parts of basic sniper doctrine were flawed.

For instance, snipers are taught never to expose themselves to the enemy. In Mogadishu, we ignored that; we arrived quickly at the front edge of a likely fight and worked out in the open, shielded only by a masonry wall. With other Marines around, we had plenty of protection, and without having to worry about whether or not the enemy could see us, we dominated the battlefield.

Mobility would be the key to the sniper remaining an effective combat tool.

Using traditional methods, just reaching a good shooting position could be extraordinarily complicated. Sometimes we humped along with a patrol and dropped off at a specific point to find a hide and set up shop. Or we might cling like leeches to the back of a tank and roll off when it passed a certain location. Or a helicopter might drop us several miles from the target location and we would sneak forward on feet, bellies, hands, and knees.

I dreamed of the day that we shooters would have wheels, but the time had not yet come for that. Bringing about that change became my beacon, and I intended to hurry things along any way that I could. The problem with evolution is that it is too damned slow.

During World War II, snipers who fought in Europe worked much as their forerunners had on many of the same battlegrounds twenty-five years earlier. The Germans and Russians both used snipers to great effect, and in the Pacific, Japanese snipers were deadly shots. However, the primary tactic remained the same: hide and shoot.

In Vietnam, the craft was forced to adapt to a jungle environment, which proved that it could change to meet new conditions. Then, creative Marine marksmen such as Carlos Hathcock and Chuck Mawhinney proved that snipers could be much more aggressive and effective by getting out of their holes and going on the hunt. These guys refined the ability to stalk and shoot, and showed up where the enemy least expected them to make a kill. Hathcock's stalking and assassination of a Vietnamese general was a classic piece of work.

Perhaps they were too good, because their methods became embedded doctrine. Hathcock's story, *Marine Sniper*, was not only a best seller but became a bible in sniper school. Students can often pick up an extra ten points on an exam by answering a bonus question that almost always comes from *Marine Sniper*.

Our planners apparently believed that if Hathcock and Mawhinney did it, then it must be right, and they adjusted their training to include the conditions imposed by Vietnam. That meant they were still mistakenly basing their teaching upon historical patterns, albeit more recent history, when they should have been looking into the future. What the modern tacticians missed was that Hathcock and Mawhinney were not only good shots and scouts but were also very thoughtful men who would have been among the first to insist that what was right for Vietnam would be pretty useless outside of the jungle.

Most people go through life without ever seeing a dead body, unless it is laid out on coffin silk. Cops and first-response emergency workers wade in carnage but usually arrive after the violence has been committed. Even in the armed forces, death frequently is not seen, and much of the killing is done from a great distance. A ship can launch a missile that will fly hundreds of miles before striking a target. Airplanes drop their lethal loads, many times at night, from a great height and are long gone before the bombs even hit the ground. A tank firing at another tank is a duel of machines, and most infantry skirmishes are brief, wild firefights in which everybody shoots at something, somebody, somewhere, and hopes he hit it.

My job is very different. Through the powerful telescope on my rifle, I see the expressions on the faces of my victims at the moment I quench that spark of life in their eyes. You don't dwell on that point, because you are just doing your job, and the sniper's one true commandment is "Thou Shalt Kill."

We soften the ultimate severity of what we do in vague terms such as "removing the threat" and "controlling the battlefield," which puts us firmly into the military matrix, where national security interests easily scrub away any personal guilt, like soap and water removing a spot of dirt. When I "smoke-check a target," as we call killing someone, I feel nothing at all, other than a bit of professional satisfaction.

I never enjoy taking a human life, for only a homicidal maniac would do so. An experienced sniper can hate what he what he does when he pulls the trigger, but at the same time, he understands the important fact that he is involved in something much larger than himself. I always knew there was a good reason for what I did—if I didn't get him, he would get us—so I put him in my crosshairs and squeezed the trigger without remorse.

With that mindset, a good sniper, over time, becomes almost immune to sharp emotional reactions. I never have nightmares, at least not the usual sort, but I do have the occasional surprise nocturnal visitor. Those who have fallen to my rifle will sometimes drop by in my dreams, vague acquaintances who show up for a while and then leave again. The line is long.

By the dawn of the twenty-first century, as wars changed, the sniper had become almost irrelevant on a shifting battlefield. We were no longer the marksmen who picked off the Viet Cong in rice paddies, any more than we were the seaborne Marines who fired on the Barbary pirates from the rigging of American sailing ships. We had thermal optics, night vision lenses, handcrafted weapons, satellite communications, and other toys straight out of science fiction, but our basic mission remained the same. We were prisoners of yesterday's success.

Although I was making noises about changing that, my suggestions to create Mobile Sniper Strike Teams were not warmly received by military tacticians who still considered snipers to be little more than support troops, like bakers and truck drivers. It became plain that this would be an uphill battle all the way.

Our last big war had been Vietnam, some thirty years earlier, and after that adventure was done, the whole machine remained poised for another two decades to fight the Soviet Union in a huge land battle. Advances in technology, new weaponry, plans, and training mirrored those threats until they simply evaporated with the demise of the USSR. Since then, the overwhelming majority of U.S. military deployments have been in cities and towns, not in Asian jungles or on sweeping European terrain. These latest dangerous conflicts are an entirely different kind of warfare, but our tactics were slow to change.

Tangled urban environments sharply inhibit the advantages of our smart bombs, overhead imagery, and standoff robotics, and jet fighter-bombers and aircraft carriers cannot hold territory. When a bad guy hides deep in a building or mixes in among civilians, he cannot be readily seen and identified, so his low tech beats our high tech: If you can't find him, you can't kill him.

General Robert Alexander once observed, "The infantry soldier, using intelligently the firepower of his rifle, is still, as always since the introduction of firearms, the dominant factor of victory. . . . In war the machine, while it may assist the man, can never replace him." Sooner or later, the ultimate weapon is the guy on the ground with a gun. Guys like me.

But the Pentagon's planners virtually left snipers out of their future assessments, deeming us to be irrelevant. In modern conflicts, the airpower would strike hard, then the armor would move fast, computerized weapons systems would smother all resistance, and helicopters would deliver to the battlefield soldiers loaded with specialized gear, superwarriors from Silicon Valley. The image of a sniper hiding in a hole somewhere, waiting for a specific target, virtually relegated us to the status of anachronism, and we were valued about as much as some old Army mule. It was as if our age-old craft, which had evolved from the days of bows and arrows, could not change again to meet the new challenges. What nonsense. These people apparently believed their press clippings and thought that things always go right in battle.

A good sniper is trained to think for himself, and I had spent a lot of time in the wild places and had spent countless hours considering the puzzle facing shooters like myself if we were to have a future in this game. I knew the way out was to prove the usefulness of the Mobile Sniper Strike Team concept, but how could I challenge the beliefs of senior officers and military thinkers from around the world? Just talking about the problem did no good. I was, after all, just a staff sergeant, and they were officers, and military protocol, yeah, yeah.

The difference, of course, was that they didn't have my experience, they were not Marine sergeants, and, most important, they were not snipers! Just because they had read Carlos Hathcock's biography did not mean they were right.

I wasn't feeling loved, which is never a good thing with a sniper. So, being just as stubborn as that old Army mule, I decided to stop arguing and start doing. I needed a showcase in which my boys and I could upset the groupthink mentality that was betting everything on technology, and I decided that the best way to get the attention of the strategists at the top of the pyramid was to simply go out and kill a whole bunch of people.

4

New Ideas

The chance fell into my lap during January 2001, when the Marine Corps Warfighting Laboratory in Quantico, Virginia, a think tank that prepares the Corps for the latest wrinkles in warfare, dreamed up Project Metropolis, or ProMet.

ProMet would unfold in various scenarios. Some units, known as OPFOR, the Opposition Force, would defend a make-believe city while the USFOR, or U.S. Force, attacked. When one phase was completed, a new exercise was begun to familiarize Marines with how to fight in cities, or Military Operations in Urbanized Terrain, known in the trade as MOUT. As usual, specific roles were given to the armored units, the infantry, the artillery, and the support teams, but the snipers were swept aside. When I raised hell, I was bluntly told that snipers were unimportant in a big battle because we simply could not survive in urban combat.

I was running a platoon of ten school-trained snipers and six scouts, plus myself, a medic, and a lieutenant who was in overall command. We could put a lot of trouble on the street, and I argued that to leave such firepower on the shelf was asinine. Lieutenant Bryan Ziegler, the platoon leader, was a true believer and made the same points I did, only in more polite ways, but he had no better luck. They just would not listen to us.

Finally, I had a showdown with a senior planner who told me this was to be a mixture of the lessons learned in Somalia, Haiti, the Balkans, and Central Asia. Hell's bells. I reminded him that I had been in most of those places, including spending six memorably unpleasant months in lovely downtown Mogadishu, where I had proven that mobility multiplied the effectiveness of snipers in urban environments. He was right that a prepositioned sniper was a duck that would soon be dead, but set us free to move and hunt on our own, and the paradigm changed dramatically.

They finally told me to be quiet. Lieutenant Ziegler wisely quieted things down, but our good cop–bad cop routine had worked. To shut us up, we were told to find some way to make ourselves useful and were given eight days to train independently while bigger units prepared for a full-fledged ProMet invasion. We would work with the defending forces.

Nobody said we had to play by the rules.

Marines across the country were involved in such training. On one exercise, another Marine unit in full combat gear had "invaded" North Little Rock, Arkansas, where they stopped and questioned motorists going to the supermarkets and dry cleaners. The population happily pretended to be the residents of some unknown hostile land, but it simply was not realistic. American cities were no place for a military shootout, and we didn't want an Abrams tank accidentally squashing somebody's SUV.

So the War Lab guys had decided to use the real thing and leased a couple of abandoned military bases, including the former George

Air Force Base outside of Victorville, California, some ninety miles northeast of Los Angeles. The Mojave Desert base once had been a huge facility of more than 5,300 acres, with thousands of men and women, civilian and military alike, living and working there, all dedicated to getting planes in the air. Closed in 1992, it was now almost a ghost town. We could take this place apart in combat drills and nobody would care.

I showed up for an unscheduled walk-through one morning, and the empty little town seemed to breathe, almost talking to me, as I prowled its streets, clapping my gloves together for warmth as a bitter rain lashed the area. The old base had two long runways, and although part of it had been given over to the Southern California Logistics Airport, the roosting places for airplanes were of no interest to me. Instead, I poked around the fourteen massive oblong dormitory buildings, the 1,641 individual housing units, and a hive of other buildings that ranged from what had been a hospital to routine office space. Wonderful. Cities are sniper country.

For several weeks, Marines from our base at 29 Palms had been invading and fighting in the town. Big tanks parked in the driveways of little bungalows, helicopters swooped over the rooftops, and helmeted Marines carrying rifles dashed across scraggly brown lawns. I already knew that the overall game plan called for massive assaults, platoon- and company-sized actions supported by tanks and armored vehicles that would crush enemy positions with overwhelming force. The planners believed any prepositioned sniper would be only a minor irritant, to be picked off early in the game. I wanted to teach them simultaneous lessons in mobility and humility.

People often ask why I did not try out for the prestigious Marine Corps Shooting Team, but the question usually comes from someone who does not understand that there is a world of difference between competition shooters and snipers. Pure shooting is only part of what a sniper does, for we also must master the arts of sneaking into an area, hiding, deception, and hunting. We are entirely different societies, although the Marine competition shooters are awesome to watch.

I personally didn't care about being called a marksman, winning a medal or trophy, or becoming an Olympic shooter, because a competitive rifle expert must spend so much time at the training range that his body becomes programmed to do just that. By doing so, he loses the skill sets necessary to be a good sniper. Paper targets don't shoot back, so it's really kind of boring.

It is important for snipers to thoroughly understand that what we do is not a competition. The best sniper in the world will have no success if there are no targets, but even an average shooter can rack up a bunch of kills in an environment filled with possibles, so the numbers can lie. Put an excellent sniper in a target-rich situation, and amazing things happen. One of the best was a young Russian who mowed down German soldiers during World War II like a John Deere tractor tearing through a Kansas wheat field. The soldier's name was Lyudmila Pavlichenko. That true rarity, a woman sniper, she terrorized the Eastern Front, with more than three hundred confirmed kills. For myriad valid reasons, American armed forces do not train women to be snipers, but this Russian Annie Oakley of the Steppes could stall an entire attack.

That, and more, is exactly what I planned to do during Project Metropolis, which was why I was out walking the deserted streets in a rainstorm. An attacking force has a tall order to fill when it tries to advance through warrens of buildings, maneuver through tight doorways, and run across open areas, snoop around corners, and wiggle through windows. From the point of view of a defending sniper like me, things couldn't be much better. The historical casualty rate for an attacking unit in such fighting was estimated at 30 percent, and I intended to keep it at least at that level. This was my town, and it was golden with opportunity.

After my unauthorized tour, we went to work on insertion tactics to determine ways to get into the fighting zone, and then I took the boys inside the city to set up hides. In a real combat situation, we would have gotten into position early, so why not do the same in a war game? And why not do it in secret? We would never tell the enemy what we were doing. We established excellent rooftop positions, found spots deep in the shadows inside the buildings, arranged some other sneaky hides, and made ourselves at home.

Then we practiced moving quickly and aggressively from one hide to the next, taking advantage of the cluttered urban terrain. I had no intention of being a sitting target for a bunch of tanks and artillery or being overrun by infantry troops. In this miniwar, we would be fine just sneaking from one position of cover to another, but I could not help thinking of the future. When a real fight came along, we would need solid, hardened vehicles to safely cover long, exposed distances, and I wanted other Marines around to protect us with additional firepower, so we could concentrate on dominating the battle. Moving from place to place alone or with just another sniper would leave us much too vulnerable. Without good protection, survivability became the ultimate issue, and a dead sniper is useless.

For ProMet, though, our boots would serve us fine, and by the time the other side got to where we had been hiding, we should already be gone. Let them try to find us. Urban sniper movement can be a bitch to solve, and combat in tight quarters can be a terrifying business. Streets and alleys are ready-made kill zones, and closely packed buildings are obstacles for troops and vehicles alike. We could pop somebody from a rooftop and two minutes later be shooting from behind a bunch of street junk, staying on the move.

Instead of real bullets, everyone would be firing lasers and would be festooned with MILES gear, electronic devices that simulate shots from the various weapons. A hit triggers buzzers on the web gear and helmets of the "enemy" soldiers, and a person who is hit immediately lies down and pretends to be dead. He cannot give advice, talk on the radio, or participate in the fight in any way. All he can do is lie on his ass and wonder what hit him.

Our targets, I reminded the boys, were not the grunts in front. We wanted to reach over their heads and touch more important targets. Get the officers first, then any enemy snipers who might threaten us, then go after their forward observers and senior sergeants. In other words, decapitate the leadership. Next would be the crew-served weapons like big machine guns and rocket launchers. In a real war, we would also shoot the radios themselves. Put a bullet in the operator, and someone else can pick up the handset and make a call. Put the radio out of commission, and the operator makes no difference whatsoever. There was a whole long list after that, but the important thing for them to remember was to shoot priority targets that could make a difference, then get away from the advancing troops and do it again.

By the time I finished my final walk-through, visualizing the coming battle, and returned to my room, I was satisfied that we indeed had found something useful to do. I gathered the lads and gave them a final talking to. We all knew exactly what was expected—nothing less than changing the way some of the most influential people in the Marine Corps thought about the way snipers could be used in combat.

Dawn on the day the exercise began brought more cold, wet weather, and we were hidden in our positions, waiting, hours ahead of time. The attack force gathered outside of town, and after a nice breakfast, the USFOR leaders came out to play. Officers from foreign armies had been invited to observe ProMet and see how Marines could take a city. There were final briefings, equipment checks, and a lot of engines revving to life. The noise was incredible as they moved into position. Stealth was never a factor for them, but it is everything to a sniper. That's what the manual says, so it must be true.

The defending force was already positioned inside the city, but we snipers, unloved little bastards that we are, were operating independently. Our positions were marked on the map grid lines of the commanders, but those were going to be obsolete after the first shot. I would not be playing fair today, because I believe it is sometimes better to beg forgiveness than to ask permission. We were in our hides long before the first attacking unit of Marines crossed the starting line. Welcome to my world.

It didn't take long. I was in a prone position, rifle at my shoulder, far back in the shadows of a room, with a table and some other junk stacked in front of me, invisible to anyone looking in with powerful binos. Thanks to having done this sort of thing for much of my life, I had hardly moved since wiggling into position hours earlier and clearly heard the noise of the advancing units. Jesus, they might as well have broadcast "Hey! Here we come!" on our radios.

A helmet peeked around a corner, and the game commenced.

I let their lead squad go and held my position until one of my favorite targets came into view, a platoon commander talking on his radio. *Zap! Zap! Zap!* We laser-shot the lieutenant and his radio operator, then took down a squad leader, too, and the whole attack ground to a halt. Miss Lyudmila Pavlichenko would have been proud.

That's when I kicked in the second half of my plan. The book says that a sniper's progress must be careful and slow, measured in feet and often in mere inches. Screw that. We hauled ass. By the time the attacking force figured out the source of the original shots, my boys were gone, and the USFOR wasted a lot of time sneaking up on empty houses.

Movement. Mobility. Aggressiveness. We shifted from hide to hide, from one place of concealment to another, and poured beeping electronic death on our fellow Marines. We made a flank attack. We snuck into their rear area and shot anybody who even looked like an officer. Machine gunners atop Humvees were nice targets. And by increasing the pressure in one spot, we herded the ground-pounders into other kill zones, where we could shoot more of them and move on. It got silly after a while.

By afternoon, the exercise was in chaos, and the senior planners were, shall we say, pissed off. A lot of time and money and effort had gone into running this show, and my boys and I were making a mockery of it. They said we couldn't survive in an urban environment, but we seemed to be surviving just fine. They couldn't find us, much less stop us.

One young platoon commander in particular got the message. Second Lieutenant Casey Kuhlman, a linebacker-sized engineering graduate from the University of Illinois, was only three months out of the Infantry Officer's Course and had been doing pretty well winning his spurs. After participating in Steel Knight, a thunderous live-fire desert training exercise, he had found the ProMet drills completely different and somewhat quieter. I had him in my scope from the moment he rolled into town atop a tracked vehicle, and I watched him dismount and walk cautiously forward. He was doing everything right, leapfrogging his boys forward with good cover, establishing bases of fire, and coordinating with the units on his flanks. Then I shot him; his buzzers erupted, and he had to lie down. The radio operator right behind him was the next to go, and then the platoon stopped, because there was nobody to command them and they couldn't communicate. We turned our fire on the heavy weapons people next and debilitated the platoon's firepower. I leaned from the window of my hide for a moment and waved broadly to Casey so he would know exactly who nailed him, then ran for a new location.

Casey lay there for a while and considered what had happened. His people were adding nothing to this make-believe war, since several more of them had been tagged and had come to a beeping stop. With nothing else to do, he made a note to look into the situation when it came time to debrief. He learned fast and would later become my guardian angel when we started running sniper strike teams for real in Iraq. I never apologized for shooting him in ProMet.

We kicked so much butt that day that after a few hours of beeping and chirping MILES belts, the game was stopped and my sniper platoon was divided, with half of us being given to each force. That only made things worse, because now we were doing it to everybody instead of just one side.

The commanders grew agitated. If they couldn't get rid of the pesky snipers (the ones who couldn't survive in an urban environment), this war game would never get played, so the bigwigs finally called each other on the radio and swapped the grid coordinates of my various teams. Finally they knew exactly where we were, and they sent units out specifically to squelch us.

It's bad enough when the enemy doesn't want you around. It's worse when your own guys don't want you either, and we started feeling unloved again. As soon as I figured out that we had been given up, I radioed word for all of my boys, on both sides, to free-play — just go out and kill as many people as possible before they get you — and we took off like a bunch of cockroaches.

By the time they weeded us all out of the game, my small team had "killed" more than sixty men, including many of the important players, and had staggered both the attacking and defending forces. After I got beeped, I went over and sat on the porch of a small house to get out of the rain, figuring I could be just as dead dry as I could be wet. Casey and a whole bunch of other Marines were resurrected and sent back into the fight, and ProMet resumed.

I was filthy and exhausted but happy with the job turned in by my boys. I could not have asked for a much better demonstration of my arguments for unlocking snipers from fixed positions and setting them free to roam. Our run-and-gun tactics had altered the geometry of the battlefield by turning us into a totally unexpected force, and I could easily imagine that the trouble we caused would have been greatly magnified if we had been able to increase our range by using fast, high-performance vehicles.

Before I could delve too deeply into my recollections of the day, a high-ranking officer sloshed through the mud to find me. He was one of the foreign observers and wore the badges of a special operations unit that I knew well. He planted a big black boot on the porch, looked me in the eye, and said with a thick accent, "You're good. Oh, you're good." Then he walked away, chuckling.

My boys had proven some things that day, and the overall tactics that Marines would use in taking a city had to be reconsidered. Snipers still had a place in war, and the ways to use them had increased. The experiences of ProMet in the neighborhoods of George AFB were important.

It didn't make me too popular with most of the planners, but it did make me right, and I liked that better. We had proven that snipers had a valuable role in modern warfare, with possibilities that could not be ignored. We had brought an attack to its knees, and even when the enemy knew where we were, it was hard to snuff us out. Give us wheels and we would be only more deadly.

ProMet was in January 2001, and the world had not yet collided with the horror of mass terrorism, for 9/11 was still nine months away. We had no idea that the lessons learned on the tidy streets of an abandoned Air Force base would soon be put to use in other towns in another desert. The War Lab swamis had called it right.

5

Winds of War

Twenty-nine Palms, California, is a company town, and its business is the United States Marine Corps. It has more barbershops than convenience stores, and apartment leases run month to month instead of by the year because Marines are transferred at a moment's notice. Fast-food joints stay open late, knowing that we may be in the field long past normal closing times, and the dry cleaners keep their doors open on Sunday nights so we can pick up pressed uniforms after a long weekend. Despite the name, it is an arid desert so devoid of majestic palms that we call it "the Stumps."

I am stationed there as part of the 3rd Battalion of the 4th Marine Regiment, attached to the 7th Marine Regiment of the 1st Marine Division. The reasons for this numerical soup are complicated and confusing, even to those who understand them, and make little difference anyway. We are called "the Three-Four"—it's written like a fraction, 3/4—and because of our aggressiveness, our nickname is "the Bull."

Out here, in nine hundred square miles of emptiness, we have as much room to play as the mind can imagine, and roaring, thunderclapping, live-fire exercises are common as we train to the breaking point. We fire our weapons in a totally tactical environment that we make as realistic as we dare: Real bullets are fired right over the shoulders of the troops, tanks attack with real cannon fire, and planes drop real bombs. Then we do it all over again because we never consider ourselves ready enough. There are no days without gunfire or Marines running in the sand at 29 Palms, although only a few miles away down Highway 62, the rich folks play golf and enjoy a champagne brunch in Palm Springs.

Other units are sent here for specialized training, but this is our home turf, and we know every inch of it. An area called "Range 400" is considered one of the scariest stretches of territory in the Corps for training, but that range is so familiar to us that it is no longer challenging, so we devise different, and more difficult, scenarios to practice. The result is a unit so razor sharp that we walk with a swagger and are always ready to be the opposing force in some war game. The Bull is the home team, the varsity.

But it didn't feel like that on September 11, 2001, when terrorists drove two hijacked airliners into the Twin Towers in Manhattan, crashed another into the Pentagon, and sent still another spiraling down into the placid countryside of Pennsylvania. Thousands of American civilians were murdered that day, and there wasn't a damned thing the Bull could do about it. Not yet.

Only the month before, in August, most of the battalion had packed up and departed for Okinawa. This small island in the Pacific had been one of the most contested battlegrounds of World War II. Now Japan owned the place again but allowed the United States to keep the 3rd Marine Division, our official parent unit, on the island to respond to area threats. The 4th Regiment headquarters was also out there, along with a rotation of its fighting units. It was the Bull's turn to go sit on the Rock for a while and do some jungle training. Among those who made the trip was Lieutenant Casey Kuhlman, the platoon commander I had "shot" during ProMet. We still barely knew each other, because we were in different companies within a large organization, and while he went to Okinawa as the executive officer of a rifle company, I stayed in the Stumps.

Colonel Steve Hummer, the commanding officer of the 7th Marines, was what we call a warfighter, the highest accolade an enlisted man can bestow upon an officer, and he was always preparing for the fight he was sure was coming. Hummer didn't know exactly who, when, or where—only that it was coming and that he would have his Marines ready.

He had become a fan of my idea for a Mobile Sniper Strike Team that could yank snipers out of the shackles of yesteryear, and his eyes would almost glow when we discussed turning such a team of highly trained killers loose on a battlefield. A sniper platoon with fast-attack vehicles would give him a valuable new asset that would combine reconnaissance with a lethal strike team. So while the rest of my battalion went to Okinawa, Hummer kept me in California as his regimental chief scout/sniper, gave me bankers' hours, and told me to stop talking and bring my idea to life.

With the colonel behind the plan, pushing and cajoling and opening doors, things actually began coming together. I needed special weapons, and a fellow sniper at another base was maneuvering that paperwork for me. For vehicles, I wanted to leapfrog over the available Humvees in favor of quicker desert-rat dune buggies. Hummer said, "Do it."

I also needed men for my plan to work. Not just any troops, but those finely tuned overachievers from advanced schools such as

Recon and Sniper. I wanted to take five to seven men from each battalion, personally train them in the new tactics, then have them train others. That's where I ran headlong into the regimental operations officer, a bear of a lieutenant colonel named Bryan P. McCoy. Since Marines don't grow on trees, any men I gained for my team would be subtracted directly from McCoy's roster of combat personnel. He didn't like that.

Casey once described me as not being very subtle: "If Jack likes you, he curses and insults you. If he doesn't like you, he does the same thing, only nose-to-nose and louder." McCoy and I had a number of spirited discussions.

While I could bully a lot of officers, he was a stone wall. He stands about six-six, weighs a muscular 240 pounds, keeps his light brown hair high and tight, and usually has a big cigar stuffed in his mouth. He tried to stare holes in me with his beady hazel eyes. McCoy is brilliant and kept cluttering up our arguments with quotes from Napoleon and Rommel. Nevertheless, the Boss supported my plan to put snipers on wheels, and I wasn't going to let some S-3 regimental operations officer, even a tough dude like McCoy, stop me. I didn't think anything could.

On September 11, 2001, our eighth wedding anniversary was less than a month away. My wife was in the kitchen, and I was getting out of the shower to start another day in Marine paradise. We would take our kids to day care, then Kim would go to her teaching job and I would head off for another argument or two with McCoy.

The telephone rang, and I picked it up in the bedroom.

No hello. "Turn on the television set!" It was the battalion commander's wife, who was running the home front while her husband had the troops in Okinawa. "We're being attacked!"

I snapped the power button on the remote, and New York swam into view on CNN. A tower of the World Trade Center was on fire, and as I watched, a big jetliner slammed into the second tower. I was stunned into disbelief and silence for a moment. "OK," I said, and hung up the telephone, then jumped into my uniform and sped to the base, growing angrier by the minute. I didn't know who had done this, but they were not going to get away with it.

A savage typhoon had stalled over Okinawa, where it was now about nine o'clock at night at Camp Schwab, the northernmost base on the island. A few poor bastards were pulling outside guard duty in the storm, while most of the battalion's senior officers were in Korea for a conference. One major and a bunch of lieutenants were left in charge at the camp, including Casey, the executive officer of Kilo Company. He finished checking his e-mail, went to his room, and turned on the radio. At first, he thought he was listening to some *War of the Worlds* kind of fake broadcast. He quickly called his four platoon leaders together for a briefing, and someone found a television set in time for them all to see that another plane had crashed into the Pentagon.

Soon after that, Threat Condition Delta was ordered by President Bush. That meant Marines were to "man the lines," but there was little that the men of the mighty Bull could do other than snarl at the television set and check in by radio with the near-empty battalion headquarters. The word came down to just sit tight until things got sorted out, because it was pretty unlikely that Camp Schwab was going to be attacked that night. The twenty-five-year-old lieutenant and his fellow officers settled down to watch over their flock as the bad news unfolded. They felt helpless. It was a strange feeling.

Casey had come a long way to reach the Rock, on the far side of the world from his home in sunny Florida. He had grown up in the northwest section of Orlando, between the ocean at New Smyrna Beach and Disney World. As a kid, he visited the magical universe created by Walt Disney so many times he was almost on a first-name basis with Mickey Mouse.

Great distances did not trouble him, for Casey was almost migratory by nature. His father was from Michigan, his mother from Tennessee. Casey had been born in Chattanooga on September 3, 1976. A few years later, the family, now including a younger brother, moved to Florida, and from the third grade until he left for college, he lived in a 1,500-square-foot three-bedroom home that his mom had decorated with Mexican tiles. The family pets started small, with a basset hound, but by the time Casey left home, their pet was a 180-pound Newfoundland named Bailey, who liked to rest his huge head on the dining room table.

Casey once told me, "When I think of my childhood, it was complete normalcy." His mother was a nurse, and his father became director of budgeting at a hospital and was fascinated by the early wave of home computers. He provided his boys some nifty games while he worked up a business in computer consulting for medical practices. That was Casey's first step into engineering, and he never stopped.

He enjoyed sports but was more of a bookish kid, and reading Hemingway and Kerouac was more appealing than learning to surf.

With a swimming pool in almost every backyard in the neighborhood, he and his friends didn't need to go to the ocean to while away
a summer. What he was really good at, and enjoyed, was the math
and science classes in school, where he could make intricate sets of
numbers add up, the formulas made sense, and attention to detail
paid off with correct answers. A physics teacher guessing the future
occupations of some students looked at Casey and said, "Engineer."

He followed that very path, and narrowed his college choices to the
University of Illinois and the University of California at Berkeley,
although he had also been accepted at the Massachusetts Institute
of Technology and Georgia Tech. His parents, both Republicans,
quickly weeded the free-spirited Berkeley out of the possibilities,
and Casey went to Illinois. He would graduate cum laude from the
top structural engineering school in the country.

That's also where his life changed dramatically and what he calls
"the duality of me" emerged. He was paying his way through college
with a Naval ROTC scholarship when he realized there was more to
life than calculus and physics. It's hard for me to believe today, because Casey stands more than six feet tall and is a muscular 190
pounds, but he was small in high school. Reading all of those books
had instilled a yearning for adventure, and in his sophomore year he
decided to test himself physically and to become a Marine—not just
any kind of Marine but an infantry officer, a grunt.

He graduated in 1999, into a world that was generally at peace,
and started his climb through the tough Marine training schools.
Now, on this historic day, that was all over, and he found himself on
Okinawa, with a typhoon howling outside, watching burning buildings on television and hearing President Bush tell the nation that its
military forces were at the highest state of readiness. He had wanted
adventure, and now, he had found it.

Nine-eleven put an end to my dream for a Mobile Sniper Strike Team, at least for a while, and I didn't care. Even had it been authorized that day, it still would have taken another year to get off the ground, and now there was a risk that it had become my own personal albatross. We were suddenly planning for war, and I worried that I was going to be left behind, shuffling papers, while a shooting scrape was going on.

I went into a big staff meeting that day where contingency plans were being thrown down, changing hourly as more information arrived. Twenty-nine Palms was never far from alert status anyway, and things started clicking together rapidly. Afghanistan quickly rose to the top of the list of potential targets because it was the home nest of the Taliban, which supported the terrorist network that staged the attacks on America. Out came more maps, more studies, more plans.

In a quieter moment, I cornered Colonel Hummer to make my pitch to get into the fight, but before I could say anything, he told me, "Calm down. You're going to Afghanistan with us as my chief scout/sniper." That was just what I wanted to hear.

The Afghanistan campaign started in early October 2001, and Northern Alliance forces supported by U.S. advisers took the capital of Kabul in November. Kandahar, the last stronghold of those Taliban nutcases, fell in December.

Meanwhile, far above our pay grades, another sort of war was being waged within the polished hallways of the Pentagon in Washington. Secretary of Defense Donald Rumsfeld had come into office in 2001 with a burning desire to restructure the U.S. military into a more mobile force, and the Army generals were balking at the rapid-deployment scheme. Afghanistan became a laboratory in which each side would try to prove it was right. While some Army Green Berets had helped direct air strikes in the north, and elements of the 10th Mountain Division came over from Uzbekistan to secure two northern airfields, the first regular American combat unit to enter Afghanistan was the Marine Expeditionary Force that flew in from five aircraft carriers parked in the Arabian Sea to capture a southern base on November 25, 2001. They had been parked offshore with everything they needed for a long fight, from armored attack vehicles to water purification facilities. Rumsfeld and his top civilian assistants saw the swift, effective deployment of the Marines as proof of their argument for radical changes. The Army chain of command was not impressed.

Ultimately, the Afghanistan campaign did not involve our regiment. Our job was to get ready for whatever came next, and we set about training like we had never trained before. President Bush, in his State of the Union speech in January 2002, labeled Iraq, Iran, and North Korea an "axis of evil" and accused them of supporting terrorism and having weapons of mass destruction.

When the 3/4 battalion returned home from Okinawa in February, new and secret contingency plans were already showing that the next big strike probably was going to be in Iraq, just the kind of sandbox terrain the Bull knew so well. While the 3/4 had a good idea of where they would be going, I still wasn't sure that I would be with them, because my regimental assignment left me in limbo while my buddies were preparing to fight.

Then, in early May, I almost had a heart attack when the battalion got a new commanding officer, none other than my old nemesis Lieutenant Colonel Bryan McCoy. All of those arguments we had had over the mobile sniper teams rose to haunt me, and my spirits sank like a rock. McCoy did not help things by hooking me back into the fold to be the gunnery sergeant for the battalion's Headquarters and Supply Company. I recoiled at the thought. Me, the combat veteran who wanted nothing more than to be out in front of the action with my sniper rifle, held back as the "Gunny" of the Hotdog and Soda Company, to shepherd those freaks and geeks into making sure all the real warriors had everything needed to fight a war, from rifle ammunition to toilet paper.

The only person who felt as bad as I did was Casey, who arrived back in 29 Palms only to be snatched away from his rifle company and named the H&S executive officer and its interim commander. But he was immediately dispatched to still another school, and I was handling the company on my own.

In reality, being a Marine company gunnery sergeant is a prestigious job and a good position for promotion, and I might have been more than willing to do it—if we had not been heading for war. Now I was frustrated and hated the idea, so I marched over to confront McCoy. His desk was the size of an aircraft carrier, but he was so large that it seemed a perfect fit. Early summer sunlight blasted through the windows as I sat down, wondering just how much damage I might have caused by arguing with him so much during the past months.

"I want some other job, sir, not H&S," I said. "Anything but H&S."

"Sorry, Staff Sergeant Coughlin. I need you right where you are," he said, chomping the cigar.

"I'm a sniper, sir!"

"You're my H&S Company gunnery sergeant!"

I paused a moment, then played my ace. "Sir, I've got enough time in that I can still shift to another battalion." I was ready to walk, to actually leave the battalion, something I never thought I would say. But if it would get me into the shooting war, I would do it.

McCoy can be something of a Jekyll and Hyde character, and he let his more reasonable side take over rather than giving vent to the warfighter side. He had a job to do, he needed me, and anyway, he already was a step ahead and had plans much different than I had imagined.

"I've got an H&S company that doesn't have a commanding officer right now," the lieutenant colonel reasoned. "Your executive officer is gone for the Mountain Leaders Course, which leaves the company understrength and leaderless. That means you take over. We're getting ready for a war, Staff Sergeant, and we both have a lot of work to do. Don't let your vanity get in the way of what's really important."

"But it means that I'll be back in the rear with the gear when we go over, sir. I can't do that." I could almost feel the sniper rifle being taken from my hands.

McCoy blew a big cloud of smoke. "Look, Jack. You work with me here, and get us to Kuwait, and I promise to let you go play when we go to war. I know and respect your abilities as a sniper, and when the bullets start flying, I promise that you are going to shoot people."

I took the deal.

6

The Wait

The massive American military juggernaut was beginning to stir, and although our powerful 3/4 battalion was but one of the players, we trained as if we were the only unit involved. Our lives depended on it. The early plans called for a fast-moving war in Iraq, which meant our Headquarters and Supply people would move right along with the front line and sometimes would be in the midst of the shooting. So by early August 2002, when Iraqi dictator Saddam Hussein warned that any attackers would "carry their coffins on their backs," we were well along the road to turning our freaks and geeks into a team of fighters.

Marines are taught from their earliest days that their rifle is their most treasured possession, for they stake their lives on it, and they become so intimate with the weapon that they can take it apart and put it back together blindfolded, and do so with precision. Then they progress up the chain of arms to become equally adept with a bewildering armory of other weapon systems—from the M249 SAW (a light machine gun) to the M203, M9, SMAW, M240G, AT4, Javelin and TOW missiles, and hand grenades. A Marine loves to pull a trigger.

That had become our baseline assumption when Casey returned

from the Mountain Leaders Course and joined First Sergeant Norm Arias and me in getting the Headquarters and Supply Company ready for combat. You should never go to war with anyone who cannot cover your back, and having someone you trust around during a firefight provides a sense of peace unknown in the normal course of life.

Our men were supposed to be Marines, not secretaries, although they *were* secretaries. And truck drivers. And mechanics. And radio operators. We laid out training packages that demanded they could use their specialized skills when on those jobs but also could stay alive in a combat environment.

A small tactical headquarters team, the "Tac," would move at the front to direct the fight and would be closely followed by the "Main" headquarters, which was linked to the higher commands and other units, controlled the medical evacuation procedures, and did the battle planning. Then came the "combat trains" of supplies and backups needed to keep the whole thing rolling. The best way to stall a military attack is to destroy the leadership, communications, and logistics, which meant that our H&S Company, which had all three, was prime meat.

We sent nine of the guys off to school to learn how to handle the heavy machine guns, and our drivers were drilled in how to get in and out of their trucks while under fire. If someone bitched about sweating while we were training out in the 29 Palms desert, Sergeant Arias jumped on them, barking, "Quit whining like little bitches! Get your warrior hat on and get ready to kick some ass. You're going to be right up front, and you've got to protect yourselves." When Normy speaks, people listen. He is a tough little Filipino with a stocky body sculpted by weight lifting, and his dark eyes can be filled with humor or malice, depending upon what he thinks of you.

There is little nuance with Normy, and he can be as intimidating as hell. Iraq would prove that he was exactly right about the dangers, because the country's long and empty roads became fertile killing grounds for guerrillas who ambushed American convoys with road-side bombs that tore apart both trucks and bodies. We wanted to be sure that our Marines knew how to fight back.

The bureaucracy worked against us, since every hour we had our guys training was exactly equal to an hour taken away from their specialties. A delicate balancing act was necessary to weigh their vital support jobs against the need to polish the skills that would keep them alive long enough to do those jobs. By the time we were done, the 228 Marines of H&S were fully competent trigger pullers.

In the final months of 2002, everyone became familiar with the dreaded term "weapons of mass destruction," and we stepped up the training needed to meet the threats posed by nuclear, chemical, and biological agents. There was no doubt in my own mind that Hussein, who had used poisons to quell a rebellion among his own people, would also use them against us.

"Simply stated, there is no doubt that Saddam Hussein now has weapons of mass destruction," Vice President Dick Cheney told the Veterans of Foreign Wars in August. A few weeks later, President Bush challenged the United Nations to confront what he said was a "grave and gathering danger" by giving Hussein a final deadline to abandon his WMDs. If Hussein did not comply, the president warned, the United States was prepared to act, alone if necessary.

Iraq responded by offering to allow UN weapons inspectors un-conditional access to suspected weapons sites, but Washington dismissed the offer as merely another stalling "tactic that will fail." The

Bush administration sought quick congressional action on a resolution that authorized U.S. military action against Iraq.

On November 8, the United Nations Security Council unanimously adopted Resolution 1441, which demanded that Iraq disarm. In early December, Iraq delivered to the UN a monstrous twelve-thousand-page document that stated the country had no WMDs nor any current programs to develop them. A week later, while the massive document was still being analyzed, Secretary of State Colin Powell told the press, "We said at the very beginning that we approached it with skepticism, and the information I have received so far is that skepticism is well-founded. There are problems with the declaration."

To me, all of the political crossfire meant only that war was by now a virtual certainty and that it was drawing closer. We received our deployment orders to Kuwait over the Christmas holidays.

Following a leader you do not personally trust in wartime can be as frightening as facing WMDs, so it was too bad that we had a junior staff officer that I shall try to forget for the rest of my life.

I'll call this guy "Officer Bob," and his greatest talent seemed to be an ability to get lost, even while using a global satellite-positioning device. This was not someone we wanted leading our convoys across a battlefield, but there he was, talking loud, nodding his head, and constantly needing somebody to hold his hand. We determined that the best way to get things done was to make sure Bob was not involved.

We had to move the battalion from California to the Middle East, which meant solving a logistics equation that would get us to foreign soil, ready to fight. Everything from tanks and missiles to sunglasses and tubes of sunscreen and lip balm was going over, and precise instructions preceded every single item. An identifying dog tag was to be tied into the laces of each soldier's left boot. Not the right boot, but the left. Private Smith was issued an M-16 with a specific serial number, and there were thousands of privates just like Smith. Overheated computers spat out reams of rosters and lists, and we added little things such as baby wipes, which help clean sand off our faces, among other things, and funnels to prevent life-sustaining water from spilling while being poured.

Our battalion alone had to keep track of some $19 million worth of gear. The one thing McCoy did not want to run short of was bullets, so it was good that a shooting scrape eventually broke out. While training back in the Stumps during that fiscal year, we were about a million bucks over budget on ammunition. War trumps accounting.

Despite the work, getting ready on the professional side of the ledger was easy when compared to saying good-bye to my family. It's the hardest thing any serviceman or woman has to do, for deep in your mind you know that it may be a real good-bye—you might never see them again.

The evening before I left, I made some special "alone time" with each of my girls. With little Ashley, my younger daughter, who could only comprehend that Daddy was going away again for a while, it was playful and fun. But Cassie had not been immune to the dire news all over the television broadcasts, and although Kim and I tried not to discuss it in front of her, she clearly understood that this time could be different. Cassie knew that I was going to war. She tried to be brave but cried on my shoulder as I held her tightly and promised that everything was going to be fine and that I would be back as soon as I could. Leaving her like that made me feel like shit.

It was difficult for my wife and I to console each other. Our marriage had always been a roller coaster of highs and lows, and this time turned into one of the lowest lows of all. We owned a horse and a pony that we kept stabled outside of town, and she was worried about how my leaving would affect her plan to attend an upcoming horse show. I felt that my wife viewed this war as an inconvenience, not something that might claim the life of her husband.

I woke up at one o'clock in the morning, kissed my sleeping wife and children for a final time, got into my jeep, and drove off to begin still another journey to another war. As the house grew small in my rearview mirror, I began to morph from father and husband into my alter ego of remorseless and cold-blooded Marine sniper.

I joined the advance party and climbed aboard the big birds for the long flight over to Kuwait, which was totally boring and uneventful, other than the grousing about not being able to see the Super Bowl game. We would not be landing to the sound of guns, only to the requirement to get the camp set up for the rest of the troops. When we stepped off the plane, a stiff, chill desert wind whipped us, but other than that, it almost seemed as if we had not really gone anywhere. We lived in a California desert ourselves, so the flat vistas and dry weather were familiar. The weather was only about ten degrees hotter or colder than it was back home.

The Kuwaitis had been busy. Buses took us to a vast plain some thirty miles south of the Iraqi border, where a city of white canvas tents had been erected for us. The land was virtually flat as far as the eye could see, except for the occasional dune and the great fields of pointy-top tents. It looked as if a giant circus had come to town.

The drooping tents were the type Bedouin tribesmen had used for centuries in this hot, sandy region, not crisp military style, only ours had wooden floors instead of Persian carpets. Since I was in charge of assigning spaces for everyone in the battalion, I gave myself one of the best and created a private area, walled off by pallets of bottled water and rations, in one corner.

Everything that had been disassembled back in 29 Palms began arriving and had to be put back together and readied. Once in place, the battalion bulked up with a trade that swapped a company of our riflemen for a company of tanks from the 1st Tanks Battalion. We all watched with awe when the fifteen huge M1A1 battle tanks of Bravo Company rumbled over to live with us. The things are huge! With those and our own assault amphibious vehicles (AAVs), better known as "Amtracs" or just "tracks," we now had quite an armored punch. Then we added units of engineers, artillery and air-strike spotters, guys who specialized in detecting chemical weapons, the translators and intelligence dudes of the "Human Exploitation Teams," and miscellaneous other support personnel. All of them came to us eagerly, because getting attached to the 3rd Battalion of the 4th Marines was like being drafted by the New England Patriots. Our job was to move and attack, not hold and pacify, and we had a reputation for getting the job done.

"You're all gonna die," called the skeptics. "No," we corrected. "We're going to kill people."

Joining the Bull carried a price for these newcomers, however, because we worked them like dogs. It was not unusual for me to storm into a tent before dawn, yelling, "Get the hell up, you sons of bitches!" I would grab some lazy bastard out of the sack and force him outside for an exhausting physical training exercise in full combat gear. The newbies kept waiting for us to lighten up, but we never did, and slowly they adjusted to life in an elite combat unit. We knew that being brilliant in the basics would keep them alive when the shooting began.

We trained in every conceivable format, and when we learned that our first target in Iraq would be the southern city of Basra, we scripted that battle as if we were planning a Super Bowl, right down to watching Falcon View computer imagery that exactly painted the route to the city. A Dragon Eye unmanned drone gave us real-time aerial pictures until somebody goofed with the automated controls and rammed it into the side of an Amtrac during a training exercise. It seemed that we had everything but the home telephone numbers of the defending soldiers.

Casey and I worked the troops hard in shooting, moving the convoys, and getting into and out of dangerous dispersal areas on a crowded and shifting battlefield. A sense of urgency seeped into the training, because after months of practice, we were running out of time.

Chairman Mao Tse-tung wrote that power grows out of the barrel of a gun, but I had found that sometimes it also grew nicely out of a typewriter. While rummaging among the paperwork and personnel problems, I had uncovered a jewel: the Table of Equipment, the bible that spells out who gets what. It specified that the Headquarters and Supply Company was authorized to have several hardback, armored Humvees. It did not say exactly how the vehicles should be allocated, so Casey and I figured that it was best that the company executive officer and gunnery sergeant should each have one for his own use. Who was going to argue? The Humvees

were parked outside the tent at that very moment, each with a powerful Mark-19 belt-fed automatic grenade launcher mounted in a
turret. Presto, through a little administrative magic, we had firepower and mobility.

I had readily surrendered my plan for a fast-moving sniper force a
year and a half before, on 9/11, and thought the idea was dead. But
now that we were within a stone's throw of war, I realized that I had
all of the ingredients at my fingertips: my shooters, some good wheels,
and a battalion commander, Lieutenant Colonel McCoy, who believed in the concept. The final piece of the puzzle fell into place
with the steady development of Casey. In the old days, a sniper was
never to be directly exposed to the enemy, but my plan was to be
right up front with the crashing strong fist of the 3/4. I would need
protection so I could concentrate on my job. Casey had my trust,
plus the rank, the desire, and the ability to grab some Marines by
their collars and not only get me to the hot hinge of battle but to protect my ass while I worked. By forcing me to take this job, Bryan Mc-
Coy had given me everything I wanted.

The familiar *crack* of high-powered precision rifles was music to my
ears as I took both my personal M-16 and my sniper rifle out to Target Range Ripper, which actually was just a big mound of dirt about
a thousand yards to the left of our camp. As the company gunnery
sergeant, I had been so busy training others that I had not gotten
much personal shooting time, and I needed a final turn on the
range to zero my scope to my eye for the terrain and climate we were
in. I squeezed off enough shots to satisfy myself that everything was
perfect, then took a walk down the firing line.

The rest of the battalion sniper platoon was also zeroing their weapons, and for one last time, I looked over this stable of thoroughbred studs. Although many had only high school diplomas, the instructors at Scout/Sniper School had challenged their intellects by cramming into their heads such arcane but important subjects as advanced ballistics (mathematics), cardiopulmonary functions (anatomy and biology), air density (meteorology), and enough data to send an advanced college student running to the nearest bar for relief. Unless our guys sucked the lessons into their very souls, they would not become snipers.

They learn that the surface of a pond is much more than that, for it is a plane separating two mediums, air and water, and creates a mirage so that a stick protruding above that surface appears bent when it really is not. How will that affect your view of the target? What happens to your shot pattern if there is not perfect concentricity in the bore of your barrel? What is the formula to compute your range to the target, and how much lead do you give a moving target, regardless of the target's speed, range, or weapon caliber? Which way does the bullet go when you shoot through glass? All that and much, much more was drilled into them. And that was just to teach them how to shoot the damned rifle!

The scouting and stalking side of the business is just as difficult to learn. One myth that gets debunked along the way is that it is unsporting, even downright un-American, to shoot an adversary in the back. Snipers will pull the trigger on an unsuspecting enemy in a heartbeat.

When I became the company gunny, I handed off the sniper platoon to other leaders, but although the snipers were no longer under my direct command for their daily tasks, they were still mine, and I would participate in or make every major decision involving them. They were always coming by to ask questions, and everybody knew that when the shooting started, I would be carrying my sniper rifle.

I demanded more from them than just textbook learning and shooting skills. They would be distributed in teams throughout the battalion, and the lives of other Marines would depend on them. Were they ready? Hell, yeah. They were confident, tough, and itching to fight. A few of the arrogant little bastards even thought they could outshoot me.

My M40A1 sniper rifle lay in pieces before me on my poncho as I gave it still another thorough cleaning. In the Marines, you always take care of your own weapon, and I would never trust someone else with the job, because my life might depend on the task. It was a mechanical marvel, from the Pachmayr recoil pad on the McMillan fiberglass and epoxy stock to the modified Winchester Model 70 trigger guard, to the Remington 700 receiver, and the Atkinson heavy, free-floating barrel, all topped off with the 10-power Unertl scope that makes a target a thousand yards away seem to be right next to my eyeball. The package weighs fourteen and a half pounds, and it is my long arm of justice. It is a common misconception that we work with just one weapon until death do us part, but gone are the days of Davy Crockett and his Kentucky long rifle at the Alamo. This rifle just happened to be the one I would be using for a while, and the armorer had adjusted it to perfectly fit my grasp, so I treated it kindly.

I was tired, but feeling good after calling home and talking to my kids, for their girlish chatter lifted my spirits. The babysitter said my wife was at school, where she was working toward a doctoral degree, and I paid her absence no mind. I was receiving a lot of letters and packages from friends and family and figured the low volume of correspondence from her was because she was simply overwhelmed taking care of the girls, running the house, working, and going to school. Being a Marine wife is not easy.

Casey ducked into my cubbyhole on a bitterly cold night in early March 2003 as a hard wind beat against the sturdy Bedouin tent. He heated up some Spam on the little propane stove, grabbed some lukewarm coffee, and settled in for a bullshit session while I cleaned my disassembled rifle, up to my elbows in gun oil, patches, and rags. He was thoroughly capable in his job, although Officer Bob frustrated him almost to the point of mutiny. A couple of times I had to stop the staff guy from trying to replace Lieutenant Kuhlman, carefully explaining that we needed someone who knew what the hell he was doing to take this unit into combat.

"I hate everybody and everything," Casey declared. "I hate Bob. I hate this fucking country." Everybody hated Kuwait.

He was a kindred spirit, and I recognized his jumpiness as nothing more than a case of prebattle jitters. After months of training and tense expectation, he wanted to get into it, to see how he stacked up as a combat Marine, but he wanted to be leading a rifle platoon, not babysitting Bob. I knew he would do fine, but Casey would reach that conclusion only after enduring his trial by fire. It's always a one-man graduation ceremony.

"You need a day away. Go down to Doha and get a hamburger." Camp Doha is a rear-area paradise that had been established near Kuwait City during the last Gulf War and then was built up with millions of U.S. dollars. Between the shopping mall and the restaurants, you can get anything you want at Doha. It was not like life at the front.

I had my boots off because my feet were always itching. Outside our little office, Casey and I observed military courtesy and addressed each other by our ranks, officer and enlisted man, but in private, it was Jack and Casey, an equality that is not unusual among Marines.

"A properly trained monkey can do my job," Casey complained.

"A properly trained monkey *is* doing your job, asshole," I said. He didn't smile. "Cheer up. We'll be going soon."

"Why do you think that? The politics still suck. If we go, we risk our credibility as a player in international diplomacy. If we don't go, we risk our credibility as a military powerhouse. We got a hundred thousand Americans sitting out here and we're at a standstill."

We are not robots, and with newspapers, radios going constantly, laptop computers with Internet access, and telephone calls back home, everyone had been keeping up on the latest developments. We also received classified information that the media did not. We knew exactly what was going on. The rhetoric for war had risen in intensity, and the belief that Saddam Hussein was hiding weapons of mass destruction was universal among our leaders. The White House spelled out that we faced twenty-five thousand liters of anthrax, thirty-eight thousand liters of botulinum toxin, enough material to produce five hundred tons of sarin, mustard, and VX nerve gas, and mobile biological weapons labs. But the time for high-level discussions was over, for the command structure of the United States had all but made the decision to send us over the line along with a "coalition of the willing." Our job was not to question our orders but to carry them out.

My personal viewpoint had only hardened since the terrible attacks on the United States on September 11. I wanted to hunt down and kill every terrorist I could find, to make them pay tenfold for what they had done, so they would think twice before trying it again. I considered Iraq a logical target in the war on terror and believed that by fighting in someone else's house, we would occupy their interest and their focus. It would be better to fight the terrorists in Iraq than in Boston. I make no claim to be a national security expert, although I know how it works better than most people. While I don't make policy, I implement it by stepping onto the battlefield. It's what I get paid to do, and I was ready to do it.

"Oh, we're going," I told Casey. "Even as we speak, Officer Bob is getting all soldierly by watching *Gladiator* over in the movie tent, and he's reading a Tom Clancy book."

The wind thumped the canvas tent, cold and steady, and armored vehicles growled by outside, on their way to some night exercise. "What if we don't really get into the big fight?" Casey asked. "The Army gets to take Baghdad, and if we get held up in Basra, I don't want to be stuck in the rear."

"Not to worry. The Army may get the first bite at that apple, and the more people we have killing things, the better. Don't sweat it, you're going to see plenty of action." I put down the cleaning cloth and gun oil for a moment and looked over at my eager friend. He still wasn't convinced.

"But don't believe all that stuff about being welcomed by kids tossing flowers and herds of Iraqi soldiers surrendering," I said. "Everyone knows what's at stake this time, and they are going to fight. We're going to have to fight in Basra, then with the Republican Guard, with those fedayeen crazies, and guerrillas in every little ten-cent town all the way to Baghdad, and then within the city itself. We will win, but it's going to cost us. This is going to be a bloody business." I had been here before and knew from hard-won experience that the game plan goes to hell when the first shot in fired. Some of my Marines would not be coming back. I just didn't know how many, or who.

7

Safwan Hill

"My idea of a fair fight is clubbing baby seals!" Lieutenant Colonel McCoy, whose radio call sign was appropriately "Darkside Six," was atop an Amtrac, giving some final fighting words to his battalion as they stood beneath a broiling midday sun at Camp Ripper on March 17, 2003. "We're going to slaughter the 51st Mechanized Division!" he said, balled fists on his hips. "We're going to kill them! We're going to make an example out of them!"

He confirmed that our part of the war would start by attacking Basra, the second largest city in Iraq, and the intelligence guys predicted that an entire division of the Iraqi army would be waiting in our path. Thousands of enemy infantry troops, supported by a couple of hundred tanks and armored vehicles galore, had spent months preparing for our arrival. We would be outnumbered maybe eight to one. Some may have wondered just how our single battalion was going to demolish a full division all by our lonesome, so McCoy explained that the enemy had no idea how we were coming at them. How the other guys had planned and trained did not matter because this was going to be our kind of fight—a one-sided, nasty, eye-gouging, kick-in-the-nuts, bullet-in-the-ear, smash-mouth Marine-style brawl, and he promised that we would stomp their asses right into the sand. Fight fair when outnumbered eight to one? Fuck that. "We will hit them with everything we have," McCoy said.

Fifteen huge M1A1 Abrams battle tanks, the best in the business, stood nearby like brooding steel racehorses, eager to run. Fifty-four armored Amtracs were scattered about, each twenty feet long, eight feet high, and able to carry twenty Marines safely inside while tooling around at forty miles per hour. Sixty-three camouflaged Humvees dotted the sands, several of them specially modified with souped-up engines and armed with a staggering array of missiles, machine guns, and automatic grenade launchers. These vehicles, which traded some armor for speed, were known as CAATs (Combined Anti-Armor Teams) and would race around the desert to protect our flanks and probe enemy weaknesses. This was going to be a war not only of bullets but also of tracks and wheels and gasoline, of rapid movement and space-age mayhem.

"When other Iraqi units see what happens to the 51st, they might just go ahead and surrender," McCoy shouted, and the confidence of Darkside Six was infused into his 1,004 Marines. Although most had never seen combat, they whooped as if they were at a Super Bowl instead of in the middle of the Arabian Desert, and the smell of war rose in their nostrils. Few considered that some would not be coming back, for their blood was hot, their knives sharp, and their guns ready, and nobody felt the least bit sorry for Saddam Hussein's goddamn doomed 51st Mechanized Division.

The formation ended, and everyone got back to work, tearing down the camp and getting ready to move out. The heavy metal band AC/DC wailed "Hell's Bells" from a boom box. It was a terrific speech. Too bad Casey and I missed it. We were already gone.

_____

We had gotten up hours earlier, about four o'clock in the morning the same day that McCoy would give his pep talk, to tune in the radio and hear President Bush give Saddam Hussein and his two weird sons forty-eight hours to leave Iraq. "Their refusal to do so will result in military conflict commenced at a time of our choosing," the president warned.

Once those forty-eight hours were up, we had to be at the starting line, because no one really expected the Hussein gang would leave. So beneath the glow of a full moon, Casey and I had our boys load the Humvees with enough ammunition, communications gear, fuel, food, and water to get us through five full days, and we went tearing out with the advance regimental quartering party to find our battalion's assigned staging point in the Kuwait dirt.

In any major military movement, somebody has to go in first and stake out an area that is defensible, is accessible by vehicles, and has good lines of communication. With tens of thousands of men and vehicles on the move, the job of the quartering party is not very sexy, but screw it up and confusion reigns.

Our designated dispersal area was several miles from Safwan Hill, a big pimple in the desert on the Iraqi side of the border with Kuwait. The Iraqis used this dominant geographical feature as their southernmost observation post, and as dawn broke on March 17, they had a superb view of the powerful American force that was growing before their eyes. I knew this place only too well, as did other Marines and Army grunts who had chewed Iraqi sand before. When the fight started, Safwan Hill was to be pulverized.

We guided in the rest of the battalion that afternoon, and for hours, wave after wave of Marines arrived in convoys that trailed sky-high rooster tails of dust. The Iraqis up on the hill must have been putting down their binoculars and packing their bags to get the hell out of there. It was after dark before our final elements arrived, and before anyone slept, we were lined up with all of our guns facing north.

"MISSILE LAUNCH . . . MISSILE LAUNCH . . . MISSILE LAUNCH!"

We thought it was the fucking end of the world. *Shit! Where's my gas mask?* We had gotten up after a few hours of brief, exhausted sleep and were still stumbling about in the darkness when the banshee cries from an Army Patriot missile defense battery's loudspeakers erupted about two hours before dawn on March 18. The missile boys had set up shop a few hundred yards from our position without our hearing a sound and had just scared the hell out of us.

We jumped over and onto each other in a mad scramble for gas masks and jammed them down tight over faces still lathered with shaving cream, believing that Saddam was about to hit us. Then came a loud *"ALL CLEAR . . . ALL CLEAR!"* and we stripped off the masks and happily took deep breaths of clean air. Our new neighbors played that game all day long, until we eventually stopped reacting.

Even so, we all believed Iraq would probably smack us at some point with chemical and biological weapons. Our leaders had built much of the reason for this preemptive war around those weapons stockpiles, and we had trained hard for surviving them. For us, it was not a question of *if* . . . just *when*. Therefore, while we grew casual about paying attention to the frequent Patriot warnings, I was still glad to be wearing my MOPP (Mission Oriented Protective Posture) suit, which would give us some protection during an assault by un-conventional weapons.

The suit consisted of a jacket and matching overall pants, worn over our T-shirts and shorts. The activated charcoal lining provided an extra layer of insulation that was welcome on chilly nights. We carried masks and heavy rubber gloves that we could put on in less than eight seconds. Bulky booties completed the ensemble but were so clumsy and hot that we seldom wore them for more than a few minutes. Oddly, the MOPPs were of a mottled green pattern, so after wearing desert camouflage for months in Kuwait, we would enter Iraq in jungle colors.

If Saddam tried to chem us, it would be no more than an in-convenience, because our suits provided good protection for our lungs against any aerosol weapon. Being slimed during a biological/persistent-chemical attack was worse, because those agents might eat right through boots and skin. If a nuke fell, then nothing would help, but we knew our deaths would result in Baghdad becoming a radioactive hole in the ground.

We weren't frightened by any of it, but we always wore the suits, because they took too long to put on when a warning came. They also took a long time to take off.

Answering calls of nature meant you had to take off your flak jacket with its ceramic tile plates, then your bulky MOPP jacket, then the suspenders that held up the pants and the various clips that held everything together.

As extra protection against WMD attacks, we had our Poultry Chemical Contamination Detectors, five pigeons named Silent Bob, Jay, Crazy Pete, Little Bastard, and Botulism, that lived in cages strapped to the hoods of our Humvees. They were to ride into combat with us under the theory that if they died suddenly, we should probably put on our masks. The same scheme had worked during gas attacks in World War I, and with canaries in potentially poisonous coal mines, so why not now? Chickens had been tested in Kuwait, but they tended to die for too many different reasons, so the great Kuwaiti Fried Chicken experiment was abandoned. Instead, our battalion saw Saddam's WMD bet and raised him five pigeons.

The day was spent in final preparations, since the Iraqi dictator had not been seen waving farewell to his loyal subjects. The battalion nudged even closer to the border, our vehicles were refueled, ammo was passed out, breach points were designated in the berms, and we arranged covering fire from other units. Then the intelligence staff dropped the news on us that the 51st Mechanized Division might not be alone in the Basra area. Somehow, the Medina Division, a well-trained armored unit of the elite Republican Guard, had been trucked in with their assload of tanks during the last several nights.

McCoy took the development in stride. "Well, good on 'em," he said. "We'll slaughter them, too." His staff scrambled to dramatically change the attack plan only hours before the scheduled departure, because it seemed that a huge armored battle was looming.

McCoy gathered his officers for a final pep talk and pointed toward the setting sun, which dimmed as it lowered into a mist of dust. "Look at that sunset," he told them. "Remember it. That might be the last sunset some people see." He had been a rifle company commander in Desert Storm and knew what was about to happen when the talking stopped and the fighting began. He wanted to be sure his officers understood that they were expected to lead, not follow, and that they must not yield to panic. The motto was "Slow is smooth, and smooth is fast." Casey came out of the meeting less nervous over going to war than he had been when he had braces put on his teeth as a kid.

As the minutes before the invasion ticked away, the desert around me seemed alive with men and machines. My sniper rifle rested in a drag bag in my truck, for giant armored vehicles were about to go to work in this big sandbox, and a sniper has no business in a crossfire of tanks. I would get my shots in later.

I retreated into myself to be alone with my thoughts. This war was unfinished business, and we considered Saddam Hussein to be our Hitler. We would not be beating up on Mother Teresa tomorrow but taking down a sadistic brute and a whole army of evil people. After Desert Storm, we felt the job was incomplete; we were pulled up short after achieving the rigidly defined objective of kicking the Iraqis out of Kuwait. If we had finished the job then, we wouldn't be here now. That was Hussein's tough luck, for this time we were turning the pit bulls loose and the only order was to go get the fucking rabbit.

There was only one possibility that really brought a lump to my throat: that the attack might be called off and we would be left stuck in the Kuwaiti sand for another six months while diplomats dithered and the press and the liberals tried to turn this whole thing into another Vietnam.

Surely they wouldn't call if off now, with thousands of American soldiers and Marines, a British armored division, and other allied troops all poised and ready along a border that was nothing but a couple of sand berms and barbed-wire fences. Aircraft carriers and ships from the U.S. Navy and other nations were on station, and warplanes were rolling out on runways around the globe. From the Pentagon to the campaign theater headquarters at Camp Doha in Kuwait, staff officers of different services and nationalities were working closely together without animosity or rivalry.

Much had been made about America going into combat virtually alone and without many of its traditional allies. In my opinion, that was for the best. I was glad the Brits were with us and didn't care that the French and some of the others were not around, because all they would do was take up space, suck fuel, and slow us down. The Russians were disappointing, because I had long felt that we would someday be toe to toe on a battlefield, but as allies, not as enemies — and what a combined force we would be. I wanted them to stand tall with us in Iraq, but they didn't, and so what? I didn't want anyone tagging along who did not want to be here.

The kind I wanted around was exactly like the ragtag collection of six Marines that made up the crews of our two armored Humvees. These boys, professionals all, had become our immediate family, and Casey and I, as the designated parents, personally trained them and shared with them our meals, tents, and trucks. The bonds of brotherhood were strong, because we all understood that someday it might be just the eight of us against a large enemy force. We had not picked these guys by accident; we chose them because we believed they would be reliable in a firefight.

My driver, and the truck leader, was twenty-two-year-old Corporal Orlando Fuentes, who had gown up in a Puerto Rican barrio until he was thirteen, then moved to Pennsylvania. The first time I saw his big eyes and round face, he reminded me of one my girls' stuffed animals, and I exclaimed, "Hey, you look just like a panda bear!" The nickname stuck, and the Panda was cool with it. Trained as one of those suicidal idiots who drive the CAATs, he knew only two speeds—fast and faster—and philosophically did not believe in the brake pedal. I sat up front in the passenger seat, usually scared out of my wits that he was going to kill me before Saddam had a chance.

Private First Class Daniel Tracy, a Missouri boy who was one of my reclamation projects, rode in the back to handle the radios and provide security. Only twenty years old, Daniel was an old-school Marine with a gift for brawling and getting into trouble. He stacked up an impressive record of being belligerent and hard to control while in 29 Palms, and when he blew off a corrective program, we court-martialed him, busted him in rank, and sent him to the brig to cool off. When he came out, I pulled him into the company office so that I could personally step on him now and then, and I learned that he was a loyal and tough kid who did not suffer fools gladly. My kind of guy. He was also valuable because he honestly thought he was bulletproof anywhere beyond the Baghdad city limits. "I know I'm going to get whacked in Baghdad," he had complained for weeks. "I'm not going in there. Put me back in the brig, I don't care. I'll fight everywhere else, but I won't go into Baghdad." I figured he probably would.

Standing on a platform between the front and back seats was our gunner, Mexico-born Sergeant Luis Castillo, whose upper body protruded above the Humvee in a turret that mounted either a Mark-19 automatic grenade launcher or a 240-Golf medium machine gun, weapons we would mix and match to the mission. Castillo was very reserved and had been a sergeant for several months although he was only twenty years old. The tall, slim Marine was content to let other people give the orders and leave him alone to shoot his gun.

Another member of our crew was Corporal Clint Newbern, the communications guy in Casey's truck. He had a knack for being able to dial in God or anybody else we needed in times of wicked stress, although his southern drawl on the radio never hinted that something of interest might be happening. Lean and wiry and newly married, he was born near Savannah, Georgia, to parents who were martial arts experts and raised their son to earn a couple of black belts of his own. Newbern wasn't scared of anything and was given to us because his former boss thought the sarcastic young Marine was going to beat him up, which was a distinct possibility. He fit right in.

Handling the gun on Casey's truck was tall, tough Sergeant Jerry Marsh from Bakersfield, California. He had been a grunt in Kilo Company when Casey was the XO, and he was a machine gunner with exceptional eyesight. He really knew his shit when it came to handling that automatic weapon, and he kept it meticulously clean, even in the worst weather. The soft-spoken Marsh, however, was beset by personal demons, and I handled a lot of calls before we left 29 Palms about how things were not going well around the Marsh household. It was good to get him overseas.

Casey's driver was another story. A short and pudgy corporal, he excelled during training and was a gear queer who liked to play dress-up and wore every piece of modern fancy combat equipment he could lay his hands on. But once we all started living together, we learned that he frequently lapsed into taking like a small child. We began to wonder how the meticulous youngster, whom we called "Corporal Baby," would hold up under the stress of combat. We would just have to wait for that verdict.

At 5:34 A.M. on March 20 in Iraq (9:34 P.M. EST on March 19 in the United States), Operation Iraqi Freedom began when a barrage of cruise missiles and smart bombs fell on a Baghdad location where

American intelligence teams thought Saddam Hussein was hiding. He wasn't there, but the dictator had ignored the demand to step down, so the game was on, and "shock and awe" would be the theme for the day.

Out in front of us, Safwan Hill lit up like a birthday cake in hell. Big Tomahawk missiles swooshed into deadly dives and exploded with earthshaking suddenness, artillery rounds roared overhead like freight trains, and planes howled in to drop loads of bombs. The continuous explosions turned the night sky crimson and yellow and orange as a piece of everything in our arsenal slammed into that pile of dirt. The ground shook, and the concussions of exploding bombs thudded against our ears. I don't remember exactly how tall Safwan Hill was before the bombardment, but there wasn't much left by the time Marines went up to secure it. The Iraqis were long gone, and the observation posts lay in smoking ruin.

The sights and sounds of impending battle are incredible. Fire flashed from the bombs and rockets, radios buzzed, the sky grew thick with helicopters and planes, and machines clanked around in the darkness. Everything seemed to be happening at once. Engineers operating huge plows tore holes in the sand berms, and thousands of Marines, armed to the teeth, began to move.

If wars were always this much fun, we could sell tickets, like to football games, and I would be the richest man in the world.

8

First Kills

There's nothing like a good war to get your adrenaline pumping, and giant butterflies were bumping around in my stomach. Like tens of thousands of other men approaching battle that day, I was scared, but having been in combat before, I knew this was only normal. Stepping into the unknown makes everyone nervous. The butterflies were nothing but pregame jitters and could be controlled. I was very aware, however, that just because someone has done this kind of thing a thousand times before does not mean you are going to get it right this time. The past does not matter in this situation, only the present.

Before dawn on March 20, 2003, American ground forces finally went charging into Iraq. To the west of us, the Army's massive 3rd Infantry Division swept forward in long snakelike convoys plunging into the desert in what would become a huge left hook toward Baghdad. The Marines would take the eastern route through Basra and fight through the cities located along the two major highways that led north to the capital. The highly mobile 101st and 82nd Airborne

Divisions and the 173rd Airborne Regiment were pouring forward in their helicopters, and the British armor was on the move. Air power was plastering targets throughout the country, and Special Forces teams were already at work on specific targets. From a standing start, we all gladly joined the attack, although we had hundreds of miles to go, against unknown opposition and the ever-present threat of an attack by chemical or biological weapons. There was no hesitation.

Our own big Abrams tanks thundered through the breach into Iraq at 5:45 A.M. What had all the makings of a cavalry charge turned quickly into a massive traffic jam.

The original plan for our entry had been for just the 1st Tank Battalion to go through this particular breach while our unit went through a different one. But the reports of the bulked-up Medina Division being in the area forced the planners to redraw their maps overnight, and they chose to send us both through the same hole in the sand walls. Instead of spreading over a front of three miles, we would hit with a clenched fist of immense firepower that would match any opposing Iraqi armored force.

In the revised plan, 1st Tanks still led the way, but then the heavy combat power of armor and infantry belonging to our battalion would follow right after them. The support train of 1st Tanks would be next in line, and our own support train would then enter Iraq. It was a complex battlefield attack choreography in which hundreds of vehicles and thousands of men would weave into one continuous braid.

It took only a few minutes for things to get snarled. Before we could fight this war, we first had to get on the other side of the border, and as the sun rose, its bright redness dimmed to orange by a hanging, shifting curtain of dust kicked up by our advancing vehicles, the single breach grew busier than a bridal-gown sale day in Filene's Basement back in Boston.

The front echelon of heavy armor made it through without any problem, but then their support trucks ignored the plan, broke into the line one by one, and became tangled within our advancing armor and infantry. Soon everyone was madly dashing simultaneously for the breach. But there was only so much room, and the various hard-charging elements slowed to a crawl, reduced to trudging slowly through about six inches of loose sand. Colonel McCoy was livid with anger. Before even firing a shot, his attack was caught in a desert traffic jam that took about forty-five dusty minutes to unsnarl.

The invasion was exploding forward all across the country, but all I could see was the back end of the truck directly in front of me and sand, sand, and more sand. It hung in the air like a great dirty curtain, clawed at my throat, and went into every crack and crevice of the trucks. My Humvee was at the tail of the battalion main headquarters trucks, which were sandwiched between Kilo and India companies. From there, I could easily fly up to the front or out to the flanks if anything happened, but it meant eating a lot of dust. We pulled down our goggles and wrapped scarves around our faces, feeling like the cowboys who brought up the rear of the herd. When I finally passed through the first berm, I picked up the radio and called out to Casey, "Welcome to Iraq!"

"We're not there yet, jackass," was his reply, from the lead truck twenty vehicles ahead. As a precise engineer, he did not count us as technically being on Iraqi soil until we crossed the second berm, not just the first. We got through that one soon enough and put Kuwait in the rearview mirror.

By the time we were through the breach, the tanks up front had skirted what was left of Safwan Hill and were surging north along country roads toward a paved highway that was designated Route Tampa. It was the main road to Basra, and once we reached it, the pure khaki desert gave way to scraggly wintertime brush, and then to more green than I had expected. It looked a lot like 29 Palms in California, only without the mountains. This was our kind of terrain. The Bull could fight here.

Basra, one of the natural gateways into Iraq, lies at the southern edge of a vast marshy area. The fabled Euphrates and Tigris rivers empty into those savannas and then race down the Shatt al-Arab waterway to reach the Persian Gulf. The Caliph Omar, an adviser to the Prophet Mohammed, founded Basra in A.D. 636, and according to legend, it was home port to Sinbad the Sailor. It is even mentioned in *The Arabian Nights*.

Here and there, a few Iraqis emerged from low-walled mud huts in isolated hamlets of three or four buildings and waved, just as their Mesopotamian ancestors had greeted other invaders over the centuries. The Persians had come through in 539 B.C., and Alexander the Great and his Greeks in 331 B.C., then Muslim Arabs in A.D. 636, the Mongols out of Central Asia in 1258, the Ottoman Turks about three hundred years after that, the British four hundred years later, and the U.S.-led coalition back in 1991. Throw in the Sumerians, Akkadians, Assyrians, and Hittites, and the invasion routes into Iraq are littered with the graves of armies.

Modern-day Basra's claim to fame was the nearby Rumaylah oil fields, where a thousand wells sprouted like grim desert flowers, plus refineries that had the potential of producing about 140,000 barrels a day. Postwar planning envisioned using the revenue from that oil to pay for rebuilding Iraq.

The city, with a population of almost 1.4 million, was Iraq's major port; it had an international airport, and rail lines reached out from it to other cities in the region. As an oil and petrochemicals center, a transportation hub, and the second-largest city in Iraq, Basra was the biggest target outside of Baghdad itself.

Our job was to blunt any attempt to reinforce the defense of the oil fields. While we slammed the 51st, and possibly the Medina, other U.S. and British Marines were assigned to take the vast tract of oil wells. We sailed on, through lowlands that steadily became more populated; dirt roads careered every which way, and long pipelines reached across the sand. The place looked like a Texas oil patch.

"All Darkside units, this is Darkside Six! Gas-Gas-Gas!"

McCoy's chemical detection alarm had been triggered, and his radio call again had us grabbing our masks. Although we had neither heard nor seen anything unusual, we were on the turf of the infamous Ali Hassan al-Majid, the merciless butcher known to the outside world as "Chemical Ali." Square-faced, with a Brillo-pad mustache, Ali was the first cousin of Saddam Hussein and the maniac responsible for killing tens of thousands of Iraqis, having murdered Kurds in the north and Shi'ites in the south with equal enthusiasm. He coldly laid waste to 280 villages with deadly gas, with the intention of killing every man, woman, child, plant, and animal in them. Ali was now the governor of southern Iraq, and we knew that if anyone would launch the most poisonous substances known to man against us, Chemical Ali was the guy.

The warning turned out to be another false alarm, but it was a sobering reminder that this was no joyride.

———

We had encountered only some occasional mischief from the Iraqis so far, and by the time the distant skyline of Basra rose out of the flat landscape, the intelligence guys had determined that the fearsome Medina Division was nowhere about. Then things began to get serious.

Rocket-propelled grenades swooshed past the lead tanks, and minor fighting sprang up with some enemy soldiers who were trying to blow up an oil well. They did not last long under withering fire from the armored column.

We soon what we found what we had come for, the 51st Mech, and we set about destroying it. Our Abrams tanks opened up with their 120 mm main guns on enemy tanks, which returned fire, and the Amtracs and artillery were engaging whatever they could find. The deep-throated anvil chorus of explosions was joined by the stutter of heavy machine guns and the thump of grenades. Cobra helicopters viciously roared in with rockets and guns to attack targets we could not see.

The sky was black with smoke as we moved our Humvees among burning hulks of freshly destroyed enemy tanks and armored vehicles. Our tanks were bellowing thunder only about a hundred meters to the west, TOW wire-guided missiles pounded a target fifty meters to the east, and the nearby explosions convulsed the air, shook the ground, and made concrete buildings vibrate like tuning forks.

Casey and I temporarily parked the main battalion headquarters' trucks about six hundred yards to the rear of the major fighting and then drove forward in our Humvees to find a more permanent site. Before leaving, we gave Officer Bob firm instructions to hold there until we came back to get them. But as the battle moved forward, and Normy was away for a moment to check on a problem, Bob decided to push the Main up another two hundred meters, and suddenly the thin-skinned trucks, containing the incredibly valuable men who ran the brain of the battalion, and their important communications equipment, came under fire.

"Hotel Seven! Hotel Seven! They're firing at me! I need you back here!" My radio call sign was no longer "Gabriel" but "Hotel Seven," and the panicky words of Officer Bob cut through the crashing of battle. People, tanks, and armored vehicles were getting smoke-checked all around us, and now the Main was under attack! The Panda Bear, driving my Humvee, stomped the accelerator, and we roared away to find Bob, with me yelling for Casey on the radio, although I knew that the surrounding noise might prevent him from hearing me. I stripped the sniper rifle out of the drag bag and checked the loads.

As the old, familiar sniper rhythms kicked in, the Panda skidded to a stop and we piled out of the Humvee. The Main was strung out like a disjointed worm over about two hundred yards near a cluster of refinery buildings, and Marine infantrymen were already out of the vehicles but could not see who was shooting at them. They could have countered by spraying the entire area with heavy machine gun fire, but that would have risked unacceptable civilian casualties, and nobody wanted to start the war off by whacking a bunch of civilians.

Bob saw us and pointed to one of the multistory buildings. I braced against the front hood of the big vehicle, leaned into the stock of my rifle, brought the scope to my right eye, and dialed the focus ring until the blocky oil refinery building stood out in sharp relief. Somewhere over there were the guys who were spraying the

Main, and I could change this ambush in a hurry by taking out whoever was behind their machine gun. It would only take one shot, but first I had to find him.

Panda made a laser check for the range from our position to the building: "Nine hundred and eleven yards, boss." That distance was almost perfect, because my M40A1 bolt-action rifle was zeroed at a thousand yards—the length of ten football fields. I adjusted the elevation fine-tune ring on the scope to nine plus one, which would make the bullet strike exactly 915 yards away, almost exactly the distance to the refinery. A thread of dark smoke drifted by, telling me that the wind was no more than three miles an hour, and therefore not a factor. There is an intricate formula to accurately determining windage and elevation, but any good sniper can solve the equations in his head.

I did a hasty search because time was being measured in the rattle of machine gun fire; bullets pinged off of rocks and the road and kicked up gouts of sand. Sooner or later, this guy was going to get lucky and hit somebody. I started at the bottom left-hand corner of the building and went straight up to the roofline, so crisp in the bright sunlight that it seemed almost painted against the smoky morning sky. Then I scanned back down to ground level, where some thick bushes were clumped in a tangled mass, and that's where I found possibly the stupidest man in the Iraqi army. He was hiding behind a thick bush and firing with an RPK light machine gun.

He thought he was safe. At that distance, he was invisible to the naked eye, and the bushes and light obscured any muzzle flash. But through my scope, he appeared in full color, as if on my private television set, although this TV had crosshairs with tiny mil dots along the axes for adjustments. He wore a green field uniform that blended well in his shadowy hideaway. He had a thick mustache.

The huge battle raging around us no longer mattered to me, for he and I were now in a special zone, all by ourselves.

The soldier had made an elemental mistake by confusing concealment with cover, assuming that being hidden in the shadows protected him from a bullet. Leaves and twigs cannot do that. Two seconds after I locked the crosshairs on him, I took a breath, partially exhaled, and gently squeezed the trigger. Almost instantly, my 173-grain round of Lake City Match ammunition exploded in his chest, and he spun around and was thrown backward as if slammed by an invisible baseball bat. He was dead, my first kill of Operation Iraqi Freedom.

A sudden movement caught my attention three stories above him, and the Panda Bear saw it, too. Someone had ducked back behind a wall. "That one's gone," said the Panda, examining the position with powerful binos.

"Nah. He'll be back." Part of my job is to study human nature. It's like playing poker; if I know what the other guy is likely to do, such as blinking when he is dealt a pair of aces, I own him. Everyone has the flaw of curiosity. "He'll want to see what his buddy downstairs is doing." Without removing my eye from the scope, I focused to the edge of the wall where the mystery soldier had last been seen and remained locked in a solid shooting position. I used the thumb and two fingers of my right hand to work the bolt, eject the spent cartridge, and reload a fresh round.

A group of prisoners huddled beside the narrow road and watched us work. They had not been searched since giving up and were not really guarded, except for being under the gun of every passing Marine. When I took out the machine gunner, they probably thought they had made the right decision in surrendering. The thunder of the overall battle—tanks and missiles and artillery—had not diminished, but that was not my concern. My scope did not move, and the edge of the building remained so sharp that I could have counted the bugs crawling on it.

"He got away clean, boss," said the Panda, keeping his binos on the same spot. "He ain't coming back."

"Oh, he's still up there, Bear. Curiosity kills." I increased the pressure on the trigger, taking up about two of the three pounds needed to fire, and slowed my breathing, confident that another of Saddam's soldiers was about to make an appearance. I felt, more than saw, the picture in my scope change, as if a cushion of air were being displaced, and a man's head came slowly around the corner. Ear, cheek, eye, nose. I fired, and his head snapped back sharply as he was blown off the building.

Game over. With those two shots, the ambush of the Main was done.

We had been in Iraq less than a day and it already seemed like a lifetime, for no one had gotten any real rest since leaving Camp Ripper. The night before, a Hellfire missile zoomed in and exploded against an Abrams tank, wounding several crewmen—our first casualties of the war—and no one slept after that. The sleep deprivation combined with the exhaustion of battle was pushing us to a ragged edge, and I was getting surly.

In combat, my sole purpose is to kill the enemy, and I will not tolerate half measures on a battlefield. Violent supremacy works just fine for me. This was the first time that Casey and most of my other Marines had seen me with my real war face on, and they were startled by the sharp change in my attitude, which was totally focused and almost unreasoningly critical.

My mood was not improved when I heard a strange exchange of words on the Tac-1 radio net. The commanding officer of the Bravo Tanks Company that had been attached to our battalion was talking to Colonel McCoy, who had expected those tanks to be at a certain spot on the map. They had not shown up.

"Bravo Six. Darkside Six. What's taking you so long?" McCoy wanted to know.

"We've got some infantry trying to decide if they want to surrender," responded Captain Bryan Lewis, Bravo Six.

"What do you mean?" McCoy sounded as confused as I was.

"We're seeing if they want to surrender."

I was ready to go find Lewis's tank and kick his ass. We were here to kill the Iraqi soldiers, not let them take their time deciding whether or not to fight! Thousands of leaflets had been dropped onto Iraqi troop positions that had been very specific about exactly how they should capitulate: drop their guns, put their hands up, and walk toward us. In my opinion, if they did not do it exactly that way, then fuck them, and boom, boom, boom, for they remained a threat. This captain of our tankers had some Iraqi soldiers in his sights but was not shooting them. I told Casey that there are no second chances in combat and wondered aloud if Lewis had the right stuff. "The guy's a fucking coward if he won't engage," I growled.

"Jeez, Jack, give him a chance," Casey told me. "You're not up there with Tanks, and you don't know what's going on."

Of course he was right, but I was in no mood to cut anybody slack, particularly officers, even if they had been in ferocious combat most of the day. Most of my anger had nothing to do with Lewis or his tanks, and, in fact, I grew to admire Lewis's skill as a warrior. I was mad because I wasn't in the fight.

9

Left Out

Few things are more mind-numbing and worrisome than a strike of
"friendly fire," in which your own troops or noncombatants somehow become the targets of fire from your own side. The trigger in
such incidents is never pulled to inflict such harm, but war scram-
bles reality, and at the end of Day 1, March 20, 2003, I almost killed
a whole bunch of people by accident, then almost got killed myself
in a separate incident. On either end, friendly fire is never fun.

The invasion of Iraq was roaring ahead with astonishing speed,
and our 5th Marines and British Royal Marines captured the Rumaylah oil fields virtually intact. A few rolling columns of red and
orange fire rose out of the wrecked metal of the destroyed wells and
sent thick black smoke ballooning into the sky, but the defending
Iraqis somehow had been caught so off guard that they were able to
blow up only nine wells before they were killed or ran away. There
would be no repeat of the ecological disaster of the 1991 war, and
the backbone of the Iraqi economy, the second-largest oil reserves in
the world, was in Coalition hands.

With McCoy pushing hard, our battalion secured bridges into
Basra and was maneuvering to take the Basra International Airport.

The trade-off for the brisk advance was that everyone was exhausted by the continual effort. About an hour before dusk, Casey and I and our boys came upon an abandoned "Roland," an antitank missile launcher mounted on something that looked like a golf cart. The enemy weapon had been forsaken by its operators but was still in usable condition, so we had to destroy it.

Casey took station with his Humvee about a hundred yards to the left, and I was on the ground, looking to the right down a road that made a turn about fifty yards away. I saw that everything was clear and told the Panda to arm an AT4 rocket launcher. He hefted it to his shoulder, aimed, and waited for my command to fire. I was just about to give the order when Luis Castillo, up in the turret of our Humvee, and therefore with a better view, alerted me that shooting the Roland right now might scare "the enemy prisoners." I thought he meant a group that I knew was safely behind us. "Fuck 'em," I said.

The normally quiet Castillo persisted. "Boss, they're gonna get hit by this."

"No way, they're out of the danger zone." I was ready to let Panda take the shot when some unexpected motion down the road caught my eye, and a line of Iraqi prisoners under guard by an escort of Marines came around the curve, moving straight toward the Roland that was our target. When they saw Panda aiming a rocket launcher right at them, the prisoners and Marine guards alike stopped in their tracks. I yelled quickly for everybody to stand down, but coming so close to fucking up royally had left my heart pounding hard. Had I given the order for the Panda Bear to shoot, a lot of people would have died because I had made a stupid mistake.

After we let the astonished prisoners and guards file safely past, I called in some engineers to blow up the Roland. I had seen enough of that damned gun on a golf cart.

Snipers are trained to endure extreme fatigue, but it attacks your critical thinking like a live thing, and I cursed myself for carelessness. My body was working faster than my mind, and I recognized that I might be reaching my physical limit. But as the poet Robert Frost wrote, we had miles to go before we slept.

Rest was not in the cards, and it was not long before I was on the other side of a friendly fire incident, which was no more fun than the first one. The skies were filled with hundreds of warplanes flying attack missions from bases as far away as Missouri and Guam, and low-flying Tomahawk cruise missiles growled in from warships out in the Gulf. Explosions decorated the horizon, and a major fight loomed at the airport. Who could sleep? Who would even want to sleep at such a time?

While McCoy zipped around the battlefield in his Humvee to oversee the tactical situation, I was up to the brim of my Kevlar helmet helping set up the Main headquarters about three miles from the airport, the sniper rifle at rest while I attended to my other job as company gunny. We created an instant office by parking two command Amtracs back-to-back, flopping down their rear ramps, and throwing a lightproof cover over them, since night had fallen. Radios crackled, maps were unfurled, computers were booted up, and the battalion brain trust got to work in their mobile, claustrophobic dungeon, figuring out what had to happen next to keep this drive alive. We had done severe damage to the 51st Mech, which had been our primary foe, but remnants of the division were still around and were still dangerous. The British were coming up right behind us to take over this space, freeing us to push on up the road, and we were handing over responsibility while fighting was still under way nearby. The planners had a big chore ahead.

Ragged streaks of bright fire flashed into the darkness all around as our artillery batteries pumped out rounds in preparation for the airport attack, and the concussions of the great cannons shook the ground. Tornados of dust were kicked up by every blast.

Suddenly there was a loud *POP* in the nearby sky, followed by numerous smaller *pop-pop-pop-pop* explosions. Oh, shit. That was the signature firecracker sequence of one of the most lethal artillery rounds in the U.S. arsenal, and if you're close enough to hear it, you're already in trouble. The first noise from the incoming 155 mm rounds comes when the warhead opens about fifty meters above the ground and showers out dozens of antipersonnel bomblets, and the following little *pops* are the cluster bombs detonating upon impact. They can cause incredible damage.

There is no time to hit the dirt once the firecrackers start, so I closed my eyes and leaned hard against an armored vehicle, trying to meld my skin with its metal armor. Another loud *POP* followed the first by microseconds, and then another string of fireworks rattled off about 150 yards from where Normy Arias and I were working.

Our guys were on their radios even before the popping stopped to tell the cannon-cockers not to do that anymore, and we didn't take any casualties, but a certain junior staff officer was spooked. He thought the Iraqis had our number.

"They're bracketing us!" he shouted, running up as Normy and I brushed ourselves off. With the sort of sixth sense about such things that combat veterans have in their bones, both of us had realized instantly that the errant rounds were Dual-Purpose Improved Conventional Munitions (DPICM), which meant they were from American guns that were not really trying to kill us. The danger was already past, and since no one had been hurt, there was really nothing to talk about.

"No, sir," Norm replied, going back to work. "They're not bracketing us."

"Yes, they *are*, First Sergeant." Officer Bob was adamant that we were all in grave danger.

"No, sir, they're not," Norm repeated, very slowly this time, in his most polite tone. "Those are DPICM rounds. The enemy doesn't even have DPICM."

"How can you be sure that was DPICM?"

Norm stopped what he was doing. "Sir, I was in artillery for eighteen years. Only one thing makes that sound. Take it from me, those were our own DPICM."

Bob stood there for a minute, then hurried away.

McCoy's personal promise to his battalion came true. Not only did we utterly destroy the Iraqi 51st Mechanized Division, but we also bagged its commanding general.

Night means nothing to American combat forces, because our high-tech and thermal-detection gear lets us see through the darkness. Throughout the early witching hours of Saturday morning, the battalion maneuvered closer to the airport and hit it just before first light, killing eight Iraqi tanks and some suicidal infantrymen fighting from bunkers.

Since I wasn't involved, I had pulled a cot out of one of the ambulances and tried to get some rest, but my mind could not shut down. I got up when the attack started and walked around, listening to the gunfire and watching the flashes. I felt left out.

This was a built-up section of the city, and during the four hours it took to plan the attack, I could have easily infiltrated in the darkness, found a snug hide, done some real-time observation, and been in position to support the attack with some good old-fashioned snip-ing. Enemy soldiers were dying out there, but I hadn't killed any-body since yesterday. Seemed a waste.

One of my boys at the airport took out a target with a nice long shot, and if he got one, I could have gotten ten, not because of a vast difference in our shooting skills, but because I had more experience in finding targets. There would have been plenty of work for me, but I missed the boat on this one. I was still the unofficial commander of the sniper platoon and needed to be working with my rifle, not tied down with the Main. An uncomfortable thought nibbled at me: *Is this the way it's going to be?*

Dawn broke with us owning the key bridge across the Shatt al-Basra Canal. We resorted to brute force for the next step and pummeled the remaining airport defenders with sustained artillery barrages, bombardment by the tanks, slashing .50 caliber machine gun fire, and missiles from Cobra helicopters. The grunts moved in to finish the job and had an old-fashioned room-by-room shootout in the Sheraton Hotel, which separated the military and civilian sides of the airport. The Iraqi soldiers, outgunned and outclassed, soon began giving up, walking into the open with their hands up or waving white flags. Those who ran or continued to fight were killed. Our firepower was simply more than they could bear.

By the middle of the day, the fight was all but over. A dozen civilians who had been caught inside the terminal made their way out to surrender after a morning in hell. Our only casualty was a Marine who was wounded when he tossed a grenade into a room at the Sheraton only to have some metal fragments blow back through the wall and hit his hand.

About an hour after we took the airport, a bright yellow Nissan Pathfinder sports utility vehicle bearing a white flag of surrender drove onto the airstrip and cautiously approached some guys from India Company. When the four-wheel-drive SUV eased to a stop, a man in a crisp uniform stepped out and identified himself as the commanding general of the 51st Mechanized Division. He had nothing left with which to fight and wished to meet with our commanding officer. The astonished commander of India Company called for Colonel McCoy and suggested, "Darkside Six, this is India Six. You may want to come over here."

McCoy was there instantly, and in an oddly formal moment reminiscent of a time when wars were fought by more gentlemanly rules, the Iraqi general politely declared, "I am surrendering to you." McCoy accepted the surrender and then hustled the general back to higher headquarters for questioning. The Bull had taken a terrific trophy, but there was still some fighting going on.

By nightfall of March 21, the second day, the shooting was over and the approaches to Basra were secure. We had broken through the main defense cordon, had captured the airport, held three vital bridges across the big canal, and were in position to stiff-arm any resistance that might try to emerge out of Basra.

Casey and I escorted senior officers of our battalion and our replacement unit, the 1st Fusiliers of the British 7th Armored Brigade, the famed Desert Rats, on a tour of the vital points of the quiet battlefield. All night long, their companies moved in and took over from our units. Having come up the marshy Al Faw peninsula and battled for the oil fields, the Brits were more than capable of taking over and were tasked to conquer Basra itself.

Kipling once wrote how a cheap bullet fired by the lowest enemy soldier can erase an important officer, and as a sniper, I love taking out the big guys on the other team. The leaders are not supposed to take chances, but nobody could put a leash on McCoy, and he stumbled into doing something foolish in all of the excitement.

As I sat on the hood of his Humvee and ate my dinner of MREs—Meals Ready to Eat—that night, the colonel ducked out from under the tent of the Main headquarters, took a seat on an ammunition crate across from me, and lit one of his big cigars. We were developing a habit of getting together after a battle to compare thoughts on what had gone down, both right and wrong. He looked tired, not having had any sleep since Kuwait, but his spirits were buoyed by the two good days of work his Marines had turned in. "So, how'd you do?" he asked pleasantly, preparing me for a special ration of shit.

"I only got two, boss," I said, lighting a cigarette and describing the ambush of the Main. The man soaked up information of all sorts, and every piece of battlefield data helped him clarify the overall puzzle, so he listened to me describe working as a sniper in a shifting combat environment.

McCoy nodded, then grinned, a crease of white teeth through a dust-caked face. "I got a tank," he announced. "Pretty cool, huh?"

McCoy and his driver, driving off the road to let some of our armor rumble by, had found an Iraqi T-55 tank dug into the sand, with only the turret, its big cannon, and a machine gun showing above ground. The colonel decided to attack it. With his radio operator, he checked out the surrounding trenches, then climbed aboard the tank and yanked on the turret hatches, which were locked from the inside. Frustrated, they ran back to their armored Humvee and opened up with their rifles and machine gun. The bullets just bounced off the steel hide of the monster, so McCoy ran back to the tank again and flung a fragmentation grenade at it, then ran back to cover again. Finally, he got out of the way, and one of our Abrams tanks popped a high-explosive round into the Iraqi tank with a volcanic detonation.

It was a stupid thing for a commanding officer to do, but now I know that he had another purpose in mind rather than killing a piece of Iraqi armor that may or may not have had a crew inside. With that little adventure, McCoy solidified his credentials within the battalion as Darkside Six, the tank-eating commander, our own Darth Vader, and as word spread, his Marines puffed up with pride at the Old Man's audacity.

I was pissed. This guy was the heart of the baddest Marine battalion on the planet, and he had placed himself at great risk. For what? I was steaming, and I sat there on his Humvee and bitched at him that he was paid to lead and to think, not to go throwing grenades. What if he had been smoke-checked by some *hajji* soldier?

He just laughed, unapologetic. I stormed away from him, trailed by his booming laugh. In the middle of a freakin' war, was I supposed to be having some kind of weird competition with Darkside Six?

God, we were tired, but we plunged into hours of getting the battalion refueled and rearmed, and what normally was a totally routine job became complicated and dangerous at almost every step. Men who had been up for at least forty-eight hours were moving like zombies as they handled enough gasoline, ammunition, and explosives to destroy us all. We could do it because our totally realistic training had drummed the pure routine of these very jobs deep into our minds and muscles.

Then we were told to push ahead. Rest would come as soon as we reached our next dispersal area. Casey and I again were to lead the way with the advance quartering party, so we herded our vehicles together in a tight group, and instead of sleeping, we hit the road at 2:30 on Sunday morning, March 23. As we pulled away from Basra, bright flares of artificial light danced in the darkness over the city, and streaks of tracer fire arced into the smoky sky.

The roadside was littered with discarded Iraqi uniforms and weapons thrown away as the enemy soldiers vanished back into the city to become instant civilians. We passed the burned-out hulks of armored vehicles, but there was no gruesome carpet of maimed and shredded bodies. As our British friends noted, it was not an untidy battlefield. The fight had been a good sparring session to get our feet wet, but this was not the battle royal we were expecting.

That fight would fall to the British, and it would be another two weeks before they could enter the city, where many of the same Iraqi soldiers who had vanished at our approach had reappeared to fight alongside Saddam loyalists and fanatical fedayeen guerrillas. Vice President Dick Cheney had pledged, "We will be welcomed as liberators," but Basra remained an untamed hornets' nest, with the million-plus residents of the city hiding in their homes, waiting to see how it all turned out. Twelve years earlier, after Operation Desert Storm in 1991, they had responded to a call for revolt by President George H. W. Bush, only to have Saddam crush their rebellion with his usual cruel tactics and put Chemical Ali in charge. This time, the citizens were understandably wary.

10

Midnight Ride

Everyone was familiar with the visions of Iraqi soldiers surrendering en masse during Operation Desert Storm, but that was not happening this time. We had a real shooting war on our hands.

The danger was not confined to the rapidly shifting front line. With every turn of our wheels that moved us deeper into Iraq, the supply lines reaching all the way back to Kuwait became more stretched out and vulnerable. Enemy troops and irregular forces started chewing on those exposed convoys and slowed the vital river of ammunition, water, food, and fuel needed to maintain the forward momentum across the entire front.

Far behind us, hard fighting was going on in the important port town of Umm Qsar, which had been expected to fall like a ripe apple, and the British had stalled outside of a hostile Basra. To the west, the Army's V Corps out in the desert was encountering heavy resistance around Najaf, and an entire squadron of Apache helicopters of the 101st Airborne would be shot up during a night raid close to Karbala. Plans for a two-front strategy crumbled when Turkey refused to let the sixteen thousand troops of the U.S. 4th Infantry Division cross its territory to enter Iraq from the north.

Iraq is as big as California, though, so what was happening in one section often was not even noticed elsewhere, just as a car wreck in Los Angeles is unknown in San Francisco. The sudden developments in other flashpoints of fighting would not have been good news, had we known about it, but we didn't, so we kept moving. After Basra, our own battalion had to go hunting for the war.

We were part of an overall dash by the 1st Marine Division toward Baghdad, and we soon passed the junction where Route 8, the main highway running northwest out of Kuwait, split into Iraq's two major highways, Routes 1 and 7, almost parallel corridors that would take us all the way to the capital. For us, things had been going well. We were trained to be nimble and move swiftly, and we were carrying enough of our own supplies to fight for several days, so despite shortages elsewhere, slowdowns, and ambushes, the advance, from where we sat, still had the shape of the proverbial irresistible force that had not yet met an object that could not be moved. We were making bold, breathtaking jumps forward into enemy territory, and lines of tanks, armored vehicles, Humvees, and trucks of every sort were thundering along the wide roads and through the untracked desert. Speed was our rule. Use your wheels.

It was still Sunday, March 23, the same day we had pulled out of Basra, and although we were exhausted, sleep was still not in the cards. The bright daylight seared our weary eyes by the time we pulled into a dispersal area some thirty kilometers east of the city of An Nasiriyah, a tangled sprawl of buildings and three hundred thousand residents near the southern end of Route 7.

Another Marine unit was tasked to go into the city and capture two bridges, and when they did, they crashed headlong into an unexpectedly strong force of Iraqi paramilitaries and fanatical fedayeen guerrillas who locked them into a blazing gunfight. The enemy hid among civilians, so casualties among average citizens rose steadily during what became a bloody Sunday for both sides. The bridges eventually were captured, but at the cost of twenty-nine dead Marines and an unknown number of Iraqi casualties. Nobody had expected such fierce resistance.

Even before the Marines went in, an eighteen-truck supply convoy of the Army's 507th Maintenance Company was ambushed when the drivers, exhausted after almost thirty-six straight hours on the road, somehow blundered into An Nasiriyah. Eleven of the soldiers were killed and seven more taken prisoner, including nineteen-year-old Private First Class Jessica Lynch from West Virginia.

We were only a few miles away from An Nasiriyah during the big fight but were not involved in it and didn't even know about it until later. When our quartering party reached the dispersal area in advance of the battalion, we took a break to air out the vehicles, clean weapons, grab some chow, and wash our hands, feet, and faces. But only fifteen minutes after coming to a halt, Casey got the unexpected call to move out immediately, forcing us to throw our gear back together, gas up, reload the two trucks, and take off for the regimental headquarters. We were about to roll out on a daring and dangerous mission into bad-guy territory and would not see our battalion again for four days.

Gunner Chris Eby, a weathered veteran of twenty-two years in the Corps, was the gruff leader of the regimental quartering party, and he assembled the advance teams of all the battalions to move forward as a single unit and find a place large enough to accommodate all of Regimental Combat Team 7—three combat battalions and the attached engineer, reconnaissance, tank, and artillery units—so we would all be together for the next push. The Secret Squirrels of the intelligence teams once again thought that they had pinpointed the location of Saddam Hussein's powerful and elusive Medina Division, and we were going after them. The powerful division, which was said to have perhaps two hundred tanks, hundreds of heavy artillery pieces, and maybe up to ten thousand men, officially was named the "Medina the Luminous Division," and we intended to illuminate it even more.

Casey and I returned to our trucks after the briefing and told the guys we were about to hit the road again.

"Speed is the thing here," Casey emphasized.

"Where are we going?" someone asked.

Casey unfolded a map on the hood of his Humvee and explained that we would be going 175 miles farther up the road, to the railroad city of An Numaniyah, where we were to cross the Tigris River. He pointed to a spot and said, "That will put us seventy-five miles from Baghdad."

He did not have to explain that making a leap of 175 miles through enemy-held territory would be a dangerous undertaking, but looking around at our traveling buddies made the task at least seem possible. This was no lightly armed Jessica Lynch convoy, for we had about thirty hardback Humvees, manned by combat Marines carrying everything from machine guns to antitank missiles and radios that could put us in instant touch with aircraft. Gunner Eby, who drank more coffee than the tasters at Maxwell House, would lead the parade, and he intended to roll right through any enemy ambush with guns blazing and not stop until we were at our destination.

This was no meandering, touristy jaunt through the interesting countryside of the Euphrates Valley, but deadly serious business. We were trying to lead the regiment into position for a huge fight with one of the major divisions guarding Baghdad.

The weather was perfect for a long Sunday drive, and during the first part of the trip, we barreled along the six-lane highway at about fifty miles per hour, and cool wind blew through the windows. As haggard and sleepless as we were, we had to stay awake and alert, and it was on this stretch of deserted highway that I noticed for the first time that Jerry Marsh, Casey's gunner, was no ordinary mortal. In my truck, the boys took turns standing in the machine gun turret as we jounced over the long miles. But in Casey's Humvee, Marsh just stood there, locked in position behind his gun. He would keep that position hour after hour, day after day, with bugs hitting his face and sand grinding his eyes, knowing that if anyone was going to die, it was most likely going to be him. He reminded me of Granny tied into her rocking chair atop the Beverly Hillbillies' truck. With his exceptional eyesight, it was good to have him up there.

We had made about seventy-five miles when the speed factor vanished at a narrow bridge across the Euphrates River, where we hit a traffic jam of colossal proportions and came to a grinding halt. The sun was setting by the time our turn came to cross, and it took another forty minutes to get over and regroup. The blue canopy of sky changed into soot darkness, so we went to night vision goggles and rolled on into uncharted territory.

The good road gave way to construction as we struck out almost due north, and our speed dropped off dramatically to a maximum of fifteen miles per hour. We were passing fewer and fewer other vehicles, and the fields around us were deserted, eerily dark and quiet. This wasn't good. Where the hell was everybody? Trigger fingers rested on guns.

Midnight came and went and still we drove, and sleep pulled at our eyelids. About two o'clock on Monday morning, March 24, one of our tracked vehicles bogged down in a marshy area beside the road. When we stopped to pull out, a heavily camouflaged Marine from a Force Recon platoon materialized out of the surrounding darkness and wanted to know what the hell we were doing up here.

"Moving north," Gunner Eby told him.

"You guys know there's nobody in front of you?" asked the Marine with the blackened face. His team was scattered about at the northernmost edge of the advance, and he said they did not know what was going on farther up the road.

Somehow we had jumped to the lead position of the entire Marine advance and were basically out on our own. That was only a minor concern to Gunner Eby, so he thanked the Recon dude for the information and cranked us up again.

Sleep was quickly forgotten as we moved deeper into the unknown. There were no stars, and we heard helicopters buzzing overhead, heading for targets up ahead. We waited expectantly for a sharp crack of gunfire or the sudden blast of an ambush, but none came.

Eby kept us rolling for two more hours before pulling us to a stop. We were so far out on a limb that we could no longer even see the tree, but both Casey and I argued that we should keep on pushing. *We don't know where everybody else is, but we know where we are, so let's keep moving!* Gunner Eby rightly ignored us. It was senseless to step much farther into the great void without supporting forces; the last person we had seen was that lone Marine advance scout, and he was now far behind us.

Except for our radios, we were out of contact with any friendly units, isolated and exposed. All of a sudden, those thirty Humvees bristling with weaponry didn't seem quite as powerful as before. If we were jumped by a bunch of enemy tanks and troops tonight, we would put up a hell of a fight but stood a good chance of being annihilated.

Nevertheless, I had reached the end of my rope. Our convoy coiled into a defensive position beside the road, and guards were posted, but I passed out in my seat even before my Humvee coasted to a stop. For the first time since Kuwait, I got more than forty-five minutes of shutdown time, and the boys had mercy on an old man and let me sleep.

Fortunately, our luck held and nothing happened while we were parked out there on our own beside the road in the middle of the Iraqi night. I awoke two hours later, at daybreak, to see the Abrams tanks and the Amtracs of the 5th Marines grinding past, which meant the big boys had caught up and we were no longer alone. I got out and stretched, feeling as if I had been asleep in a cushy hotel bed for a week.

Thousands of Marines and hundreds of vehicles were pounding through the red grit in the brilliant light of a clear morning. Gunner Eby received orders from our own regimental headquarters, still far back down the road, to tuck into the 5th Marines column for a while. We got back on the road.

Desert sandstorms are not weather phenomena but evil things that rise up from hell. One of the extra-large variety brewed up and dropped on us on Monday, March 24, and the war came to a halt. The sheer power of the hurricane of dirt made all of our weapons look puny by comparison. When those breezes start to whisper against your ear, you had better take shelter and button up, for you won't be going anywhere for a while, and you are going to come out of the experience feeling like sand has been ground into your very soul.

We had begun to feel cocky because of the speed of our midnight ride and believed that the Iraqis could not stop us. We thought that nothing could. We were wrong.

Our convoy was taking a maintenance break when the first gentle breezes began to hum around the vehicles, raising the talcumlike loose sand and swirling it about in small funnels of dirt. The velocity increased, more sand jumped into the air, and visibility fell as dirt colored the sky. Within a few hours the wind was howling, and the giant sandstorm covered everything in the Euphrates River Valley. There was nothing to do but button up and stay put until the storm passed, because telling directions had become impossible.

Our heavy Humvee was being rocked on its springs by the wind, and from my seat in front I couldn't see a damned thing. I lowered goggles over my eyes and wrapped a thick bandana around my mouth, but it made no difference. Sand seeped into every crevice, including those in my body, and choked me with tiny dunes that piled up at the back of my throat. We shut the trucks tight and stuffed rags into every crack, but the harsh wind, keening at a banshee pitch straight out of a Halloween movie, seemed to push sand right through metal.

Outside it was worse, but a few Marines had to be out there on security patrols, and their exposed flesh was lashed with whips of grainy sand. Risks increased with the bad weather, and all along the line, dreadful accidents happened. A guy fell from an Amtrac and had to lie injured in the swirling storm because medical evacuation was impossible. A tank drove off a bridge and plunged into the Euphrates, drowning its crew, and no one knew about it until the next day. A bulldozer ran over two sleeping men, killing one and severely injuring the other.

It was like being trapped inside a deadly sunset, and the rushing clouds that surrounded us changed from orange to red to purple as the wind changed speed and direction, then stacked high into the dark scarlet sky until we could not tell when day turned to night. There was nothing to do but sit there and endure the pounding as the windblown grit chipped paint from our big metal machines. Sleep was impossible. The millions of dollars that we had floating around the battlefield in advanced optics and sighting systems couldn't help us, so we sat there blind.

"The storm was worse than anyone imagined," the battalion historians would write later. Mother Nature did what the Iraqi army could not do—stop the 1st Marine Division. The fucking dirt was everywhere, the wind would not let up, and for ten hours, we sat there and suffered.

The sandstorm finally eased about three o'clock in the morning of Tuesday, March 25. Then it began to rain, the water pouring down in cataracts that slammed us for the rest of the night, churned the dust into pasty mud, and further ruined the already sloppy road. Despite the weather, we started moving again even before the sun came up over a yellow horizon. None of our boys had been hurt, but days would pass before our conversations could start with something other than a cough that visibly expelled dust from our bodies.

A herd of camels, saddled but riderless and separated by the storm from their owners, serenely strolled past at daybreak, their heads held high, haughty princes of this terrible environment.

I had hoped that by being out front, we might bump into some action, because I was feeling hamstrung. Once the battalion caught up with us, we rejoined the Main and continued to roll. Iraq seemed endless, and the odometer on my Humvee was ticking away the miles to Baghdad.

Were we ever going to find some fighting? "Is this what we're going to be doing for the entire war?" Casey asked me one afternoon, and although I wanted to give him my usual optimistic song and dance, I was having some doubts myself. The days of the war were falling from the calendar at an alarming rate. It wouldn't last much longer, and I had not been involved in any real fighting, including the dustup back at Basra. In moments of doubt, I wondered if Mc-Coy had forgotten our deal, or had lost confidence in me.

11

Send In the Bull

There had been a major shake-up in the Pentagon over the past months, as Defense Secretary Donald Rumsfeld, wanting a thorough overhaul of the Army and new strategic thinking, won a decisive victory over the generals. Rumsfeld argued that a relatively small, fast-moving attack force could slice right through the Iraqi defenses and reach Baghdad quickly, making the war short. The generals argued for the more traditional doctrine laid down by Colin Powell, the chairman of the Joint Chiefs of Staff during Desert Storm and the current U.S. secretary of state: the combination of overwhelming force, a specific objective, and a clear exit strategy. Rumsfeld and his civilian deputies outmaneuvered and overruled them, and as a result, this offensive was being carried out with about half the manpower used in Desert Storm. Early in the planning, they had considered using only fifty thousand troops, but since Iraq had a population of twenty-four million people, including more than six million in Baghdad, that one was discarded.

Shortly before the invasion began, Army Chief of Staff General Eric Shinseki told Congress that several hundred thousand troops would be needed in Iraq. He was upbraided by the Pentagon's civilian leadership and retired. Army Secretary Thomas White supported Shinseki and would be fired. Rumsfeld and his acolytes were clearly in control.

But now, their novel war plans were in jeopardy. Moving fast and keeping unrelenting pressure on the enemy meant that the advance could not slow down and that support troops had to keep pace, just the opposite of what was happening. Maps and reports showed the Army was struggling out in the desert, and the big Marine drive along the two big highways was sputtering. The unexpectedly tough enemy opposition, ambushes on convoys, bad weather, the sandstorm, and an increasingly dire fuel and supply situation had the top commanders second-guessing themselves. On television, former generals said the war wasn't going well because we didn't have enough troops involved. The whole enterprise had reached a critical point, and the leaders were about to order a three-week halt in place to refit, reorganize, and rethink.

Out in the sand, we were totally unaware of all of the bureaucratic fighting in Washington. I was just hanging around in the desert with Casey and my boys, and all we wanted to do was to get into the fight. Our trucks were packed with everything we needed, and there were Marines as far as we could see, lines of tracked vehicles and trucks and thousands of men, all moving in the same direction.

We were so firmly on the sidelines that except for some local patrols for security, we were snoozing, getting haircuts, doing laundry, cleaning weapons, and servicing the trucks. In fact, from where we stood, we thought the war was going quite well.

More than a week had elapsed since we had invaded Iraq, and my butt was sore from spending so much time bumping along in the passenger seat of my Humvee. I stomped around the sand and bitched out of frustration with being useless in the middle of a war. I was a sniper, and I needed to get into the fight.

About four kilometers directly ahead, the 5th Marine Regiment was bogged down on Route 1 outside of Ad Diwaniyah, a town of about a quarter million people on the central Iraqi plain. Every time the 5th Marines battled through one patch of ambushers, another bunch was waiting for them, and they had been taking casualties for almost two days. We were some four kilometers back and could hear a bit of battle going on, *bang-bang, thump-thump*, but it didn't involve us.

And about fifty miles to the east, over on Route 7, another regimental-sized Marine unit called Task Force Tarawa had ground to a stop. They were blocked outside of Al Kut, a town where, back in the distant era of World War I, Turkish defenders held up the British drive on Baghdad for 143 days. We couldn't wait that long, but TF Tarawa, which had been bloodied in An Nasiriyah, was fighting on fumes. They were just about out of everything, and the supply convoys trying to bring up water, ammunition, and fuel were being shot up in the south.

Finally, on Saturday, March 29, my luck changed and we got back into the game. Sergeant Major Dave Howell drove up, unfolded his stocky frame from the Humvee, and took me aside. "John, get your ass over to the command tent," he said. "We're getting out of this cluster fuck. They've decided to send in the Bull, and the Boss wants you."

Dave had come out of Force Recon, and although he was the senior enlisted man in the battalion and a trusted tactical adviser to

Colonel McCoy, he would always be just a fuckin' grunt at heart. He loved to go tearing across the battlefield so he could guide a fight, and I had assigned two good snipers, Staff Sergeant Dino Moreno, a dark-haired Italian who had been placed in my slot as the sniper platoon sergeant when I moved over to be the H&S gunny, and Corporal Mark Evnin, a New Englander, to ride shotgun with him. When Howell's regular Humvee driver decided to become a pacifist just before we went to war, Dave kicked his ass out of the truck and Evnin became the driver. The fourth seat was given to one of our more popular embedded reporters, John Koopman of the *San Francisco Chronicle*. We called him "Paperboy."

Dave Howell was the only person in the Corps who called me John, instead of Jack, but usually only did so when he was angry, just as my father had done. Now I felt like my surrogate dad had given me a Christmas present. I grabbed Casey and headed for McCoy's command post.

The new mission would have a totally unexpected result for me. Not only was I finally going to get into the shooting war, but since necessity breeds invention, a flat tire on a Humvee was about to become a stepping-stone to an important new variable in my craft, something that had never been taught in sniper school. My concept of a Mobile Sniper Strike Team, shelved long ago, was about to be reborn. The answer had been right under my nose the whole time.

Radios provided a low grumble of background noise in the large tent as McCoy sketched out his plan with a black grease pen on a whiteboard. Marines were tied down in independent struggles on Route 1 and on Route 7, but a thin east-west road called Highway 17 linked those two main highways. We were to go and capture that road to open a new supply route over to the beleaguered Task Force Tarawa, but the road was dotted with towns and villages, any one of which could be an enemy strongpoint, and we would have to tackle them, one after another. Since it was not in our nature to be passive, McCoy ordered, "Go in like you own the place. We're going to kick over the beehive and see what comes out."

McCoy and his staff had come up with a way to counter the Iraqi ambush teams that fired their barrages of rocket-propelled grenades, or RPGs, from the second row of buildings in a town, not the front row nearest the road on which the convoys were passing. That gave them some extra concealment and cover. So the Boss decided that if those turkeys wanted something to shoot at, we would give it to them.

We would stick a big sword right into the heart of any organized resistance by having our heavy armor bust straight into a town like a penetrating arrowhead. Then the tanks would sit there, intentionally presenting huge targets, begging to be shot at. An Abrams tank can shrug off a hit from a Hellfire missile, so while an RPG may go *bang* against its sides, actual damage is usually slight.

While the Iraqi ambushers took potshots at the virtually impenetrable armor, our infantry would hit the first row of buildings, then attack the ambush teams in the second row and create a wide buffer zone under our control, right in the middle of town. Our fast-moving CAATs and air strikes would seal off the escape routes.

After McCoy had given his orders, a small group of us gathered around a small table to hear Officer Bob lay down his own interpretation of the plan, which I considered a harebrained scheme that was almost sure to get me killed. Suddenly, I wasn't happy anymore. Bob said that when the armored column crashed into the hostile and unsecured towns, "I want Coughlin and his spotter to gain access to some high ground to cover the Main."

Had I heard him right? "Sir, you want me to go up into a building?" I asked as the other Marines, officers and enlisted men alike, looked over at me. Having snipers up front was one thing, but I would not run a suicide mission.

"Yes. I want you up on a roof. We'll stay with the vehicles to provide local security."

"Wait a minute. You want me and my spotter to clear a whole fucking building all alone? Just us?" There was stunned silence around the table.

He nodded dumbly, and I lost it. "*Are you fucking crazy?* This is a deliberate daylight attack, and every motherfucker in a twelve-mile radius is going to know exactly where we are. Ain't no fucking way we're going in there by ourselves."

I looked over at the battalion executive officer, Major Matt Baker, to see if he was going to nail me on the spot for insubordination, but J-Matt, a forty-year-old officer who was wickedly intelligent and had the calmness of a Buddhist monk, said nothing. Only a few days earlier, he had banned Bob from even speaking on the radio for issuing conflicting orders that hopelessly snarled one unit. Baker did not interfere, and Bob stood there and took my shouting in his face without a word. What was he going to do, send me to Iraq?

Casey pulled me aside to ratchet down the situation, and in a matter of minutes, the two of us constructed a beefed-up security squad that would provide cover for me. That was a formula that I could literally live with: machine guns, grenades, and Marines.

While getting ready to move out, our battalion lost our first Marine, a lance corporal who died when his Humvee flipped into an aqueduct while he was driving around in the darkness to update the codes in command net radios. It's not good to start the day with a casualty, for such a glitch could screw up the entire timeline, but while his death would be devastating to his family, it could not be allowed to impact the mission. This was war, and war does not stop just because somebody gets killed.

Our raiding force started moving before first light, working our way through the jumpy 5th Marines outside of Ad Diwaniyah, who were worn out by their own fighting during the past few days. They gave us quiet looks of pity as we passed, like "You're all gonna die, suckers."

At the big highway cloverleaf outside of Ad Diwaniyah, we hung a right onto Route 17 as dawn illuminated big blue and white highway signs spelling out the names of towns that were our targets for the day—Hajil, Afak, and Al Budayr—in both English and Arabic. Tanks were in the lead, followed by Kilo Company, then McCoy with his tactical headquarters team. Casey and I were next, with the armored Main, and were followed by India Company. The CAATs circled the column like protective wolves, leaving triangular flags of dust fluttering in the air behind them.

I was on the edge of my seat in the armored Humvee, holding my sniper rifle tightly with both hands. We were rolling, and all thoughts except the coming combat were banished. This was where I belonged, and the familiar prebattle calm, almost a serene disconnect from the surrounding world, flowed through my system, energizing and focusing my senses. I became aware of the steady beating of my heart and willed it to slow down, because in a fight I did not want it to vibrate through my body and wobble my scope. A good sniper pulls the trigger at that momentary lull between heartbeats, and it is best not to have your heart thundering like a trip-hammer with excitement.

A makeshift barricade had been thrown across the road less than a mile beyond the cloverleaf, a hodgepodge of big rocks and metal junk that provided cover for some Iraqi militiamen manning a group of technicals, those ubiquitous third-world weapons that are just pickup trucks with machine guns mounted in the beds. Those jackasses might scare the locals, but they were nothing more than an inconvenience to us.

Our tanks smashed through the barricade without slowing down, and the big, bad militia technicals scurried away like cowardly cockroaches—but not fast enough as our guys opened fire. Within minutes, the steaming carcasses of a couple of pickups, and the corpses of their drivers and gunners, dotted the roadside.

Just beyond the barricade, on the left side of the highway, was a string of low-walled houses, a village so small that it wasn't even on the map. We named it Bonus Town. Empty desert surrounded the place, giving it a Martian-colony look. Although it was too tiny for a full assault, we had to take care of it, so our entire column pulled off the road. The tanks went into a covering position, the snouts of their big cannon swinging from doorway to doorway, while the CAATs zoomed about the outskirts to seal off any exit. Then the rear ramps of the Amtracs were dropped, and the grunts hustled out for a house-to-house check.

I climbed from my Humvee, and Casey fanned the security unit out around me as I laid the rifle across the hood to steady it, and glassed the area through the scope. Dun-colored homes that were not much more than stacks of mud building blocks moved past my rifle in quick montage, and I examined a few civilians, plus some dogs, cats, goats, and chickens. Everyone else apparently had abandoned their homes until things settled down. Fortunately, no one fired a shot at us, for had they done so, we would have returned a thousand. After thirty minutes, the place was clear and we got ready to move on.

I was disappointed that Bonus Town had been so easy and that, once again, I had not been a factor. Was I ever going to find some way to earn my salary? But there were bigger places just down the road, where there had to be some soldiers, paramilitaries, fedayeen guerrillas, and other guys with guns, and I wanted a piece of those clowns.

As I walked around the Humvee to continue toward what was sure to be a fight, I found a glittering four-inch-long piece of metal sticking out of the right rear tire, which had gone as flat as a dirty penny on a railroad track. I filled the desert air with my entire vocabulary of obscene words, and other Marines actually laughed at me as they saddled up to head for the next village. I had been taken out of the war again, this time by a fucking flat tire!

We could not fix the tire on the road, for while we had plenty of combat stuff, spare tires were few and far between in the Marine Corps. The Army had plenty, but we didn't. We were stuck and could neither hold up the advance nor stay where we were alone, so we had to head back to the safety of the cloverleaf, six hundred long yards away. I watched with dismay as the armored column set off to attack the next village; then my Humvee headed back to the big intersection, bumping along on the steel tire rim, and Casey's truck followed to provide security.

As the gap between the raiding force and ourselves got wider, Route 17 immediately grew dangerous. That stretch of road, only recently so totally under our control, was turning back into bad-guy country right before my eyes. If we didn't sit on it, we didn't own it. The bad guys could easily reemerge and assemble another roadblock, plant a roadside bomb, or prepare an ambush. An officer's voice came on the radio, telling us not to try to rejoin the column because it would be too dangerous. Casey turned him off.

But when we reached the cloverleaf, we got the full NASCAR pit crew treatment from the men of the 3rd Battalion, 5th Marines, who seemed to have been waiting their whole lives to change that tire. They stripped one off of a destroyed Humvee, and with captains and first sergeants working side by side with corporals, they got that tire on in record time. It went flat, too.

While I paced nervously, they wrestled still another one onto our limping Humvee, and that one also went flat.

If we wanted to get into the fight, we had to come up with a Plan B, so we decided to leave my truck and stack everyone into Casey's single Humvee. We replaced Casey's driver, Corporal Baby, with the Panda Bear and were about ready to roll when I counted noses. We had too many people.

The Panda was at the wheel, Newbern was inside with the radios, and we definitely needed Jerry Marsh standing behind his Mk-19 automatic grenade launcher. One of the Secret Squirrels from a Human Exploitation Team also was jammed inside, along with Casey, who was in the passenger seat. That meant there was not a place for the final member of the group—me.

The only place I could figure out to ride was atop the slanted rear deck of the Humvee, so I climbed aboard and braced myself against the packs and gear that hung on the sides. Off we roared, with the CAAT-trained Panda stomping the accelerator for all the speed available from the fuel-injected diesel V8 engine. We had to cover approximately fifteen miles over a dicey road to catch up with the raiders, and this was one of those times that it was better not to ask permission. The answer would have been either "No" or "Are you insane?"

A Humvee, fifteen feet long and seven feet wide, makes an inviting target, and as the war progressed, they would sustain a high rate of loss. The trucks had not originally been made for use in combat but were supposed to be troop carriers and ambulances. The thin-skinned versions had canvaslike doors, and one of those that I rode in during a shootout back in Somalia picked up twenty-six bullet holes. I definitely preferred this newer type with its sporty seventy-thousand-dollar armor package.

As we rocketed along Route 17, Casey turned the radio back on to let the assault force know that the vehicle coming up fast behind them was us, not the enemy. Meanwhile, I discovered that my little nest was pretty nice. I was up high, relatively firmly in place, with a machine gunner over my head and a protective detail of Marines inside the vehicle. I pushed with my hands, elbows, knees, and feet, and I found enough points of resistance to convince me that this might be a stable enough platform from which to shoot.

For the Mobile Sniper Strike Team concept, I had been thinking about putting snipers aboard snazzy specialized vehicles, but those ideas never got off the drawing board. The common Humvee had been right there the whole time, and on the dash down Route 17, I concluded that the boxy truck would do just fine. *Eureka!* We had wheels, and sniper doctrine changed.

12

Decision

Sometimes, the hardest job of a sniper is *not* to pull the trigger. In an urban environment, the battlefield is a 360-degree place, with a potential threat around every corner, in every doorway and window, on every rooftop. During a pitched battle in a city, everybody is considered a possible enemy until proven otherwise, and great care must be taken to determine that a target is legitimate. You cannot, as the old dark joke claims, kill 'em all and let God sort 'em out. Professionals don't work that way, but neither are we in the business of dispensing compassion. So the scariest moments come not when someone is shooting at you but when you have to make a life-or-death decision about a person who may just be in the wrong place at the wrong time. Snipers walk that thin line of taking or preserving life every time they put a scope on a target, and some people will never know just how close I have come to shooting them dead.

Within the hour after the tire change, I was home again, out of the shepherding role and into the fight. I had waited through sandstorms, long road marches, and even that flat tire, but finally I was across the threshold and back in the war. I lay content in my new perch atop the slanted rear deck of the big Humvee, brought my sniper rifle to my cheek, and got ready to shoot.

The raiders had already finished with the town of Hajil by the time we caught up with them after changing the tire. It had been a pushover. After some sporadic firefights cleared a few pockets of guerrilla opposition, the village elder accepted some rations in trade for a weapons cache, a military radio, information about the other towns down the road, and some posters that identified different types of American vehicles—such as those parked out in the front court-yard with their big guns pointed down the street. Unfortunately, a couple of civilians had been hit during the brief fight and were being evacuated for medical treatment as we rolled by. It is horrible and frustrating when innocent people are killed in a firefight, but I steeled myself against the sight of the blood and bodies, because we could not stop the mission or lose focus. War sucks.

Ten miles later, we burst into the middle of Afak, a much bigger city of about one hundred thousand residents, where prickly palm trees needled above the ragged, dirt-brown buildings surrounded by low cement block walls.

Armored units normally avoid such narrow streets, for once inside those corridors, mobility is lost and the advantage can go over to the rocket-propelled grenades of the enemy. This time, though, we threw so much muscle into the town that the buildings shook. Abrams tanks weighing seventy tons rumbled across a bridge built to handle only automobile and truck traffic, and the rest of us followed in an armored convoy. As soon as we hit downtown, the Amtracs dropped their rear ramps and the grunts poured out to secure the nearest buildings. I heard the familiar sound of gunfire. The Iraqi soldiers and fedayeen paramilitaries were fighting back.

Our Humvee came in right behind the tactical headquarters, and Casey had the boys spill from the truck and fan out for security. I stayed in place atop the Humvee and locked into a tight shooting position, with my boots braced against the combat packs that hung around the edge of the truck. My breathing slowed, my movements were smooth and economical, and I put my mind totally at ease as I swept my scope over the rooftops, windows, and doorways of the brown buildings.

Almost immediately, I spotted motion in a third-story window about two hundred yards away. Two men were setting up an RPK light machine gun with a two-hundred-round drum of 7.62 mm bullets and pointing it toward the tactical headquarters, which was easily identifiable by the forest of radio aerials. About a third of the machine gun barrel was already sticking out of the shadowy window by the time I found them, and if they opened up on the Tac, it would be a turkey shoot and Marines would die. I knew the Marine who was in the turret of the Tac headquarters Amtrac, unaware that an enemy machine gunner was about to open up on him, but if I yelled a warning, the Iraqis would start firing. I had to act.

The two Iraqi soldiers were crowded so closely together in the window that I could not tell which one was the actual gunner, but it didn't really matter, because both of them had to die. I did a quick laser range check, brought my rifle to a stop, and saw the dimness change into a complete outline as I dialed in exactly 212 yards. They looked like the old cartoon characters Mutt and Jeff, one tall and one short. I framed Jeff, the little guy on the left, and squeezed the trigger. *Boom!* My bullet went in two inches below his heart, and the soldier's knees buckled and he slumped over, dead, exactly where he had stood, wedged between the second man and the edge of the window. Shit. Wrong guy.

When the first one went down, I could see that the other soldier was the real gunner and was about ready to open fire. But instead of shooting or jumping aside to safety, Mutt delayed for a fatal moment to look down at his fallen buddy, as if to ask, "What happened to you? You've got an unsightly hole in your chest." Then he compounded his mistake by turning his attention away from the Tac to look for me, the guy who had shot his friend. That gave me a small pause for the cause, time enough to manipulate the bolt of my rifle, see the spent cartridge pop out, and slide a new one in. I knew the windage and range were accurate, so I locked the crosshairs on the right side of his neck. *What are you looking at, asshole?* He was totally ignorant of his precarious position, standing perfectly still for a sniper, so I again squeezed the trigger and this time watched as the bullet exploded from my rifle with a muzzle velocity of more than 2,550 feet per second. It slammed the soldier completely around, a sure-kill shot, and his machine gun toppled back inside the room. The entire episode of taking out Mutt and Jeff had lasted no more than three seconds.

The loud echoes of my shots bounced around the walls, and the Marine in the Tac turret yelled, "We're taking fire!" Casey shouted back that those had been my shots and told him not to open fire.

Over the noise, I heard McCoy asking loudly and sarcastically whether I was killing anybody or just shooting for the hell of it. Even with a fight going on, the sonofabitch would not pass up a chance to rag on me.

I stayed right where I was, locked into position and glassing the other buildings. Mutt and Jeff were already history, worthy of no more thought whatsoever.

———

Seven minutes later, a sharp-eyed corporal called out, "Staff Sar'nt! I got some people on a roof a little more than two blocks away."

I followed his directions and shifted my aim up to the roof of a three-story building where two figures were moving behind a low wall. That gave them a substantial height advantage, since I was still on the truck and could only see above their thighs. That was enough, because they loomed large in my scope. One was in an Arab headdress, the other wore a scarf over his face, and both carried weapons, which meant they were fedayeen and definitely up to no good. I had them cold.

They moved toward a door that would lead them off the roof, so I centered on the closer guy, fired, and put the bullet in the middle of his chest. As he crumpled out of sight, his pal dove for cover before I could jack another round into my rifle. Damn. One got away.

Three shots, three kills, the fight was still going on, and I was in my zone, testy and irritable. I took a moment to manually reload, putting one in the chamber and four more in the magazine, then went looking for new targets.

That was when I confronted one of those dreadful do-or-die moments when I was faced with giving an unsuspecting Iraqi civilian a brush with death. Only my training and years of experience in this job, plus Casey's good sense, kept the guy alive. It would have been so easy to blow him away, knowing that nobody would ask any questions.

Casey and his security team had dragged me off the Humvee, ignoring my complaints, and took me up to a nearby roof, which put me about fifteen feet off the ground—not really very high, but every foot of altitude increased what I could see, and what I could see, I could control. We were in the center of the city, and streets wheeled out to all points of the compass. Casey posted the boys around the building, then crawled over beside me on the roof and took out his binos for a better look. Things were busy down below; files of yelling Marines were plunging into buildings to clear them and running along the sidewalks to protect the flanks of the big tanks. Instead of being terrified, residents began to venture onto the streets, and they gathered in small crowds once they realized a general bloodletting was not in progress. Soon civilian vehicles were going every which way, taking care to stay out of the sight lines of the tank gunners.

The amount of activity looked suspicious because it had neither the shape of a brewing conflict nor that of a welcoming committee. Braced solidly on the knee-high wall that edged the roof, I swept the streets below with my scope and came upon an Iraqi man standing rather calmly near a corner exactly 127 yards away, according to the laser range finder that Casey put on him. He was talking to other people moving through the area, and cars would pull up to him, then speed away after an exchange of a few words. We watched that happen over and over, and as I studied him through my scope, I saw the butt of what appeared to be a pistol sticking from his pocket. Casey saw the same thing through the powerful binos.

Elsewhere around the town, I heard the bark of machine guns, but that did not mean I could just start taking target practice. My task was to take out only legitimate threats, not to blindly murder innocent people, but deciding whom *not* to shoot isn't always easy.

This mystery man was an obvious target, but who was he? I kept him in the crosshairs and rested my finger lightly on the trigger. Was he an enemy commander who had thrown away his uniform and was now working in civilian clothes? Or was he a city councilman, a respected member of the local mosque, or perhaps the mayor? Confused citizens would naturally ask questions of such a person, and if that were the case, shooting him right in the middle of a crowd could seriously damage our cause. That pistol I thought I saw might easily be something else, maybe a wallet. There was too much doubt, so I held my fire, but I kept the rifle on him as sweat burned my eyes. This man was obviously high up the food chain and might be an officer, which would make him a big-time target for me.

I was so focused that I can still remember his face, the straight black hair and the thick Saddam-like mustache. He wore a light blue long-sleeved shirt, greenish-brown pants, and good shoes that were neither a peasant's sandals nor a soldier's military boots. No clues were available from the clothes. They were not spit-and-polish clean and showed some wear, but they seemed like a tailored Armani suit compared to what everyone around him was wearing.

I was oblivious to everything else, and in my head he had crossed the line from being a man to being a target. I left it to Casey to figure out the bigger picture. If he told me to shoot, I would, and I began to snarl at him to make the damned call before the guy simply walked away.

The minutes stretched longer, slowly expanding, and several times the sheer fatigue of concentration and the bright sun made me pull away from the scope to blink—something I always hate to do, for it gives a target time to escape. Holding this guy's life in my hands was the hardest thing I had done since the start of the war.

My mind reeled as I studied his unhurried chats with passersby, his open stance, and the easy way he was waving his hands. He looked like a leader and acted like a leader. *What if he is somebody we want on our side? I pull this trigger and all those people are going to think we murdered him in cold blood. Who the hell are you?*

Several times I took up two pounds of slack on the trigger, which only takes three pounds of pressure to fire. Each time I eased off again, in a game of cat and mouse with the mouse unaware that he was being stalked.

When the man reached into his pocket for the suspicious object that had originally attracted our attention, I tightened the trigger pressure once again. It was a cell phone, and with that, Casey decided that without a positive identification we would pass on this one. I put the rifle down and closed my eyes, panting for breath as if I had just run ten miles. My muscles had been locked in place for so long that I had cramps when I tried to unfold and stand up. The guy would not die by my hand and would never know that two Marines had watched him for fifteen solid minutes, deciding if he would live or die.

Word came to move out, and we scrambled over the edge of the roof. The Panda made the fifteen-foot drop first, and I carefully dropped my rifle to him, then jumped down. When Casey tried it, a section of the roof broke away beneath his feet and dumped the arm-waving lieutenant unceremoniously onto the dirt. He hit on his back and almost had the wind knocked out of him. The mighty Casey popped right back up, embarrassed, swearing, weapon in hand, looking ready to charge up a mountain. The only bruise was to his ego, as our XO, J-Matt Baker, was laughing his ass off and accused Casey of delaying the mission.

With the moving firefights and the action, it was easy to push into the back of my mind the fact that ordinary people lived in these homes and buildings. They were just men and women and kids who played no role in the conflict other than enduring the savagery that was passing through their neighborhoods. We had to examine each of them as a potential threat and make a decision, just as I had done with the fellow I didn't shoot. Most of the time, they were bypassed, minor characters in a great drama, as we stayed locked in on our military mission. Then a little Iraqi girl broke my concentration and sharply reminded me once again of the human side of war.

Casey and I were to take a patrol deeper into the city and were briefing the rest of our boys when an older guy walked up and asked if he could go along. "Who the fuck are you?" I demanded.

F. J. "Bing" West introduced himself, said he was from the Marine Warfighting Lab, and added that he had permission from the top dogs to roam the battlefield, giving advice and taking notes.

That did not make me happy. This was a combat patrol, and having some think-tank weenie along, particularly one of his age, only added to the things that I would have to worry about. "I don't care about their permission," I said. "They're not leading this patrol."

West smiled at my stubbornness and said, "I was at Hue in Vietnam." That made me feel a bit stupid. This guy had been in one of the biggest urban battles of the Vietnam War, and I learned later that West had also been an assistant secretary of defense at the Pentagon. The guy had more credibility than I could ever ask for, so not only did I put him on the team, I offered him a pistol to carry. He refused.

"If we have some contact, you may need it to protect yourself," I said.

"Do your job right, sniper, and we won't have to worry about my safety," West replied. After the war, Bing West and retired Marine Major General Ray Smith, a walking legend in the Corps, would write *The March Up*, one of the definitive books on the conflict in Iraq.

But in the Marines, it is unseemly to give anyone too much respect, so we dubbed West and Smith "the Muppets." For the rest of the war, I would occasionally see them riding around the battlefield, a couple of real Marines easily distinguishable by their confiscated vehicle: the yellow SUV that had once been the property of the defeated general of the 51st Mechanized Division back in Basra.

The patrol set out with the Panda Bear on point, Casey at the rear, and me in the middle with our Muppet and five other Marines. Since bullets follow walls, we kept about three feet away from the sandy buildings and moved very deliberately. Not fast, but safe. Slow is smooth, smooth is fast.

About twenty minutes later, we found a multistory house with a high roof from which I could increase my view, and Chief Warrant Officer Steve Blandford, one of our translators, approached a man standing behind a metal gate. The man, in his midthirties, agreed to let us go up and swung open the gate in the five-foot-high wall that surrounded the house. Although we had permission, we all remained combat wary, because we did not know who else might be behind that door. We left some of the guys outside for security while Casey, the Panda, Blandford, and I went in.

The place was modest, but the furniture was clean, although old. Colorful plates flashed brightly in a china closet, and a small piano was against one wall. Grandpa, in a long robe, was seated in the main room, and Grandma showed only a mild interest in the four Marines who were moving through her home, carrying weapons. Three kids played on wide rugs in the cool dimness, and a big-eyed little girl looked at me with a smile that could break a heart. The impulse was to lay down my weapon and comfort her, knowing she was disturbed by the big foreign men with guns in her home. I could almost see the same look on the faces of my own daughters in a similar situation, and I know I would want the soldier to be gentle with my children.

We did a tactical sweep as we went along, checking out a kitchen at the rear and a couple of bedrooms with mattresses on rug-covered floors. The family had been warned by Saddam's henchmen that Marines slaughter everyone they see, but they were treating us like neighbors. They made welcoming gestures, and although they spoke a language I didn't understand, their attitude was totally friendly. Amid that kindness, we had to fight our emotions to remain alert.

We went out the rear door and then up a stairwell to the roof. I did a brief visual check of the surrounding area but found nothing of interest, so we retraced our steps.

I could not help feeling that we were intruding into a private sanctuary. These good people were not frightened and were obviously glad we had arrived in Afak; they acted if they truly had been liberated. I thought about the men I had killed earlier that day and persuaded myself to believe they had bullied this and other families for years. I wanted to tell them not to worry, because I had smoke-checked some of the neighborhood thugs and those bad guys wouldn't be coming back, but I couldn't, and I wouldn't.

On the way out, I paused a moment to reach down and pat the head of the little girl in the living room. It was my first feel-good moment of the war, and it made me homesick. I was happy to leave those people in peace and said a quick and private prayer that they would stay safe. But when I stepped back into the sunlight, I had my warrior face back on.

Our engineers had cleared the bridge at the eastern edge of town, and it was time to move out.

13

A Bench in a War

It was only a little after ten o'clock in the morning. I had already killed three enemy soldiers that day and was on the road to another fight. In the old days, a sniper never moved this fast.

I was back in my little nest aboard the armored Humvee, with my boots braced in the cargo nets to keep me from being thrown off if the Panda Bear made a sharp turn or one of his jaw-breaking sudden stops. Our backpacks, lashed to the outside of the truck, gave me a false sense of security, as if those little bits of cloth were going to stop a round. I did not feel invincible but was confident as we dashed down Route 17 toward our next target town, a place called Al Budayr. Things were going well, and I was right where I wanted to be.

We hit the village fast and hard, with Cobra helicopters taking out some antiaircraft artillery and the CAATs cutting off the escape routes. While an infantry company halted on the outskirts of town to give supporting fire, McCoy took an armored spearhead straight downtown.

Casey and I paused to plant the Main headquarters safely outside of the city, then sped into town, where civilians in a shabby open-air market watched as the Panda Bear skidded to a halt. Our tanks and

Amtracs were parked with their heavy guns pointed down every street and alley.

"You're late," McCoy growled as I climbed down. He was pacing near his command truck, talking into his radio. Saddam Hussein smiled benevolently at us from a large, tattered poster, and sunlight glittered off empty brass shell casings all over the pavement.

"How's that, boss?" I asked.

"I just dropped a *hajji* about two hundred yards down there," the colonel said, pointing down a side road. "I think I hit one or two, but more got away."

"Sounds like you're getting slow," I said with a smirk, dishing back some of his earlier sarcasm.

"How so?" McCoy rose to the bait.

"You let a few get away."

He chuckled. "Remember I'm shooting with iron sights here. Not everybody has a scope."

"Don't hate me because I'm good, boss. I'll glass the area and see if I can clean up your trash."

"Yeah. Do that." Our game continued.

The colonel's Humvee was in the middle of the square, a great location for me, so I climbed onto the hood and wiggled into a shooting position. I braced against the windshield, and the machine gunner in the turret pointed to where they had last seen the enemy troops. This was an incredible change in the way snipers worked; instead of being disguised or hidden in the dirt and the dark, I was sprawled out on the truck in broad daylight smack in the middle of the town square. Being visible to the enemy had ceased being a factor, because this was not a clandestine mission, and I was just one Marine among many involved in this fight.

I did a systematic search starting about twenty yards in front of me, scanning from one side of the street to the other, from the roofs to the ground. Civilians continually moved through the sight of my scope, and I had to decide the fate of each individual then and there. Was he a threat or not? The midday sun glared from the buildings and paved streets, but I could not stop working just because my eye felt like it was about to fall out.

After about fifteen minutes, I found something in a second-story window of what looked like an old fortress, and I fastened onto it. What had been just a moving shadow solidified into the dark image of an Iraqi soldier with an AK-47. I made a SWAG (Scientific Wild-Ass Guess) on the distance and dialed 430 yards into the scope, slowed my breathing, took up my trigger slack, and waited for his next move. This guy was already dead but just didn't know it yet. When he moved more fully into the window to point his rifle at the Marines in the street below, I smoke-checked him where he stood, and the big round kicked him back into the room. Only then did I take out the range finder and laser the window, which was exactly 441 yards away, almost exactly a quarter of a mile.

"Coughlin!" McCoy barked, looking up from his radio. "Stop shooting my targets and get out of my sandbox. Go find your own place to shoot."

I ignored him and glassed the area a bit longer to be sure there were no more threats, then politely obeyed and walked off, satisfied that I had one-upped the Boss.

I found Casey around the corner setting up protection for an Intelligence and Psychological Operations (Psy Ops) team that was using giant loudspeakers to blast recorded messages in Arabic, urging civilians to cooperate with the Americans and not to be afraid.

The technique worked all too well, because a growing crowd pressed in around them, wanting to voice complaints and point out suspicious people and settle some personal grudges. It looked like the bar scene from *Star Wars*. There was nothing that I could do to help, or wanted to.

By now, my sniper cover was completely blown, and I was walking around town with my rifle in my arms, as out in the open as a door-to-door magazine salesman. It made no difference at all on this new type of battleground.

Nearby, a tin awning hanging out from the wall of a shabby shop dropped a rectangle of shade over a battered white wooden bench, and I took advantage of the moment to escape the hot direct sun. A half dozen Iraqi men sat on a nearby stoop, smoking cigarettes and watching me closely, jabbering excitedly and pointing to the big sniper rifle and its scope. I nodded a greeting to them, and they nodded back.

Talk about being exposed.

I got back to work by putting my boot on the bench, then brought up my rifle, rested the fatty part of the back of my bicep on my knee, and leaned forward into a good tight position. I made certain there was no bone-on-bone contact, such as elbow to kneecap; that might feel solid, but it is an unstable platform because of slippage. The way I was knotted up, I controlled all of my movements. I glassed the area and visually got to know who was out in the street, scoping out every new person who appeared. After a while, confident that it was under control, I lowered the rifle and sat on the bench, taking only occasional looks through the scope at the street scene if something caught my interest. Periodically I would check out my little fan club on the nearby stoop, and they watched me right back.

Our prime rule during training is to become part of your surroundings, to stay hidden, and never expose yourself. Stealth is everything. On some missions, I had worn the traditional ghillie suit, a camouflage trick handed down over the generations from Scots gamekeepers, who invented them to make counting game and catching poachers easier. Vegetation plucked from local plants is pushed into burlap netting sewn all over an old fatigue uniform, and the irregular strips and leaves totally break up the human outline to help the sniper vanish into the background. Sniper training requires that you be able to sneak up within two hundred yards of spotters with binoculars and fire a blank round without being seen. Wearing my ghillie suit, I was the invisible man.

Now I wasn't hiding at all but rode atop a truck and operated openly within a congested urban environment. In such plain view, I was the subject of an animated conversation among the six men who had started talking at me. I warmed to these guys and even traded cigarettes with one, but I never trusted them for a second. Who knew if a weapon might appear from beneath one of those long robes?

"Hey, dude," I called out to Casey after glassing the area again. "Look at this. I'm dominating an entire avenue of approach, just me, from a park bench, like on a Sunday afternoon." I felt like an eight-hundred-pound gorilla with a gun.

Later that afternoon, with Al Budayr in our hands, we went looking for information.

Marines blew a hole in a wall to get into the local police station, where they released prisoners and picked up notebooks filled with information and photographs. A cache of weapons was found in a schoolroom.

When the regional headquarters of Saddam's political machine, the hated Ba'ath Party, was discovered, Casey and I accompanied

Steve Blandford, the same smart chief warrant officer who had worked with us in the unexpected visit inside the Iraqi home an hour earlier, into the two-story lime-green building. It turned out to be a gold mine of intelligence, for it was packed with more logbooks than we could count, and Casey even retrieved the appointment and address books from the mayor's office. Account ledgers noted payments and names. A detailed sketch of the town's defensive positions, no more than a few weeks old and frequently modified, was discovered. Beneath the empty eyes on the posters of Saddam that were in every room, we hauled away a trove of information about his corrupt and savage government.

After we left, a certain junior officer decided to bring in a squad and secure the building. Corporal Dustin Campbell, who had helped me spot targets in Afak, was moving stealthily from room to room with another Marine when they heard glass breaking and the noise of someone walking. They went to full alert and set up shooting positions to take out the clumsy enemy solider they thought was blundering toward them. A window crashed nearby, and they tensed for the confrontation—but it was Officer Bob who suddenly walked into their sights. He had gotten separated and was entertaining himself by throwing rocks through windowpanes like some adolescent prankster.

Our mission to open Route 17 as a supply corridor between the isolated major Marine units was a total success, and we had crashed through Bonus Town, Hajil, Afak, and now Al Budayr, four towns with an estimated combined population of over two hundred thousand people. By moving aggressively and quickly, our tanks, the Amtracs, armored Humvees, and about seven hundred Marines simply ran over those little towns. Taking them aggressively had minimized casualties all around. Our audacious use of force and surprise became known as the Afak Drill, and most of the bad guys chose to run rather than face us.

However, the success of a single unit did not mean the entire war was going well. We had crossed the border from Kuwait into Iraq nine days ago, and despite making major advances, by March 29 things were not moving with the lightning speed that had been envisioned and was needed. The Army was having serious problems out in the desert, Basra still defied the British, and exposed supply convoys were raw meat for guerrilla attacks. With the Marines, our tanks were only just beginning to roll with the needed resupply vehicles over to Task Force Tarawa, and the 5th Marine Regiment was still bogged down in back of us, at Diwaniyah. Our raids along Route 17 had been successful, but the offensive was falling days behind schedule.

Snipers are always looking for an edge, because we don't like to fight fair. So when Casey found me that evening after things had calmed down, I was recording my day's work in my sniper's logbook. I now had six kills since the start of the war, and I added specific notes about the weather conditions, the range, directions of the targets, windage, and a few other things. Racking up the new kills did not make me feel proud. Snipers hate what ultimately happens when we pull the trigger, but we understand that we are important fixtures in something much larger than ourselves. Out of professional habit, I entered my observations and results in the logbook. Over time, when we compare those notes, the books can reveal patterns of enemy behavior and highlight their mistakes, so we can kill more of them.

We shared some food—packages of nasty MREs. Casey was as excited as a pup, having been in the middle of some firefights, and he was clearly over the hump of worrying whether he could measure up as a combat Marine. "Is this all there is?" he asked. "I want more! Gimme more!"

"You want to fall off another roof?"

"Asshole. You know what I mean."

He said that about two dozen prisoners had been captured that day and that maybe twenty bad guys had been killed. Ever the engineer, he pointed out, "You got four of the twenty today, Jack. Twenty percent of the total for the whole battalion. Not bad."

I put away the logbook and told him that I felt as if I had finally been taken off the leash and that I was happy to be contributing to the fight, able to see some shit and do some shit. There was no telling what was going to happen next, but I sensed target-rich environments ahead. "If this keeps up, I'm going to come out of this with some hellacious numbers."

Life had been a lot simpler many years ago, when I first joined the Corps and was pulling duty as a crossing guard at Camp Lejeune in North Carolina. Simpler, but nowhere near as interesting.

That night, we decided that we no longer wanted to go into battle with Casey's driver, Corporal Baby, because he had not measured up to our standards. That would not do, so we picked Corporal Dustin Campbell as his replacement. Campbell was one of the best riflemen in the company and had impressed me with his exceptional eyesight and courage during the recent fighting.

Campbell's only problem was that he talked back to his superiors, which made him an even more natural fit for our team. Everyone recognized that Casey and I were in charge, but we encouraged what might be termed a free-flowing exchange of views. It not only taught the boys to be mentally quick, but if a guy could not hold up under our verbal abuse and dish it right back, how the hell was he going to stand up to somebody trying to kill him?

"I don't know how to do this," Campbell protested the first time we put him behind the wheel of the Humvee. "I'm just a small-town boy from Mississippi!"

Lieutenant Casey Kuhlman, a product of intense Marine Corps leadership training on how to deal sensitively with the concerns of his men, told Campbell to just shut the fuck up and drive.

14

A Call Home

Sunday, March 30, began with a brilliant sunrise and bad news from home. We had bedded down outside of Al Budayr after the long day of fighting on Saturday, and the memory of the smiling little Iraqi girl I had touched on the head had lingered with me overnight. The thought made me homesick. I missed my family.

As dawn broke, I went to find Paperboy—John Koopman, our embedded newspaper reporter from the *San Francisco Chronicle*— who had been receiving periodic e-mails for me on his laptop. All my sisters and their families, my mom, my mother-in-law, my kids, and my friends had sent warm messages, but there had been nothing from Kim.

Paperboy said there were no e-mails for me today, but he lent me the satellite telephone that he used to file his stories, and I stepped away to find some privacy as I dialed my home number far, far away. The call all the way from the battle zone to our house in 29 Palms went through without a problem, an amazing feat of technology, but the telephone was answered by the babysitter. Kim was once again away at school, she said. Cassie and Ashley filled me in on what was happening in school and at day care, and their happy voices were sounds from a different planet, a balm to me in troubled times. The babysitter sounded flustered, though, falling all over herself with apologies that my wife was not at home. The connection terminated with a forlorn little *beep*. I returned the phone to Koopman and walked off to find a quiet piece of desert.

Smack in the middle of the thousands of men of the 1st Marine Division, I felt isolated and alone, as if I were the only person out there on the desert sands. I had called home six times since I left California, and my wife had been there twice. I'd had more conversations with the babysitter than with her.

Then I thought about the time difference. California is eleven hours behind Iraq, so since it was about 6:30 A.M. on Sunday where I was standing, it would be 5:30 P.M. Saturday at home. Suddenly I realized that the babysitter had said my wife was at school, but I knew she didn't have any classes on Saturday night! Why wasn't she home with the kids? Was she out at a happy hour with some other teachers? Was she off at a library? Or was it something else? Shivers went up my spine. To me the word "wife" no longer seemed a term of endearment, home was on the far side of the world, and there was nothing I could do at the moment about the obviously out-of-whack domestic situation.

I was feeling crushed by demoralizing doubt. Killing enemy soldiers had not bothered me, but not hearing from Kim did. Churchill once called his own deep depression the "black dog," and I could hear that same sort of drooling beast panting hotly in my own ear. Hell of a way to start a day.

I needed to shake up my brain. Too much emotion was creeping into my consciousness, and I could not operate as a shooter that way.

Jack (right) and Casey (left) are outside Ba'ath Party compound in Al Budayr.
(Courtesy of Gunnery Sergeant R. P. Simpson)

Jack on the plane to Kuwait.
(Courtesy of Major B. T. Mangan)

Sergeant Jerry Marsh is at his machine gun in the turret of Casey's Humvee in the streets of Baghdad.
(Courtesy of Major B. T. Mangan)

First Sergeants
Norm Arias (right)
and Guy Rosbough (left)
rest atop a mountain
of money after we
break up a bank robbery.
(Courtesy of Major B. T. Mangan)

Sergeant Major "Uncle Dave" Howell.
(Courtesy of Major B. T. Mangan)

Our secret chemical
identification specialist—
Little Bastard.
(Courtesy of Major B. T. Mangan)

Lieutenant Colonel Bryan P. McCoy (right) addresses the men of the Bull at Camp Ripper, Kuwait. Jack is on the left, and Casey, wearing glasses, is in the middle. *(Courtesy of Major B. T. Mangan)*

Corporal Mark Evnin at Camp Ripper, Kuwait. *(Courtesy of Staff Sergeant M. S. Mattson)*

Jack shooting from atop of Casey's Humvee, Afak.
(Courtesy of Gunnery Sergeant R. P. Simpson)

Marines of the 3/4 Battalion, the Bull, move on Ad Diwaniyah.
(Courtesy of Staff Sergeant B. R. Bochenski)

Colonel Steve Hummer, commanding officer of the 7th Marines, gives the order to attack into Baghdad to Lieutenant Colonel McCoy (left), and Major J. M. Baker (right). (*Courtesy of Staff Sergeant B. R. Bochenski*)

Jack throws a grenade in Az Zafaraniyah.
(*Courtesy of Gary Knight*)

Casey goes over a wall in Az Zafaraniyah.
(*Courtesy of Gary Knight*)

A column of smoke from an air strike rises on the far side of the Diyala Bridge. *(Courtesy of Major B. T. Mangan)*

The Diyala Bridge, with the body of an Iraqi fighter. *(Courtesy of Major B. T. Mangan)*

The new bridge we built across the Diyala River. *(Courtesy of Gunnery Sergeant R. P. Simpson)*

The statue of Saddam Hussein, as seen between U.S. Marines, moments before it is pulled down.
(Courtesy of Major B. T. Mangan)

Cheering Iraqis gather before the statue falls.
(Courtesy of Staff Sergeant B. R. Bochenski)

Iraqis with Casey's flag at the base of the fallen statue.
(Courtesy of Major B. T. Mangan)

Lieutenant Colonel McCoy (center) and Sergeant Major Howell at a memorial service for fallen Marines in Iraq. *(Courtesy of Major B. T. Mangan)*

Jack is presented his Bronze Star by Major J. M. Baker, 29 Palms, California. *(Courtesy of Lance Corporal H. E. Laredo)*

As a sniper, you are supposed to be coldhearted and must be able to control yourself, no matter what is going on. But you are still human. If you don't have feelings and emotions, then you step over the line and are just a psychotic killer. It can be a difficult balancing act.

No one was allowed inside my head while I worked, and I had spent almost twenty years building my invincible gunslinger persona, and I never let my guard down in front of anybody, not even Casey. It was okay for me to bitch about other things, but I always stopped short of exposing any personal feelings.

So although I listened to other people's problems on a daily basis out in the field, there was really nobody there for me, which was as it should be. Now there probably was no one at home, either. We all have a private room in our soul for our deepest secrets, but I have a whole warehouse down there in which I keep my personal stuff, because I carry so much of it. Since I had no control over what might be happening back home, I put my girls safely on a shelf that was out of harm's way and turned my growing anger and frustration onto the soldiers of Saddam Hussein, closing off any thoughts other than those directly related to where I was and to my job. Life was easier when my worldview was narrowed to what I could see.

So far in this war I had fired six shots and had six kills, exactly the right ratio. I considered the ill-trained, poorly led soldiers of Iraq to be hamburger in my scope, practically begging me to kill them, and I was more than ready to grant that wish.

Then came the second slice of Sunday-morning bad news, and we learned that the war was about to grind to a dead stop for three full weeks! Coalition forces all across Iraq were to stop in place for a twenty-one-day "operational pause" to refit and secure the exposed lines of supply. McCoy was summoned to take a helicopter back to regimental headquarters for an official briefing.

We were stunned and almost felt the earth tilting beneath our boots, because we could not understand the reasoning behind the decision. We still had plenty of supplies and had just ripped through four towns in a single day to kick open a vital supply line. So what was the problem? To us, stopping made no sense at all, but orders are orders.

Now we believed that dusty, nowhere Al Budayr on Route 17 was to be our home for the next month, so we planned to go back into the town and set up shop in the old Ba'ath Party offices. McCoy could be the mayor for a while, and we could erase all traces of the Saddam regime. We would saturate the area with patrols for security, maybe reopen schools, get the utilities running, and prove to the locals that the dictator and his men were no longer to be feared.

It was a good hearts-and-minds program, but I found it all to be totally depressing. My boys were trained as scouts and snipers, not carpenters or bricklayers, and we had come to fight, not to occupy. Yes, we wanted to help the people, but we also needed to get on with the real job. Having my boys put down their rifles to do reconstruction work would be like hitching up a thoroughbred racehorse to pull a beer wagon.

And personally, the sooner I finished in Iraq, the sooner I could get back home, and a lot could be happening back there in an extra thirty days, none of it good. I was struggling to keep apart the two phases of my life, the professional and the personal.

Thank God that op-pause nightmare only lasted a few hours.

I was checking the Main's defenses when Gunnery Sergeant Don Houston came running up with good news. "Jack!" he announced with a big smile. "It's off!"

"What's off?"

"The stupid fucking op-pause. I just heard it on the radio."

"No shit?" I thought he was trying to be funny, and I was in no mood to get excited about a joke.

"No shit, Jack." He threw a little jab at me, tapping my shoulder. "You get to kill more people tomorrow." I could almost feel the monkeys jumping off my back.

Immediately we went back to being Marines instead of administrators. We received orders to collect the noncombat battalion units that we had stripped off for the Afak Drills, then move up to the big cloverleaf intersection and prepare to attack into Ad Diwaniyah.

As we returned along Route 17, small groups of civilians emerged from their homes to wave, a hopeful sign that they were beginning to believe that Saddam and his thugs were finally gone and that they could perhaps have a brighter future. I was riding atop the Humvee, with my rifle across my lap, watching them watch us, when among those standing in the crowd outside of Afak I recognized someone: straight black hair, light-blue-and-white-striped shirt, greenish-brown pants, white shoes, and a big mustache. It was the guy who had been down in the street, the man I had come within a kitten's whisker of killing. He saw me, too, and there was a strange moment of recognition as our eyes locked and he looked at the big sniper rifle. I patted the weapon and gave him a look of "Man, you don't know how lucky you are." He returned a look that seemed to say he understood how close he had come to dying, and then gave a slight nod, perhaps a silent "Thanks for sparing me."

Over the next twenty-four hours, the 5th Marines pulled out of Ad Diwaniyah, heading farther north. Our first units arrived at the cloverleaf before their final trucks left, so there was no break in the chain.

We smelled the place even before we could see it, an overwhelming stench of rot and filth that grew even worse as the hours passed and the afternoon temperatures rose. Bugs of biblical-plague proportions attacked us, along with swarms of blackflies and gnats and battalions of fleas. Good God, what an awful place. It had been the landfill for the city, and stinking trash was everywhere. As the day passed, it rained, and the gathering pools of water turned the disgusting area into stinking mud syrup. When the rain stopped, the saunalike humid heat returned, as did the bugs.

The final night of March was one of the most miserable points of the war for us, for the flies became absolutely unbearable. Marines looked as if they were having fits, flailing their arms over their heads as they swatted the flies while creepy little bug feet walked on their necks and snacked on their skin. Some men put on the full MOPP gear for protection.

We looked forward to morning, when we could attack the city, preferring battle to the purgatory of that stinking cloverleaf.

15

April Fool's Day

A sniper usually sees the face of his target. Although that target may be a thousand yards away, with the scope on my rifle it is as if I can reach out and touch him with my fingertips. While targets look like human beings, they remain targets, and there is no personal attachment whatsoever. Feeling a personal kinship of any sort risks having second thoughts. So it came as a shock when I met someone whom I had shot not once, but twice, and had seen him fall. Normally, that would mean that particular target was very dead. However, that was not the case with my friend Achmed, the only man I ever shot who lived through the experience.

April 1 was the twelfth day of the war, and we launched our attack on Ad Diwaniyah, leaving the cloverleaf shortly after daylight, with the tanks in the lead and two companies of infantry fanning out in support. Despite all of the noise we made, we still caught the Iraqis by surprise. Some of the enemy soldiers were still resting among the date palm groves in snug holes in which they had placed rugs and carpeting. Others were having breakfast in their mud huts, and we would later find warm food and cups of tea still on tables, with canteens and helmets and weapons nearby. Just because our predecessors in the area, the 5th Marines, had not gone in after them, they thought they were safe from us, too. Big mistake. We were the Bull.

When our tanks came highballing down the road, an Iraqi lookout jumped from his observation post and ran like hell to warn his friends, but a flash of machine gun fire cut him down after just a few steps. In minutes, our artillery went psycho and rained explosives on the enemy positions. Tank cannons, TOW missiles, heavy machine guns, and that most lethal weapon of all, the Marine infantryman, joined the fight, and gunfire lit the dark, hazy sky of the early morning. The Marines tore through bunkers, trench lines, and palm trees and shot any Iraqi soldier who tried to resist. As usual, the fedayeen ran away before things got heavy.

I was again atop my truck, and after five minutes of scoping out the mud huts on the outskirts of the city, I spotted an enemy rifleman fighting from a foxhole exactly 286 meters to the south. Easy shot, so I smoke-checked him, *bam*, and he was dead, his body twitching for a few more moments while his internal systems shut down. I noted the time, 7:47 A.M., on a green page of my sniper's log and got back to work. The place was as noisy as a steel factory; rocket-propelled grenades whooshed through the morning air and detonated on impact, and our tanks answered with volleys from their big main guns, heavy rounds that moved at a mile per second and seemed to lift the earth where they struck.

My second kill of the day was nothing less than a quick-draw showdown. We were taking Ad Diwaniyah block by block against bitter opposition, and the Panda drove us deeper into the urban area, bringing our Humvee to a halt near a group of Marines who were advancing through a cluster of huts. An Iraqi soldier suddenly appeared from between two buildings right beside the road, his weapon at the ready with the butt stock to his shoulder and the barrel pointed slightly down. I had just gotten out of the truck and was in the same basic position. This was no faraway target but a man standing only about seventy-five yards away, point-blank range for my sniper rifle. He hesitated for a moment, perhaps startled by all of the Marines in the area, and then, too late, his eyes locked on mine. That brief flicker of uncertainty cost him his life. I killed him before he could get off a shot. In such situations, only an amateur would dawdle. Professionals shoot.

As the front line advanced, the Panda moved us cautiously forward another few hundred yards to a bridge that curved to the right, arcing over another road that led into the dark heart of the besieged town. Our guys were already fighting at the other end of the span, and I was to help control this end and block any flanking movement.

I went back onto our Humvee and anchored myself into the now-familiar solid prone shooting position to get a better look at a group of scruffy mud and cinder-block buildings that lined an area studded with palm trees. I slowly glassed the rooftops, doorways, windows, and alleys, the four places where death likes to hide in towns and cities.

The temperature was a mild seventy-eight degrees, but the rising sun had taken on its normal fierce brightness and bounced off the light-colored walls with such intensity that it was like staring into high-beam headlights.

Suddenly, three targets wearing green uniforms and carrying AK-47 rifles broke from cover and ran full speed from right to left. These were straight-up soldiers, not civilians, and I kept my scope on them as palm trees danced through my field of vision, blocking my view.

The Bear did a laser range-check on the buildings where the men were heading: about 470 yards. A mirage shimmered from right to left, telling me that a slight wind was moving across the battlefield, and I fine-tuned an adjustment to compensate.

I had kept the crosshairs on them while dialing the scope, and when one paused at the corner of a building, at two minutes before ten o'clock in the morning, I put my crosshairs on his chest and squeezed the trigger. Targets rarely remain still in combat, however, and he moved at the last moment, spoiling a perfect shot. Instead of a center-mass hit, my bullet went through his throat, and the impact catapulted him back into the street.

Then came Achmed. I had just jacked another round into the chamber and was continuing to scan the area when he dashed from cover, running away but still carrying his rifle. Since I have no compunction about shooting a man in the back, I instantly fired and put a bullet in him. Somehow, perhaps just with forward momentum, he kept running, so I shot him again, and this time he went down and rolled out of view.

"I can't believe I missed," I told Panda.

"You didn't miss the second time, boss. I saw him go down," the Bear confirmed. I spent another ten minutes searching for the third soldier, who had vanished.

A little later, things quieted down and we got back into the Humvee and moved out, with me complaining the whole time. "I had the crosshairs right on that sucker. I had him! How could he have kept going?" It was unsettling, and I knew that my fellow Marines would soon be riding me about it—"Coughlin missed!" McCoy would have a field day with this. It was a major fuckup.

We were taking a break back at the Main when a rogue RPG whooshed overhead, which was enough to convince Officer Bob that the headquarters was under attack. I yelled for him to calm down, but his frenzy startled one of the Amtrac machine gunners, who opened up with a full automatic burst and thoroughly killed a nearby donkey. I scrambled to get things back in order, and J-Matt Baker, the battalion XO, gave the donkey's bewildered owner some rations as payment.

Casey and I went forward again, and I found two of my snipers, Corporal Mark Evnin and Sergeant Dino Moreno, standing along-side Master Sergeant Bob Johnson from Bravo Tanks, studying the wrecked hulk of a civilian bus about a half mile to the northwest. Smoke oozed from the blown-out windows.

"Somebody's over there, boss," Evnin told me. "Been getting some occasional fire. Maybe they're in the bus."

Top Johnson figured three Marine snipers were more than enough to handle whoever was in the bus, so he went back to his tanks, leaving us with a succinct instruction: "Kill 'em."

I climbed on the nearest Humvee and glassed the smoking carcass of the bus. For the first time in the war, I was working with fellow snipers, and we lapsed into the arcane sniper-spotter dialogue. Moreno was glassing an adjoining area, and Evnin acted as the spotter for both of us.

After three minutes of searching specific sectors, being patient and waiting for a mistake, I saw a shadow shift in the bus, and then the outline of a rifle appeared, an enemy sniper rising up for a shot. We had lased the bus at exactly 817 yards, more than eight football fields away.

"Mark," I said softly to Evnin, "I think I have movement in the bus, in the left third of the target zone."

Evnin swung his powerful scope around and responded, "I see the bus."

"Third of the way down, from back to front, left side, fifth seat, window side."

"I see it."

"Does he have a weapon?" I asked for confirmation that I wasn't looking at a civilian.

"Sure does."

"What's the wind?"

"Three minutes left."

"Elevation?"

"Eight plus one." The conversation was brief, automatic, emotionless, professional. Moreno kept watch on the surrounding area, undistracted by our discovery.

I fine-tuned my scope to match Evnin's numbers. "OK. I'll hold an inch above center chest."

"Roger. On scope," Mark confirmed, holding his spotting scope steady on the bus. My spotter had the target.

"On target," I said. The shooter had the target, and everything was in place. I exhaled some breath and tightened on the trigger. I had this sucker as sure as if we were on the practice range. He was as good as dead anyway, for he might somehow live through a meeting with one sniper, but not two, and never three.

"Fire when ready," Mark said.

My rifle barked and my shoulder took the recoil.

"Hit, center chest, target down," Evnin reported when the soldier was staggered by the big bullet and fell out of sight. Mark did not lower his scope. "Good shot, boss."

"Good windage," I told him. "Dead on." That was as high a compliment as one pro would give another. There were no high-fives or end zone celebrations, for we were professionals. We had done what we had been trained to do, so we expected both the cooperation and outcome. We switched back to assisting Moreno scan the rest of the area.

Inwardly, I was proud of Evnin. Mark was a stocky kid with brownish hair, an eager, happy-go-lucky youngster from Vermont who was hardcore into becoming a sniper. His talent level wasn't the best, because he had not yet finished sniper school when the war broke out, but he had worked so hard and had such an infectious enthusiasm that when my scout/sniper platoon went to Iraq, he came along with us. He would complete his training when we got back to the States, though it would be odd for a student to have kills to his credit before officially winning the title of sniper.

As it turned out, that was not to be. Within a few days, Mark Evnin would die in a firefight.

The battalion had finished with Ad Diwaniyah by lunchtime, having no casualties of our own but killing at least ninety-two Iraqi soldiers and taking another fifty-six as prisoners. The actual butcher's bill could have easily been three or four times what was reported, but we were intentionally lowballing the numbers, minimizing enemy casualties instead of maximizing them to avoid the Vietnam body-count habit that created unrealistic numbers and expectations.

Once again back at the Main, I was gulping water and washing some of the thick dust off my skin when a Marine stopped by to tell me the security platoon had picked up some prisoners over in the area by the bridge, including a guy who had been hit by what appeared to be sniper rounds. The Panda and I headed for the prisoner pen and found the wounded man sitting on the ground with his legs crossed and plastic flexcuffs shackling his wrists.

He was no more than twenty years old, and his cheeks were bare, as if he were just starting to shave. He had taken one bullet in the left arm, and the second had penetrated his back and emerged out of the top of his left breast. Somehow the big slug went through without ripping out his heart or hitting anything major. He was not even bleeding hard.

I checked the wounds, and they looked about the right size. Was this the guy I had shot? I grabbed a nearby interpreter and asked the boy how he had been wounded. The Iraqi refused to talk, and his dark eyes flashed in anger, but I saw some fright, too. I put on my war face, leaned close to let my own eyes pierce his, shouted a few choice expletives, then had the interpreter ask again. The kid was growing pale, and this time he answered, saying he had been trying to surrender when he was shot. Bullshit. He still had on his boots and had been carrying a rifle while he was running. "Where?" I wanted to know, and he described the area. Same place.

He said the first bullet hit his left arm and sent him stumbling forward, off balance. Then another shot went through his shoulder. I asked why, if he wanted to give up, he didn't throw down his rifle and take off his boots. He said if he tried to do that, then his own people would have killed him. I decided to ease up on him. I had the interpreter tell the prisoner that I was the one who had shot him. The Iraqi soldier glanced at my big M40A1 rifle and nodded.

Weird, conflicting emotions swept over me. I was glad that I had

not missed a target, but I was also strangely delighted that this guy
had survived. Never had I felt personal responsibility for the safety of
an enemy combatant, so this sudden kinship was unexpected, and it
was kind of cool.

The fighting was over for the day, so I didn't want him to die. I felt
he had earned a new lease on life. I called him "Achmed," because
I didn't know his real name. By doing so, I crossed the invisible line
of humanizing my enemy.

Next, I had Achmed carried to the front of a long line of other
wounded Iraqi soldiers at an aid station, and I told the doctor, an old
friend, to patch him up. "He's the only one I've ever shot that lived
through the experience," I said, and the doc balked.

He apparently thought that I wanted to make sure the kid didn't
survive much longer in order to keep my record intact. No, I explained, just the opposite. This new patient was one lucky bastard,
so I wanted him to receive special treatment. The interpreter explained to the soldier, "You're hooked up, man. You're a celebrity."

He began to lose that defiant look. As the doctor removed the shirt,
pumped in some anesthetic, and started to work, I stood there, talking
quietly to the boy.

GAS . . . GAS . . . GAS!! The dreaded warning roared through
the area in a hasty echo of shouts, and Marines dropped whatever
they were doing to put on their gas masks. Achmed, flat on his back
but not unconscious, grew frightened when we covered our heads
with the big hoods and goggles, and we must have looked to him
like a bunch of unworldly, blunt-nosed elephants. I called out to the
Panda, my words muffled, to bring in one of the masks we had taken
off some dead Iraqi officers earlier in the day. He was back in moments and tossed me the mask; I worked it down over Achmed's

face, seeing a look of pure gratitude. The other wounded Iraqis had no protection.

I removed the mask when the "All clear" was given after the false alarm. When the doctor finished working, the kid was moved to a cot. I knelt beside him and had the interpreter explain that he was going to be all right and that I would be back to see him later and bring him some food. He was woozy but never took his eyes off of me.

I went back to work at the Main for a while, then grabbed some coffee and rations and returned to the prisoner aid station. Achmed was gone, having been taken by the military police to another prisoner cage in the rear, so I tossed aside the MRE rations and dined instead on fried Spam with my friends. It was disappointing, but it was war.

After chow, I was briefed on where we were going the next day, cleaned my weapons, and settled in to get some sleep on another cold night in Iraq, banishing Achmed from my mind. He was a onetime thing, and while I was glad that he survived, my job was not to coddle enemy soldiers but to kill them. If we ever faced each other again on a battlefield, I would shoot him again without hesitation.

I now had ten kills in Iraq. Then there was Achmed, who was blessed and protected by his merciful Allah. Should have been eleven, but things had not been going quite right all day.

Earlier, I almost got my foot shot off by accident, and Casey almost committed suicide by RPG.

Gunny Don Houston and I were on patrol along a canal when a gunshot snapped out. The round impacted right at my feet, punching up a small column of dirt an inch from my boot.

"Oops," said Houston.

"Oops?" I yelled at my buddy. "What the fuck do you mean, *oops?*"

"OK. Oops, sorry."

That broke the tension, and I cracked a smile. He had accidentally pulled the trigger on his rifle, but it had been pointed at the ground. I told him to forget it—after all, shit happens in war—but I came out of the incident knowing that I was one lucky sumbitch.

Meanwhile, Casey and some of the boys had cleaned out a bunker in which they had found a cache of AK-47s, machine guns, plastique explosives, and about fifty rocket-propelled grenades, enough to arm a whole platoon. They stacked the weapons and set about destroying them with a thermite grenade, a big-league weapon that generates as much heat as a welding torch and melts through anything. Casey unwrapped the grenade, then handed it over to a sergeant who wanted to toss it.

They jogged away when the grenade was thrown, and we heard the quiet *pop* as the little bomb ignited and began to sizzle through the stacked weapons. Then came a loud *BANG* and a *WHOOSH*, and an RPG flew past Casey's ear and thudded into a nearby sand berm. The intense heat of the thermite grenade was cooking off the pile of live ammo. Casey and the sergeant crawled behind a little mound some farmer had built and hunkered down while more rocket-propelled grenades came to life and went flying. For the next five minutes, the aimless rain of RPGs zoomed about, giving the place the look of a major counterattack—or a carnival. Everyone chewed dirt. Luckily, an RPG must be manually armed in order to detonate on impact, so the actual damage was light.

"Were you really trying to shell your own troops?" I asked the unusually sheepish Casey as he was dusting off.

He gave the only appropriate response, "Fuck you." The lieutenant had just endured another embarrassing lesson about how, in combat, even doing the right thing can go wrong.

Achmed, the murdered donkey, a bullet that almost took off my foot, and Casey's attack on the rest of us made a weird kind of sense later that evening, when I realized that we had been fighting on April Fool's Day.

16

Have Gun, Will Travel

We pulled out of the rancid Ad Diwaniyah cloverleaf, which Casey accurately likened to "a camelshit amusement park for flies," at ten o'clock on the morning of April 2 for another road march that moved us closer to Baghdad. It was another day of just getting into position to fight. All across Iraq, other Coalition troops were doing the same thing. The weather had improved, supplies were flowing, and the ground attack was rolling inexorably forward beneath a sky owned by Coalition warplanes. The Army's 3rd Infantry Division finally was coming out of the desert through the narrow Karbala Gap and was within sight of the Euphrates River, while the 101st Airborne was finishing off the stubborn resistance in the strategic city of Najaf. On our side of the war, the 5th Marine Regiment was rushing up Highway 1, with our 7th Marines right behind them, and we formed a mighty column of tanks and trucks that stretched for miles over the horizon. It was time-consuming, but we had to reach the enemy before we could kill them.

The two Marine regiments made a sharp right turn off of Route 1 and onto an intersecting highway, Route 27, and caught the Iraqis flat-footed when we rolled up on the city of An Numaniyah and its important bridges across the Tigris River. Once on the other bank, we would link up with Task Force Tarawa and unify the combat power of the entire 1st Marine Division into a single powerful fist for the final push on Baghdad.

The steady movement was bringing all of us into the Red Zone, the area around Baghdad in which intelligence analysts predicted Saddam Hussein was most likely to slime us with his chemical and biological weapons. We were aware of the possibility but would not even think of stopping.

We drove all day, and as I sat and rocked and bumped along in the passenger seat of my Humvee, my thoughts drifted to how wheels were making just the sort of difference I had long envisioned for snipers. Once relegated to stationary hides and holes in the ground, we were now part of a mobile force. Shoot somebody in one town, saddle up, move on to another town, and shoot somebody else. Have gun, will travel.

Toward evening, Casey and I added a couple of CAATs for extra security to our advance quartering party, broke away from the main column, and raced ahead to find a spot where the battalion could settle down for the night near An Numaniyah. The sounds of a mighty battle, a steady drumbeat of gunfire and explosions that rolled across the desert, greeted us as we approached the first bridge and pulled to the side. Then we received startling new orders from regimental planners who wanted our handful of Humvees and CAATs to drive right through the firefight that was raging around the embattled bridge, cross it, dash through the hostile, uncleared city, and set up camp on the other side of the Tigris. It was a recipe for a suicidal disaster.

Fortunately, as we were trying to figure out some way to carry out the order without getting everyone killed, our battalion began pulling in, and McCoy was soon standing beside us. He chewed on his big cigar as we gave him the briefing, and he grew quite unhappy to hear how we were supposed to go through a ferocious battle, then drive through a totally unsecured city, and do it in the dark. The colonel grabbed his radio and laid some sharp, unkind words on headquarters about planners who did not take into account the reality of the battlefield.

At least three times, McCoy said, "I won't have a *Black Hawk Down* situation!" Since one of the raps against Darkside Six was that he liked to fight too much, the colonel easily won his point. The battalion would spend the night where it was and attack tomorrow, when conditions would have changed and we could see what the hell we were doing.

Somehow, Casey squeezed the battalion into an overnight position in a scrubby field about two football fields square, only about 20 percent of the space that normally was required, and I took out a security patrol. Our discoveries underlined the potential enemy strength in the area and confirmed that trying to carry out that idiotic run-for-the-bridge order could have gotten a lot of Marines killed.

First, there was an **L**-shaped bunker complex on the perimeter that was packed with weapons of all kinds, including antiaircraft guns. The Iraqis had left in such a hurry that the little stoves they used to cook food were still burning. We collected and stacked about seventy AK-47s, fifteen light machine guns, four heavy machine guns, thirty-five RPG launchers, and four 90 mm antitank recoilless rifles. Once the pile was arranged, an Amtrac rolled over the weapons to crush them.

Then we found pastures of antipersonnel and antitank mines that had been planted around the area in which we had set up camp. The danger from the mines was so great that the Marines who had been in their vehicles all day could not even get out and walk around to stretch their legs. Our vehicles were tightly coiled inside the circle of mines so they protected us instead of the guys who laid them in the first place.

But the major cause of nerves that night was the knowledge that we at last had hit the Red Zone and were facing the threat of WMDs. Headquarters said that if we were hit, the new conditions "would make the advance significantly more difficult." No shit.

Sure enough, word was flashed to us that night that our intel boys had intercepted an Iraqi radio transmission ordering commanders in our area to release chemical weapons. That got our attention in a hurry, and I quickly checked our brood of caged pigeons. Little Bastard and Botulism had not yet keeled over dead, but this was no time to take chances. It wasn't a drill.

We expected the real thing to be dumped on us at any moment, so we buttoned up our MOPP suits and scrambled to wiggle our feet into those terrible rubber boots. If the worst happened and we received incoming rounds, we would pull on the matching rubber gloves and the bug-eyed masks and be 100 percent protected from chemical munitions.

The boots were awful and quickly raised blisters on our feet. After sweating it out for thirty minutes while trying to work, I checked the pigeons again. They were still strutting, so the air was good. Colonel McCoy, who was just as clumsy in his boots as the rest of us, finally let us take them off rather than stumble around like a bunch of drunks. The full MOPP gear impeded our ability to fight, so we chose to live with the threat and carry on as usual. If hit, we would scramble to suit up. Meanwhile, if we died, we died.

We fell asleep to the sound of gunfire at the bridge, awoke to barking volleys of artillery, and rolled out though the carpet of debris left behind by the 5th Marines' fight for the bridge. Dead Iraqi defenders lay about in grotesque positions as we drove cautiously through the city, where shifting columns of dark smoke from burning buildings darkened the morning sky. Our little quartering party never would have survived that fight alone.

A few miles from the Tigris River, we dropped our light-skinned vehicles and gathered the armor to head south and attack Al Kut, a port and market center that was the site of another important bridge. The intel guys warned us that the enemy had a significant number of well-trained and well-equipped troops in the city, including elements of the Baghdad Division of the Republican Guard, so we had a green light to be "liberal" in our application of firepower.

That put it mildly, because we were about to pound the hell out of them, using everything but brass knuckles and switchblade knives. As we bore down on the city along one side of the Tigris, another battalion shadowed us on the far side, and Task Force Tarawa was pushing up from the south. The combination locked the paramilitaries and Republican Guard troops into defensive positions, so we battened down the hatches and jumped on the bad guys in what developed into our biggest firefight of the war thus far.

American planes slashed in overhead and smashed Iraqi tanks, armored vehicles, artillery and antiaircraft guns, and about a company's worth of infantrymen who were hidden in a thick grove of trees northeast of our position. The deafening explosions of bombs weighing a thousand pounds shook the ground as if giants were running around, and debris, trees, and dirt were flung into the air. A staccato of secondary explosions followed and lasted for twenty minutes. When the dust settled, a major threat to our flank had been obliterated.

Our Bravo tanks charged over the bridge and into a fight with more Iraqi tanks, cannons blazing only twenty yards apart, as we penetrated deeper into the western outskirts of the town. Enemy tanks and armored vehicles were hidden behind corners and would pop out to take easy shots and quickly pull back. Bravo kept attacking, and the grunts of Kilo Company piled out of their Amtracs and dove into a sprawling grove of date palms, where enemy bullets chipped trees around the ears of the advancing Marines. The CAATs swept out north and south to add their missiles and machine guns to the fray, while India Company hit clusters of buildings the Bravo tanks had bypassed.

Casey and I brought in the Tac and Main headquarters, and I watched with breathtaking eagerness as heavy fire slashed out from the palm grove where the enemy troops were dug in. The radio blurted calls for assistance from the battle commanders, and I grabbed my sniper rifle but Officer Bob suddenly appeared and refused to let me leave. "I need you back here," he insisted.

"I'm not your personal fucking bodyguard!" I shouted, but I got no response.

There was a war erupting just up the road. Up there, the big guns of the tanks were hammering away, heavy machine guns were stuttering, Marine grunts were yelling and running and shooting, tankers were calling for more infantry support, enemy fire was astonishingly heavy. Down here, Officer Bob strolled back and forth, safe behind the steel walls of the Amtrac. I was heading back to see J-Matt Baker to protest when a coded radio call broke through.

"Nightingale!" That single code word meant that Marines were down and urgent medical evacuation was needed. It was also my ticket out to the fight. Casey and I and our boys jumped into the Humvees to provide security for an ambulance Amtrac on a two-minute sprint to the front edge of the battle. We wove through debris on the road and past smoking hulks of enemy T-62 tanks in which ammunition was still cooking off in booming explosions. A CAAT came screaming back, and its commander said it was carrying out the wounded men. We cut the ambulance free to return while we kept going to the fight. Although I didn't know it at the time, lying in the CAAT was a badly wounded Mark Evnin, the eager kid from Vermont who had been my spotter only two days before when we took out that sniper on the bus in Ad Diwaniyah. He would die before I even knew he was hit.

The palm grove was alive with action, but the thick dust, flashes of fire, and flying debris made it impossible to distinguish who was who, so we pulled to a stop and I climbed atop the Humvee. Since the tanks and grunts were already at work among the trees, I glassed over to the right and found that the north side of the battle zone seemed open for a flank attack on the Marines. I lasered some ranges and yelled down that we would be staying in this spot for a while, so Casey spread the boys out in a protective cordon. The radio squawked annoyingly: Officer Bob, telling us to return to his position. We ignored him.

I lay there, still as a corpse, with my eyeball becoming part of the scope, magnifying my world in multiples. A mirage down the way tipped me about wind conditions, and I adjusted the setting, then scanned the empty streets and worked my view up to the rooftops. Accumulating knowledge of repeated behavior is a prime reason for keeping sniper logbooks. Ours had taught us that the Iraqis liked to hang out near those little doorways that exit onto the rooftops, so I gave extra attention to every one of those that I found.

Only three minutes into my search, one of them slowly opened, and an Iraqi soldier stepped out, carrying an RPK light machine gun. I let him peek out a bit more as I adjusted the rifle to a distance of 461 yards and dialed another bit of windage onto the scope. This guy knew what he was doing and was being careful, deliberately taking his time before stepping into the open, but his caution was not enough to save him. I already had my crosshairs centered on his chest. I had no intention of letting him come close to shooting.

The mathematics of the battlefield, time, motion, distance, weather conditions, and angle and speed of the bullet merged into smooth calculations that I did in my head, without really thinking about it. Do this sort of thing long enough and those factors blend together.

Exhale, slow pull of one-two-three pounds of pressure on the trigger, and my rifle fired and bucked comfortably into my shoulder with the recoil. I was concentrating so hard that I barely heard the gunshot, but the round took the soldier dead center, and I saw a hole open eight inches below his throat. The force of impact threw him back down the stairs, leaving the door swinging slowly on its hinges.

Bob continued badgering us to return immediately. "Tell him we're busy killing people," Casey instructed his radio operator.

I slid my scope around some other buildings, down to ground

level again, and along a street that ran perpendicular to our position. About a quarter mile away, several people were peeking around a distant corner. *Civilians? Troops?* I steadied up on the corner for two minutes, using the time to adjust for range and wind, and saw the barrel of an AK-47 poke into the open. The dark-haired soldier holding the weapon leaned forward, exposing only about the upper third of his body. Not much, but enough, and I owned him. I put a bullet through his chest and saw him flop down beside the building. Unseen hands took him by the ankles and pulled his body out of sight.

By this time, Officer Bob was furious and gave us a direct order over the radio to come back immediately. Casey tried to tell him that we were actively engaging targets on a threatened flank, but Bob replied with another order that gave us no choice but to leave. It meant that we were giving the enemy a wide avenue of approach.

We got lucky, because another good sniper, Sergeant Eric Meeks, showed up within minutes, recognized the threat, and took over the position. Over the next few minutes, Meeks took down another RPG gunner and four more Iraqi riflemen, effectively shutting down the street. But there had been a window of two to three minutes when the approach had been unguarded. Next time, we vowed, we would not be so obedient. If Officer Bob wanted us, he would have to come get us.

Back at the Main, I was stunned to learn that Mark Envin was one of the wounded Marines we had gone out to retrieve.

When the fight had broken out in the grove of date palms, Sergeant Major Dave Howell directed his Humvee to roar in close so he could direct the advancing grunts. AK-47 bullets were zinging about, and an RPG erupted from a trench line only six feet from the road, so they stopped their truck, and Howell got out of his Humvee with a grenade launcher in his hands. Evnin, the driver, jumped out right beside him. Dino Moreno also got into a shooting position. The job I had assigned them was to protect Howell, even in the teeth of enemy fire, and that's exactly what they did until one of the enemy bullets burrowed beneath Mark's flak jacket and tore through his femoral artery. Howell tried to stanch the flow of blood while Moreno gave covering fire, and Evnin looked up at Howell and wisecracked, "Look at this, asshole. You got me shot!"

My boy had lost a lot of blood before they could get him onto a medical evacuation helicopter, a big twin-rotored Chinook. He died in that bird before it reached the aid station.

It shook me. He was not the first, nor would he be the last, of our battalion to die, but Mark was the only man in my entire career to die directly under my command. I almost felt as if I had been the one to pull the trigger on him.

As much as I was trying to banish emotion from my thoughts, I couldn't, and a lot of guilt was added to the load. I had selected Mark for the platoon and spent hours and hours with him over the past two years, coaching him on how to realize his dream of being a sniper. War requires compromises, and when the fool who had been the sergeant major's original driver chickened out before the war, I had thought nothing of letting Evnin take over that driving job in addition to being Dino Moreno's spotter. So Mark was killed taking the place of a coward.

His death had a sharp impact on our tight little sniper community. We are used to dealing death, not absorbing it. A couple of my snipers who had been working with the tank battalion at Al Kut had come clanking back down the road after the fight, and Corporal Sean Dunn jumped down from a tank and asked me, "Who got hit?"

When I told him, Dunn, who had been Mark's best friend and had gone through school with him, almost collapsed. Standing beside that scarred road, I held the big Marine in my arms while his tears painted muddy paths down his dirty cheeks.

All the while, I wondered what would have happened if I had been able to get into the fight earlier. Could I have saved the boy? I believed the death was my fault, for I had ordered Mark into that assignment, and now I would just have to live with the terrible result. War really, really sucks. Mark was part of my family, and I will miss him.

17

Ghostbusters

We were finished with Al Kut by 2:54 in the afternoon and began to withdraw, completely changing direction in order to rejoin the push toward Baghdad, only a hundred miles to the northwest. Explosions boomed in the distance as captured caches of enemy ammunition and weapons were blown up. Our part of the fight was done, and the Marines of Task Force Tarawa could clean up the rest. We had helped kick the butts of the Baghdad Division of the Republican Guard, and now it was time to leave.

The road out, which had been empty on our way into Al Kut, was now lined with Iraqi civilians, some waving and giving thumbs-ups while others just stared with baleful eyes. They had known a battle was coming, so they had closed their shops and left their homes until the fighting was done, and now they were reappearing to see what was left. Looters were already stripping destroyed vehicles. Kids obviously untroubled by the bloody and torn corpses strewn about their scarred city kicked a soccer ball around a desolate field. To these people, we were only the latest conquering army, and they were already getting on with their lives.

Fire from our 155 mm howitzers rumbled overhead in kettledrum

staccato to light up any area that the enemy might use to counterattack as we regrouped at the edge of the city, with the armored vehicles lining up at a newly liberated gasoline station to fill their big
fuel tanks. Let Saddam pay the bill. About thirty kilometers farther
up Route 7, we went into a defensive position beside the road. A
lone, abandoned Iraqi 20 mm antiaircraft gun pointed its useless
barrel at a sky filled with potential targets as Coalition planes
roamed freely, heading north on bomb runs. The ground was covered with the gun's unfired ammunition.

April 3 had been a very long and dangerous day, and Al Kut had
been a dangerous place. Mark Evnin was the only Marine who was
killed, but several others were wounded, including a corporal who
caught a burst from an enemy machine gun—seven bullets on a di-
agonal line across his torso from his right hip to his left shoulder. He
lived because the ballistic plates in his flak jacked stopped three potentially fatal rounds.

Another casualty was Captain Bryan Lewis, the commander of
our Bravo Company tanks. During the opening moments of the battle for the palm grove, an Iraqi soldier managed to put a bullet
through Lewis's left hand before being killed. Lewis never paused
in his relentless attack, waited until after the fight to even tell anyone that he was injured, and refused to leave his command and go
to the hospital. I looked straight through the hole in his hand and
could see daylight on the other side. After a few days, it began to
scab over. Lewis was the Man. I recalled how strange it was that,
way back in Basra, I had doubted his abilities. Since then, he had
repeatedly proven himself to be the ready and reliable leader of our
armored spearhead, and by the time he was wounded, he was one
tough Marine.

Bravo Company had a warrior for a leader, but not all officers are made of such stuff. For instance, Officer Bob had sent out a patrol of only six men to clear a factory complex about 1,400 meters away from the headquarters—six Marines for a job big enough to require a company, and with no backup force and no one in a protective overwatch position.

Fighting raged nearby when he did it. Just a few minutes earlier, a Harrier fighter jet had dropped a thousand-pound bomb to pulverize some Iraqi troops. Kilo Company infantrymen were on the attack, and a platoon of tanks from Bravo cut down a half dozen silly Iraqi solders who charged the heavily armored Abrams tanks with only AK-47s. RPG rockets trailing smoky tails whooshed around all morning, hand grenades exploded with deadly *thumps*, and cars, buildings, and buses were on fire.

To me it was a dumb and dangerous move, and I went out in a hurry to get the team safely back to our lines. The patrol had found a couple of antiaircraft guns inside one of the buildings, and after checking to be sure no rocket-propelled grenades were in the room, I popped thermite grenades on the big guns.

There had been a shake-up within the beleaguered, slow-moving Task Force Tarawa. Their bravery was never a question to me, but we all knew something was wrong over there, and it came as no surprise when the commander of the 1st Marine Regiment was literally promoted upstairs to fly around the battlefield and coordinate air support. Under its new leaders, the regiment regrouped and got back into the race to Baghdad. So my question was, if they could replace a regimental commander, a full bird colonel, why wouldn't they fire someone much less important in the grand scheme of things, a screwed-up junior staff officer who I thought was giving stupid people a bad name?

After helping get the Main squared away at our new location, I had some chow, cleaned my rifle, and brought my gun book up to date. The front page is printed with standard cheat-sheet data that helps snipers remember pertinent things about the so-called average man — that he is seventy-two inches tall, the length of his head is ten inches, he is twenty inches across the shoulder, and neck to belly button is a dozen inches. Those details, part of any sniper's memorized table of algorithms, help determine how best to kill a target. This evening, I was writing around the margins of the green page.

I had smoke-checked two more men that day. I logged the details of those shootings as I normally would, then added them to a special table of results that I had created on the front page. Starting back in Basra, I had written down the numerical sequence of my kills and crossed each number out with a big X. Tonight, I wrote "11" and "12" and crossed them out. The table was not being kept out of grim braggadocio but simply as a practical tool. If I needed to prove in a hurry that I could help an officer whom I did not know, to get permission to intrude into a fight on his dirt, I could just flash that page of the gun book, like a police officer showing a badge, and save a lot of arguing.

Being in double digits meant that I now carried the best number in the sniper platoon, which was just as it should have been. How could I lead the boys if I wasn't the best among them? Although I didn't know it at the time, I had hardly begun.

When I finished with the gun book, I settled in to get a few hours of sleep, but the death of Mark Evnin still ate at me. I thought I had stabilized my dangerous emotional seesaw, but when one of my own Marines was killed, it tilted again, and I knew I had to get it back in balance in a hurry.

I was the tough guy, the stone-cold killer who was never bothered by something as absurd as personal feelings. While I freely bitched about many things to anyone, anytime, I had to remain true to my badass character of designated gunslinger. But day after day, I also had to listen to other people's problems and never really speak of my own. Doing so would be misinterpreted as a sign of weakness, and I had to stay invincible. I had to be there for everyone else, but no one was there for me—certainly not here on the field of battle, and most likely not at home either. As I went to sleep, I again slammed those mental doors shut hard and coiled into my solitary, emotionless, fuck-you-all, don't-need-anybody mode. The lone gunman felt very damned alone.

The war gave us the morning off the next day, Friday, April 4. Few things are as sweet as a couple of hours of downtime during a combat situation that allow you to put aside the psychological and physical stress for a little while. Most of the regiment's six thousand men took a break, knowing we would be back in the shit soon enough.

We had our own embedded reporters but also had inherited a gypsy group of newsies along the road, and cool jazz blared from the laptop computers they propped up on the hoods of their SUVs. They were a good group; we called them "the Jackals." Marine began caging satellite minutes on the Jackals' phones to make calls back home.

Even doing the mundane rearm and refit jobs felt almost like being on vacation, and we sank comfortably into boring routine. We hauled everything off the trucks and used a broom to sweep out the small dunes of dirt that had accumulated inside the vehicles, so much sand that we could pick it up by the handful. It was everywhere, even in the tightly closed boxes of ammunition. We field-stripped all the weapons to clean off the sand, grime, and carbon, cleaned the belts of machine gun bullets, and polished the optics systems, and we found humor in almost every situation. The lightheartedness masked the fundamental truth of this strange moment—we were all glad we were still alive.

Last, we cleaned our bodies and personal gear and washed our hair beneath warm water spilling from a buddy's canteen. Two weeks into the war, and we all stank. Casey, who had gotten new boots just before the war began, peeled them off for the first time in days, and his feet smelled like dead rats. Staying clean during a fast-paced war is always a problem, particularly when you're in a desert that makes you breathe and eat dirt. Once in a while, you might have a quick bucket of water dumped over your head, but you can never have a leisurely soaking, never anything resembling a real bath or shower. In a combat zone, just being able just to take off your boots and socks and air out your feet is a luxury. Everyone had stocked up on baby wipes and used them on faces and feet alike; at least applying moisture and taking away some of the caked-on grit gave you the illusion of being clean. Of course, you paid particular attention to the crotch after taking a dump—a relief not only because it emptied your bowels but because it was a chance to peel away the thick MOPP overalls and let some air into your sweat-soaked bottom.

The break was short. Ahead of us, Route 7 was blocked; the 5th Marines were in a hard fight to get through the city of Al Aziziyah, located at a horseshoe curve of the Tigris River. Our orders were to join them for an attack on the Al Nida Division of the Republican Guard, still another supposedly elite unit of the Iraqi army. The Al Nida soldiers swaggered around in red boots to show that they were special. Of course, the United States Marines have a reputation, too, so we looked forward to meeting them. Nobody was afraid of these characters.

While Casey was at the headquarters track to pick up maps and double-check his information, Colonel Steve Hummer, the regimental commander, came by and told McCoy to start planning a strike into Baghdad itself. If conditions were right, we would leapfrog to the front and make a nighttime plunge into the capital city.

Casey hurried back with the news, our first clue that there had been a major change in strategy. The original game plan simply wanted the Marines to be a blocking cordon south of the city while the Army secured the place. Now it looked as if we were going to get a piece of that action. "Told you so, asshole," I said to Casey, recalling my prediction back in Kuwait that we would get a bite of the Baghdad apple.

Casey and I and our boys were soon on the road again as the advance quartering party, and after traveling only about three kilometers, we got a taste of what the 5th Marines were facing. The battalion headquarters unit we were looking for was near the burning remnants of an M1A1 Abrams battle tank that had been ripped apart, and the crew inside killed, when a suicide bomber drove a pickup truck loaded with explosives into it. Our only job was to pick out a safe place for our own battalion to stay that night, and we weren't there to get involved with someone else's fight. That changed in a hurry.

Their busy command tracks were parked in a scrubby area where black smoke blossomed from a nearby burning oil pipe. I left my sniper rifle in the Humvee and was carrying only an M-16 as we walked over to the headquarters. There was a crisp burst of loud popping noises, but the officers were not bothered by it, explaining that the sound was only the creaking expansion of that burning pipe.

They told us that Iraqi paramilitaries, the fedayeen, were running around out there in the fields, wearing black pajamas and causing trouble. Black pajamas? Were they were trying to look like the Viet Cong and scare us with the shadow of Vietnam? That was a long time ago; we weren't Vietnam vets, and some of our boys probably didn't even know what a Viet Cong was, so old spooks could not haunt us. Did they really think they could freak us out with some Halloween getup?

There was more popping, and I asked again if someone was shooting at us. No, that was just the pipe. Then, closer, it happened again. *Pop-pow! Pop-pow!* Casey and I ducked at the familiar crack of 7.62 mm bullets passing overhead, and I shouted, "That's no fucking burning pipe! That's incoming!"

"No," protested their executive officer, a major, as Casey and I moved behind an armored Amtrac. "That's been going off all day. It's just the pipe burning."

"Sir. Trust me on this one," I told the XO. "I've been shot at many times, and that definitely is incoming fire." I wasn't supposed to get involved, but people were trying to kill us!

First, I needed my sniper rifle. Someone would have to grab the big gun from the truck, cross fifty yards of open ground over which bullets were flying, and bring it to me so I could start hunting. Luckily, I had just the guy. "Daniel! Bring my rifle! Now!"

Since we still had not reached Baghdad, Daniel Tracy was

immovable in his faith that he was immune to enemy gunfire. I saw him gently pick up my rifle with both hands and jog toward us. He wasn't moving in much of a hurry.

"Keep your head down," Casey shouted. Bullets showered around us, kicking up the dirt and plinking off the armored vehicles as Daniel loped across the open area, then came through a gully. He arrived unharmed and not even breathing hard, holding out my gun with a grin. "Here y'are, boss."

"About fuckin' time," I said, and we traded weapons.

I started to climb atop an Amtrac, but Casey grabbed my shirt and hauled me back. "Hold on, jackass. Let me go up first," he barked. This sudden transformation into John Wayne startled me, but I realized that he was getting the hang of that leadership thing and was addressing me not as a friend but as an asset to be deployed. Casey went up first to see if there were any immediate threats, and I followed, feeling as if I were going to war with my mother telling me how to behave.

"Hey! What are you guys doing?" the XO snapped. "There are friendlies out there. Make sure you don't shoot any of them. We don't want any friendly fire incidents."

I almost laughed. "Sir, I've got a fucking scoped rifle here. When I shoot, it will be at the enemy."

Now the commander of the Amtrac woke up long enough to notice that he had company atop his vehicle. "Hey! You can't shoot from here!"

"Why not?" asked Casey. "It doesn't look like you're shooting at anybody."

I chose the gun turret platform as my firing platform, and the gunner stood there looking at me curiously, holding the trigger to his .50 caliber machine gun. I told him not to even fucking move, because if that turret shifted, it could crush me.

"Well, we might have to shoot," the Amtrac commander protested, trying to get back in the game. Pouting little shit.

"By the time you find something to fire at, it'll be too late," Casey yelled. "Now get out of the way." It was nice to have an officer around to holler at other officers.

I put the rifle to my shoulder and my eye to the scope as Casey ignored the incoming fire and scanned the field with his binos. He pointed to the west of the road. "About a half mile away, six guys in black," he said. We painted them with a laser at 922 yards, and I dialed in the dope, thinking, *Oh, I'm gonna VC your asses, dudes. This ain't Vietnam, and I ain't afraid of no ghosts.*

I chose a target on the far left, a guy whose RPK light machine gun was merrily chattering away, and clicked two minutes right to my scope to shift the crosshairs to the middle of his body mass. Then I caressed the trigger, and the bullet hit two inches from the center of his chest, flipping him violently backward as his automatic weapon hit the dirt. I exhaled and worked the bolt to put in a new round. *That's one. Who's next?*

Daniel had gone back to the trucks at Casey's direction. Our armored Humvees were wheeling into position to fire as Castillo and Marsh got ready to open up on the bushes.

A few seconds later, I found another guy about fifty yards to the right of my first target and adjusted the scope to nine plus four, tacking on some more right windage, aimed at his center mass. Squeeeeeze, *bang,* recoil, eye still in the scope, and this AK-toting asshole took it right through the chin, the bullet drilling a hole the size of a silver dollar in his head and sending teeth and jawbone fragments flying out of the skull and onto the desert floor. *Damn. How could I have hit so high when I was aiming at his chest? He must have moved.*

Other Marines had joined the fight by now. As they moved forward to clear the area, I had to stop. The bad guys scattered or died.

Our own battalion pulled up a few minutes later, and we parked our nine hundred Marines and 112 vehicles in the median strip of the broad highway, leaving room for other vehicles to continue moving on both sides of the road.

I waited for things to settle down and then had another private little off-the-record talk with McCoy as we walked the perimeter. Despite just having come out of a major battle in Al Kut, he was up to speed on everything that had happened within his battalion, including the casualties and my problems with Officer Bob. Plenty of senior staff members had watched Bob's actions with growing concern.

I knew the Boss would never say anything critical of any officer in front of me, but I told him that I was being kept on the wrong side of the door in this freakin' war and was only getting into action almost by accident.

The colonel was as tired as the rest of us but told me to calm down. "You got how many, now?"

"Fourteen confirmed, boss. Should have been more, but I either get there late or get yanked out early."

McCoy nodded and said the time had come for that to change. He wanted my rifle where it would do the most good. I would roam the battlefield, he said, with Casey and the boys going along to cover my ass.

Finally, the green light of freedom that would get me out from under Bob's thumb, a deal blessed by Darkside Six himself! McCoy's aggressive philosophy was to get his killers in position to kill, and I knew there was going to be a lot of killing going on in the next few days.

18

Push, Push, Push

The 3rd Infantry Division had captured the Baghdad International Airport, other Army units were crunching the key town of Karbala southwest of the capital, and we were closing in from the southeast. Everyone was coming to roost at the same time, and while the Iraqis might delay us here and there, as the first week of April came to a close, they couldn't stop us. The regime's spokesman, a little fruit-cake known to every television audience in the world as "Baghdad Bob," was undeterred by reality and busily peddled the official line that we had all been rolled up like a dirty rug and were on the run. Baghdad Bob was broadcasting from a swank hotel, not on the front lines, where things were dirty and bloody. Looks like each side had its own Bob.

The 5th Marines were still involved in heavy fighting around Al Aziziyah. "The enemy order of battle included T-55s, T-62s, mechanized vehicles, air defense artillery, long-range artillery, and mortars of the Republican Guard," the regimental historian wrote. Enemy troops, dug into formidable positions, managed to destroy a couple of Marine tanks and some other armored vehicles, and several hundred fedayeen fools who had come in from other Arab countries prowled the countryside to ambush the unwary. But piece by piece, the 5th Marines took them apart—and killed a Republican Guard general in the process.

Our unit, the 7th Marines, had spread out alongside the 5th to the east, and the 1st Marines came up beside us, which meant that the entire 1st Marine Division was now grouped together, ready for the final party.

One of our forward air controllers, Captain Christopher Grasso, arranged a surprise for one persistent pocket of Iraqi fighters. We watched from a safe distance as a lethal pattern of bombs fell from a giant B-52 that was flying so high we couldn't even see it. These huge bombers with their signature swept-back wings are older than the men who fly them but have been continually upgraded with advanced avionics over the years to remain weapons of immense power. A single bomb can cause incredible destruction, which means there are few things like a B-52 strike, when such bombs fall in strings like monstrous firecrackers.

A towering fountain of dirt, debris, and dust rose into the air when the first Mk-82 bomb hit and exploded, followed in a heartbeat by another fountain overlapping the first, then another, and another, and another, and finally it seemed there would be no end to the entwined, ripping explosions, and a solid curtain of dust hung in the air. We were a mile away and still felt the wall of displaced air push against our faces and our clothes, and the dull grumble of detonations reached our ears. How could anyone survive that? The reeling Iraqis had to be wondering just how many different ways—tanks, bombs, missiles, artillery, helicopters, ships, grenades, riflemen, snipers—we could kill them. The answer was, a lot.

Early on Saturday morning, April 5, our Bravo Company armor parked their tanks squarely on a busy intersection, and we took a security platoon out to deal with a huge crowd of civilians streaming around their position. Many of those traipsing past were men of fighting age who had thrown away their uniforms and donned droopy civilian robes. Only a short while ago, some had been the strutting members of the vaunted Al Nida Division; they were still recognizable by those signature red boots beneath their robes. After we made sure they had no weapons, we let them get out of the way of our advancing battalions, because it was easier to parole them rather than have to guard, feed, and protect them as prisoners of war. If they shed their uniforms, walked south through our lines, and had no guns, we considered that they had surrendered and let most of them return to their homes. To capture so many thousands of men would just have slowed our momentum, and we had the enemy reeling.

We did take prisoner any men we thought might be dangerous or possess useful information. Just being in civilian robes did not earn them a free pass, but they were not brutalized. McCoy had written and distributed to his officers and staff NCOs before the war a printed list entitled "Expectations of Combat Leaders," in which one element stated, "Treat prisoners with dignity but do not trust them and be forceful and firm. Do not abuse prisoners, it is cowardly." In all, those of us on the front line treated them better than they had expected, and in accordance with the Geneva Convention. What happened to some prisoners later in some of the prisons, such as the infamous Abu Ghraib, startled us all. Torturing prisoners is dishonorable, no matter who does it, and it usually gains nothing of value, because a prisoner being tortured will say anything to stop the pain.

One man Casey and I bagged that morning was a pretty friendly fellow who was a lieutenant colonel in the Iraqi counterintelligence corps, and he sang as freely as a canary. He described in great detail one of those "sensitive sites" that our intelligence people had been hunting, places where it was hoped some of the weapons of mass destruction might be stored. The officer even built a model of it in the sand, like a kid at a beach, and helped us mark the position on a map. We passed him back to the rear for further questioning, although I would have preferred to keep him around as a consultant.

We pushed on up the road from the intersection until we reached a peculiar area where a bunch of abandoned and heavily weathered buildings occupied the right side of the road, a run-down collection of structures similar to a light industrial park in some small city back home. On the left was a mysterious wall of sand, a thick berm that must have reached forty feet in height, with no entranceway facing the road. McCoy sent the Bravo tanks around to see if they could find a door in the dirt.

In a little while, an ominous radio call came back from Captain Lewis. "Darkside Six, this is Bravo Six. I've got something up here that you may want to come see." The tankers had found the site described by the Iraqi officer.

Much of the argument put forward for America starting this war with a preemptive strike had hinged on Saddam Hussein's possession of weapons of mass destruction, including a nuclear capability. So far, no such weapons had been found, although we still expected to be chemed or slimed as we neared Baghdad.

Rumors had been flying that the 101st Airborne Division had discovered some chemical munitions and that the 82nd Airborne had also found some suspicious artillery rounds. Both of those reports proved to be negative. Perhaps we had finally turned up one of those mysterious caches.

Behind that huge berm of sand, our boys had come upon a complex of modern buildings that were startlingly different from almost every other place we had seen in Iraq. While obvious neglect reigned almost everywhere else, this place had been carefully maintained. It was actually clean! Large pieces of industrial equipment lay in the yards, each neatly covered with a tarpaulin and protected by sandbags from the elements and American bombs. The air inside the buildings was cool, although the electricity was off and the air-conditioners idle. Computers with blank screens sat in neat ranks on desks, wooden cabinets lined the floor, and a picture of Saddam Hussein was in every work cubicle. It was obvious that this was a workplace for skilled technical personnel and needed a thorough search.

Some of the Jackals did a search of their own and found that some of the buildings still had running water, a promise of bliss for the civilian media types who had been out in the desert with us for almost two weeks. Reporter Peter Maas later wrote about the incident in a *New York Times Magazine* story: "Along with the usual assortment of portraits of Saddam Hussein and outdated computers, Ellen [Knickmeyer of the Associated Press] discovered a shower with running water. I grabbed a bar of soap, raced inside, and stripped. Just then a Marine shouted down the hallway, 'The building is rigged with C4! Get out!' I got out." The Jackals hastily abandoned the booby-trapped building and stayed dirty, just like the rest of us.

The site eventually gave us nothing. There was no evidence of WMDs, and the exact purpose of the place remained unknown. The best guess was that the abandoned factory complex was some sort of precision manufacturing facility.

———

With only three hours of daylight left, Casey located a broad, tilled field about two kilometers away where we could spread out for the night. McCoy secured the sensitive site of mysterious buildings with an infantry company, plus the Bravo tanks and his tactical head-quarters team. The Main, the CAATs, the trains, and other units set up in the field. That night, much of the combat power of the battalion settled down within the berm of the complex itself, among manicured rosebushes, while the rest of us stretched out on farmland that had the consistency of granite.

The strange war just kept getting stranger. Enemy soldiers could become free citizens simply by dropping their guns and uniforms and walking away from their fighting positions. Their comrades up the road would still be trying to kill us, and some of those who quit made their military retirement temporary and would revert to their combatant ways in the cities and villages that we had bypassed. Who to trust?

That night, India Company was marching back from a mission to join our position when they crossed a field that we had traversed earlier, sidestepping the bodies of some enemy soldiers. The "bodies" suddenly came to life, leaped up, and started firing, but the Marines reacted instantly and returned fire, so the enemy soldiers went back to being dead, this time for real. It was another lesson that we were close to the enemy's heartland and sudden death could come from any quarter: suicide bombers in pickup trucks; fedayeen hiding in the bushes; soldiers who were dangerous one moment, then changed into civilian clothes at our approach and laid down their guns—but not their hatred. There were booby traps, deadly RPGs, roadside bombs, the threat of weapons that could deal death in massive amounts, and now people faking death to stage an ambush. It was dangerous to let down your guard.

On the flip side were the friendly little mom-and-pop stores that could be found alongside almost every road in Iraq. Sometimes, when a trove of Saddam's private cash was discovered, the intelligence guys we called the "Secret Squirrels" became our private ATM machines, spitting out money, as they distributed Iraqi dinars among the troops as unofficial bonuses so we could pump cash back into the local economies. We figured the dictator had stolen enough money, so we were happy to give it back to the citizens.

We would step into those dark little shops and buy almost everything on the shelves—bottles of 7-Up and the Arab version of Pepsi-Cola, bubble gum, and local snacks such as an odd version of caramelized corn. There would be a lot of friendly jabber about prices, and the costs skyrocketed as more Marine customers showed up. A cold drink that went for only five dinars to the first customer was suddenly five thousand dinars for latecomers who were trying to shove ten-thousand-dinar notes into the hands of the shopkeepers. They could not believe the bonanza spilling from the wallets of the young men carrying guns. Those shop owners were friendly, exuberant, and happy to see us.

Or were they? Who knew? How could you tell? To say we were on edge is an understatement.

Artillery blinked against the night sky in the north, and mosquitoes hit us in swarms as I made myself as comfortable as possible among the hardpan ruts of the plowed field. I wondered what kind of crops could possibly grow in such desolation, other than sheaves of hardship and vines of misery.

Suspense gripped us tightly, for the war was entering its final phase. All along the Marine lines on that Saturday night, recon teams were out, snooping to find ways through the last big obstacle, the Diyala River.

Over the centuries, the swift green waters of the Diyala had dropped from a lake far to the north to carve a wide and deep channel that meandered for miles through central Iraq and the eastern suburbs of Baghdad until it bled into the Tigris River. In a country that was mostly desert, we now faced a natural geographic barrier that would be easily defensible by the enemy, a big, deep river with extremely steep bluffs at the sides. By any method, getting over it would be a bitch.

The Force Recon boys can do wonders, but they can't build bridges alone in the dark. They investigated every small road and muddy cow path leading down to the river and kept reporting back that no suitable crossings were available, except for the one place that was right in front of us.

Headquarters types are nocturnal creatures who are not allowed to sleep at night, because they stay up reading tea leaves, preparing orders, and drafting plans for the following day. While the rest of us either loafed within the bermed complex of buildings or stretched out on the field, the planners filtered through the alternatives until, by default, and to the utter delight of Lieutenant Colonel Bryan P. McCoy, the primary assault on the Diyala fell to his Marines. The Bull got the job.

Straight ahead on the road that we currently straddled was the bridge, two parallel spans across the river, about 150 yards wide.

There was a slim two-lane span for pedestrian traffic, and the main bridge was a four-lane highway. Far below swirled the strong currents of the Diyala.

Worse, the bridge was located in the middle of an urban area. That meant a house-to-house fight would be needed just to reach it on our side of the river; then even more urban fighting awaited us on the far side. But if we could take it, we would be only nine miles from downtown Baghdad.

The captured Iraqi colonel had warned us that Saddam's troops had been ordered to make a stand at this bridge. Nutty fedayeen and militiamen defended the town on this side of the river, and regular troops were well dug into positions on the far side, all with orders to fight to the death. The enemy commanders could read maps, too; well aware of the vital importance of the river crossing, they laced it with explosives. They planned to blow it up the moment they saw the first American approaching.

Of course, all of this is very plain in hindsight, but at the time, I was blind as a bat and innocent as a lamb with regard to what tomorrow might bring. Nine times out of ten, the Tac, or tactical headquarters, would have been located with the Main, and I would have known what was going on. But with the discovery of the sensitive site, the Tac had stayed within the berms, and I was back at the Main, totally out of touch as the planners toiled through the vampire hours. At least four plans were debated about how to go get that bridge, and although I was oblivious to them all, I was confident that I would be in the thick of it. But when I asked Officer Bob about it, he told me there would be no attack at all tomorrow.

So we slid into relax mode and caught some shut-eye, lulled by the distant bumping of our long-range artillery guns lobbing shells at the defenders of the Diyala Bridge. Nothing going on but a war.

The next day, Sunday, April 6, began in an unhurried manner back where we were, with no sense of pending combat, although a lot of Marines and machines were moving about as the battalion lined up on the road, with the Abrams tanks up front. It is natural to have your stomach in a scramble of nerves before a fight, but this was a normal, piece-of-cake, let's-get-our-shit-together kind of morning. Our combat power was strung out in a line long enough to cover the length of about eight football fields, and from our place at the rear, we couldn't even see the front. I called Officer Bob again and was once again firmly told that the senior officers were getting together but there would be no attack. Specifically, I was to stay with the Main.

The sun jumped into the morning sky and was already burning bright with a soaring temperature that had us sweating in our protective suits; MOPP meant HOT. I found a chunk of shade on a sidewalk and sat with my back against my Humvee. Wait. Sweat. Wait. Casey came by to say that he thought that getting shot at was "a bit of a rush" and that he was considering trying out for the CIA when the war was done. I told him not to make any decisions out here: Keep your head in the game. Wait. Wait. We were clueless.

This just didn't feel right, though, and I began to fidget. I got up, stretched, and looked up the road at the long line of vehicles. Something was stirring up front, and the combat power was on the move. Were they going into a fight or just repositioning?

Little bells began to jangle in my head. Something was up. Something had to be happening! *Are we attacking?* I climbed inside my Humvee and sat there, staring through the window at the truck in front of us, as if the answers were written on the tailgate. In my gut, I had that sinking feeling again that I was in the wrong place.

At nine o'clock in the morning, we suddenly heard the clear sounds of battle ahead and watched some rocket-propelled grenades ride their hot little tails into balls of explosions. I flipped the radio to the Tac-1 net and clearly heard gunfire behind the voices. Detonations erupted in the area of the sensitive site. I tuned to the Main net and got Officer Bob on the horn. Why had I not been told about the order to attack?

His laconic reply was simply "The colonel said he doesn't need you today."

Oh, my God! McCoy himself had told me that I would be taking my gun into a target-rich environment, and now I was once again on the sidelines, literally stranded at the very back of the line and intentionally left out of still another fight. Cursing loudly, I got out of the truck, found a scrawny tree, and sat beneath it in a brooding sulk, so plainly pissed off at the entire fucking world that no one dared say a word to me. The boys had questions but asked them only with their eyes, and for once, I had no answers.

Then one of them screamed that there was some talk on the radio about me, so I walked over to the truck in time to hear the last part of the transmission. It was the unmistakable voice of Darkside Six roaring over the tactical net, shaded by a background of crackling gunshots, asking, demanding, none too politely: *"Where the FUCK is Coughlin?"*

19

The Baghdad Two-Mile

Death was just beyond my windshield. Bullets whanged against
metal, and rocket-propelled grenades zipped toward us. Marines
were running and gunning amid the chattering *pops* of small-arms
fire, and machine guns were firing full out, with a heavy, rhythmic
stomp. Artillery shells exploded and shook the ground.

On the map, this town was called Az Zafaraniyah, but on that
April morning, it was hell for the United States Marines, a raging,
brutal firefight that gave this new generation of jarheads a taste of
what the Corps had faced on Guadalcanal in World War II, at the
Chosin Reservoir in Korea, and at Khe Sanh in Vietnam. It was not
pretty enough to appear on TV, for our job was to heap casualties on
the defenders, fast and with unrelenting force, and force them to
withdraw. So time slowed down and I went on a killing spree.

McCoy had been thoroughly ripped that I was not out on the front
edge of the attack, dominating the rooftops when the fight started,
and he had barked out on the open radio frequency, "Listen, I want
Coughlin and his rifle up here *right now!*"

I grabbed the mike and confirmed that I was on the way. "Good," the colonel grumbled. "See you soon." We'd explain after the shooting stopped, but right now there was work to be done.

"Game on, boys!" I yelled. "We're back in it."

Our trucks were rolling almost before I finished telling the boys to get cracking, and we went from loafing to combat-ready in a heartbeat. As the two Humvees broke out of line and gathered speed, Officer Bob appeared in the road, waving his arms. Casey told his driver, "You work for me, not him. Do *not* stop." His Humvee dodged the captain and kept going.

I, however, wanted a few words with the lad, so I had the Panda pull to a quick stop. The officer rested his hands on the edge of my window and asked, "Where you guys going?"

I pointed north, toward the gunfire. "Right up there. You told me the colonel didn't need me in this attack. You told me there was not even going to be an attack today." My voice was shaking with anger as he dumbly nodded his head.

"Aren't you monitoring Tac-1?" I asked. "Colonel McCoy just personally ordered me up to the front, and he's more than a little pissed that I'm not there already. I'll let you explain it to him later . . . Sir."

The Panda gunned the engine, almost dropping Bob into the road as he stammered something I didn't bother trying to hear.

Our Humvees careered through the narrow streets, and I scrubbed my mind clear and loosened my muscles in preparation for combat. My fingers walked along the length of my sniper rifle, unconsciously checking it for imperfections with a sense of touch as accurate as a concert pianist playing Mozart on a familiar Steinway. The gun's magazine carried four rounds, and I slid the bolt back slightly and stuck my finger inside the raceway to check for brass.

There was already a round in the chamber. I sighed, content and ready.

Smoke floated into the sky above the flat rooftops of Az Zafaraniyah. Casey worked the radio as our Humvees sailed down a street of low-walled homes already pockmarked by bullet strikes, and he let India Company know we were coming up behind them. We were in a precarious position, because we were not directly affiliated with any of the platoons or companies, and we could easily become targets if we showed up unexpectedly on their dirt. "If anybody poses a threat to you, you kill them," McCoy had ordered his combat teams right before the attack. Violent supremacy would rule this day, and there was a chance that we might get zapped by our pals.

We stopped at a gate, at which a couple of Amtracs were firing like crazy, jumped from the trucks, and grabbed our gear. I would carry only my rifle, the sniper logbook, a pistol, and four quarts of water. Casey toted a low-power handheld radio, maps, water, and his own weapons. Then we had to break up our team. We picked Tracy and Newbern to come with us. The other guys would provide support with the guns on the Humvees. Everyone picked up a twenty-round box of the precision-made ammo to feed my rifle. At a hundred yards, those special bullets would hold within a one-inch circle; at a thousand yards, within a circle ten inches in diameter. The average human head is about twelve inchs in diameter.

The guys in the Amtracs could tell us little about what was going on, other than that there was a lot of shooting, so we cautiously stepped around them and entered the city. Newbern took point.

I came next, then Tracy, with Casey hustling along to provide rear security and radio communications. I could hear him telling India Company that we were heading for the rooftops. It was the start of an unofficial marathon that came to be known as the "Baghdad Two-Mile," an event that will never make it to the Olympics.

As soon as we were in the clear, we broke into a gallop for the built-up north side of the road leading to the bridge and rushed inside a two-story building that the India Marines had just cleared. We pounded through the darkness and up the stairs into the hot sunshine that blazed down on the roof. No wind at all. Great shooting weather.

A two-foot wall encircled the top of the small building, and I pulled a cinder block over to a corner and sat on it, arranged some gear on the top of the barrier, and pushed the rifle into a sturdy position. Then I locked into a tight shooting posture and glassed the area, looking slowly north of our position and blinking away the sweat that stung my eyes. God, the MOPP suit was hot.

My scope was drawn to a small blue-tiled minaret that rose above the surrounding brown buildings, where I saw a flicker of movement. Somebody was hiding behind a wall high above the street, an enemy fighter in civilian clothes with an AK-47, and I saw him peer down into the maze of streets below. The bastard was doing the same thing I was doing—looking for targets. I had found an enemy sniper, so this instantly became a matter of professional honor: *I'm better than you, motherfucker.*

Moving fast, to get him before he could open fire on the Marines, I painted a quick laser on his position, dialed in exactly 343 yards, and planted my crosshairs right on his chest. All the while, my mind was unconsciously wheeling through the sniper's mantra of S—Slow, Smooth, Straight, Steady, Squeeze—and the rifle seemed to fire on its own. My bullet bored perfectly into his chest, and its heavy mass penetrated his major blood-carrying organs, crushing and destroying tissue. That created a hole that is called the "permanent cavity," and then the bullet exploded, sending small, jagged fragments spinning off in erratic paths that shattered his organs. Had to hurt. I watched him slump into a fetal position. Although his body might twitch for another few seconds, this guy was dead.

I was in my zone. The protective presence of Casey, Newbern, and Tracy around me, and the advancing Marines and armor down in the streets, allowed me to concentrate totally on being a pure shooter, an ethereal feeling of being untouchable and able to reach out and control the destinies of other men.

McCoy was off somewhere ramrodding the entire battlefield, with enough radios to talk to anybody on the fucking earth. The company and platoon commanders were making sure where the rifles were pointing, platoon sergeants were hollering orders, and fire team leaders were pushing Marines into exact positions and kicking butts to make them run faster. Casey had binos at his eyes and a radio glued to his ear to guide our little team. Tracy and Newbern were in nearby protective positions. These were all well-trained military personnel who understood the grand plan of battle unfolding that morning as we bashed into the river town. The great dance was in full swing.

I didn't have to worry about that shit. I was merely a destroyer of men.

I pulled the bolt back and reloaded, oblivious to what was going on around me. That was someone else's job, and if I needed to know something, they would tell me. As Casey later explained, "Unless I absolutely had to get into his zone, I left him alone. You don't want to fuck with a man's zone, especially when he's killing people and doing good things."

My eyes seemed to magnify things even without using the scope, new smells drifted to me over the rooftops, and my hearing gathered all kinds of sounds while my brain filtered out the noise and turned down the volume, distinguishing one type of explosion from another or the whine of a passing bullet. Things seemed to slow down, and the adrenaline helped me move and think five times faster than normal. It is an inexplicable feeling that comes to warriors in the heat of a fight, and it has been described since the dawn of man. It is a cliché, it is mystical, and it makes no sense at all, but, by God, it is true.

Four minutes after taking out the sniper, Daniel Tracy called, "Boss, I got something out to the northwest." He verbally walked me across the rooftops, like a stranger in town giving directions to another stranger. *See that funny-looking building with the blue flower box? Up above that, the open window with the green curtain? Look left to the doorway.* I found the gunman Daniel had spotted, did a range check, squared up on the target, who was crouched half-seen 411 yards away, fired, and watched my bullet strike home and efficiently do its grim job at the far end of its parabolic flight. Another enemy soldier lay dead. I reloaded.

Casey was a different man. All of the apprehension and curiosity that preceded his first firefight were gone, replaced by the calmer mien of someone who had smelled the smoke, heard the bullets, and knew what do to. In the warrior's world, we called dramatic change "seeing the elephant." Once you saw it, you never forgot it. He listened to the position reports over the radio as India Company's grunts continued clearing the west part of the city. "Let's go," he ordered, stuffing his maps into his pack. "We stay up here any longer, the fight will pass us by."

We hurried downstairs, hollering, "Friendly coming out!" to prevent some skittish Marine grunt from lighting us up. India's commander had been so obsessed with training his boys to fight in an urban environment that some people had thought him a bit of a nutcase, but now the training was paying off as they worked efficiently house by house through this dangerous warren of homes, shops, and buildings. It was nice to be within their security bubble, for death could be lurking in the sewers, on the roofs, or in the bushes, and the grunts were constantly yelling to keep track of each other in this urban abyss.

Out in the street, mortar shells were detonating ahead of us, and India's Amtracs moved up the road, flanked by Marines on foot. At each window, they drew figure-eights with the muzzles of their M-16 rifles, shooting quickly at any suspicious movement from within. Individual fire teams handled different levels of buildings. To go around a corner, two men would set up, with one kneeling in front and the second resting his hand on the shoulder of the first. When the hand squeezed the shoulder, both men would pop around the corner with weapons ready to shoot. India had practiced the techniques for hours on end, and their attack moved inexorably forward with a smooth fluidity despite the continued incoming fire.

We jogged down the road, moving from one squad to another, dashing across open intersections as bullets whizzed and smacked around us. The bad guys were laying a carpet of gunfire.

There are definite things to look for when choosing a building for a sniper overwatch position, but we didn't have time to run the checklist. We just needed to get up on a roof somewhere, fast, and set up a killing field. A hundred yards down the road, we found a likely spot and dashed upstairs, but by the time we got there, the battle had already moved past. We needed to jump farther and faster, so we pounded back downstairs and rejoined the fast-paced assault.

We were sweating profusely in our MOPP gear and panting with exertion by the time we found a good building 350 yards down the road and had an India rifle squad clear it for us. Up to the roof we went, where we picked up a passenger, Italian photographer Enrico Dagnino, one of the Jackals. They had unfettered access to this battle, and Enrico wanted to follow us. Fine, we told him, take your pictures, but just do what we tell you to do, and you might live long enough to see them published. He did not explain that he had bounced from war to war for years and had seen more combat than any of us.

Rocket-propelled grenades were swooshing all over the place, exploding overhead and raining shrapnel; the rattle of enemy small arms and machine gun fire was increasing, and the return fire from the Marines was deafening. The boys took security positions in the corners of the roof, and Casey contacted the battalion headquarters to let them know we were moving across jurisdictional lines.

Once again, I settled behind one of those low walls that ran the circumference of the roof, got the rifle in place, checked that I had a full load of ammunition, and took a look around. Three minutes later, I spotted a guy atop a two-story building who was firing an AK-47 and had an RPG strapped across his back. This dude definitely had to go. According to the laser, he was 550 yards away, and in this cluttered urban environment, somehow there remained a clear shooting lane between us, an open visual channel that yawned between the buildings from me to him. I hit him three inches below his throat and watched him sink onto the roof like a deflated balloon. The jackass had gone up there alone, with no security, and allowed his attention to be diverted elsewhere, away from the direct threat to himself.

I jacked in a new round, without removing my eye from the scope, and quickly found another target in the open. The soldier was standing atop a chicken coop on the tin roof of a garage only 230 yards away, so close that his form almost filled my scope. He had his rifle in his shoulder and was popping away at Marines, so I blew him away. It was as easy as shooting a paper target in a carnival midway. A bright red flash washed over his face when the round hit him in the mouth, and his head snapped back as if he had been tagged with a heavyweight boxer's left hook. The backward momentum snatched the rifle from his hands and knocked him not only off his perch but also clear off the tin roof. The body was limp when it hit the ground.

I reloaded, took a deep breath, and swept the area again, finding nobody else to shoot. I was still in my zone, emotion suppressed, brain engaged, my actions virtually robotic. My concept of a Mobile Sniper Strike Team—wheels to get to the area of action, then roaming at the front of the advancing forces, guarded by an experienced security team—was getting a thorough workout. My reach was hundreds of yards in front of the advancing troops, and I was sowing disarray and confusion. The idea worked!

Seven minutes after we bagged the guy on the garage, as we were getting ready to leave this building and move forward again to leapfrog the battle, an enemy soldier wearing the snazzy tan uniform and red beret of the Republican Guard walked into the middle of a street, almost as if he were on parade. From only 324 yards away,

I spent thirty seconds examining him in detail and waiting to see if anyone else would join him in the open. He was calmly walking around as if he, instead of me, were the king of the world, and in his right hand he carried an AK-47 that looked almost new. Then he turned around, and that was his death notice, for it appeared that he might be leaving. I had the crosshairs precisely between his shoulder blades, and my bullet sent him slumping to the ground like Jell-O falling out of a mold.

Three kills from one any area is enough, because you don't want to draw special attention from the enemy. So we took off again, only now with an Italian photographer running in the middle of our line. The last thing we needed was one of the Jackals getting whacked while tagging along with us. I went into the lead spot because I had been in urban warfare before, but Casey kept yelling at the boys to get in front of me and finally just grabbed my shirt to stop me. "Stay the fuck behind me! I'm not messing around. You don't have anything to defend yourself with," he barked.

"Yes, Mommy," I replied.

"Fuck you," he said. "Stay behind me." He took point instead.

The battle was still ferocious, with a continuous din of explosions and gunfire, as we made our way forward. We had to get to that bridge. A Marine Amtrac parked in an intersection opened up with a heavy machine gun when we dashed across one street and almost nailed Daniel. But he missed, because Daniel was still not in Baghdad and therefore was not allowed to die yet. We decided to go into a tall house that was surrounded by an eight-foot wall and a locked pair of huge metal gates. With no India Marines around to clear it, we did it ourselves. We formed a stack along the wall; then I tossed a grenade inside, and Casey went over at the sound of the explosion, spider-dropping into the courtyard, one of his boots landing in a bucket of water and fuel. He opened the gate, and we went inside through the front door, but when we got to the roof, we discovered that tall buildings nearby shut down my sight line. We had just wasted a lot of time. The battle was rolling and booming, and we dashed back down and headed for the sound of the guns.

My mind was totally on the job now, and when I get that way, I am fucking invulnerable. Everything else faded from my thoughts; life slowed down and became a black-and-white movie. The mechanics of the craft had taken over my body and the rifle was now part of me, as my mind whirred with permutations, calculations, and scraps of knowledge picked up doing this job in many places over the years. Things automatically fell into their proper places without my even realizing that I was thinking about them.

We joined some of the India guys atop a good building, and I settled in and spent five minutes glassing the new surroundings. The scope jarred to a sudden stop, as if it had a mind of its own. Four hundred and seventy-five yards away, a middle-aged man wearing a red beret and shoulder boards on his clean uniform stood at ease between a couple of buildings. *Officer! Primary target!*

In the American military structure, we are trained to react even at the lowest levels, so if an officer goes down, someone else immediately takes over. The Iraqi army was structured so that no one automatically assumed the responsibilities of a fallen leader.

He was ready to fight, with a pistol on his hip and an AKM, the cut-down version of an AK-47, in his hands, but the only thing he was going to be doing now was dying. Without hesitation, I popped a round through his chest. It flew out of his back, and the bloodstained officer fell face first into the roadway. He would never issue another order, and if you cut off the head of a snake, the whole reptile dies. More confusion.

Two minutes later, I saw an Iraqi soldier jogging down a street and estimated the distance at slightly more than three football fields. A moving target requires new math for speed and distance; such shots have a minimum 90 percent success rate, so I decided to take it. I aimed at a point on a wall ahead of the guy and when he jogged across a specific dot engraved on the lens of my scope, I squeezed the trigger smoothly. The conscious mind can focus only on one thing at a time, and I was watching the runner, but my body was simultaneously making sure that I did not lose trigger control in my rush to take this target. The trigger must be pulled back exactly straight, because any side pressure can affect the flight of the shot ever so slightly, enough to cause a miss. A sniper learns to pull the trigger straight back, every time, so he can hold the necessary sight alignment.

My bullet hit the running soldier at kidney level. He tumbled down, his death fall tracked by a dark crescent of his blood on the wall. Kidney shots should be taken only as a last resort, since both of the organs have to be destroyed for a quick kill. There were a lot of variables, but this guy didn't have a hope in hell from the second I first saw him. I couldn't miss today, and I had to rein in the confidence that grew with every successful shot.

The hunting had been good so far, but the bridge was the decisive point of this battlefield, not individual soldiers, and we were still a good distance away. We were exhausted by the running and gunning and were sweating like pigs in the heavy MOPP suits as the sun beat down without mercy. Casey decided to get us over to Kilo Company, which was closing on the bridge under vicious enemy fire.

That meant we had to move across about five hundred yards of uncleared territory, where the chances of getting shot by Iraqis and Americans were about equal. But my rifle could help take that bridge, which was what this day was all about. "Pack up and let's go," Casey ordered, and we all took a quick drink of water and staggered to our feet, much like Boston Marathon runners who are all out of gas with Heartbreak Hill looming just ahead. This was where our intense physical conditioning paid off, because we could reach deep and find the extra energy we needed.

Casey set off at a slow trot; I came next, then the photographer, with Newbern and Tracy in the rear. Everyone knew that getting separated was probably certain death, but putting one foot in front of another was huffing-and-puffing work. Tracy was humping along, cursing, at the back of the line and warning the panting photographer not to quit. "You stop and that fucking old man'll leave you here," he said. I heard somebody puke, but we didn't stop running. I grinned and kept pushing as hard as I could. We were doing the Baghdad Two-Mile at a full gallop.

We linked up with Kilo, steadily made our way forward, and finally got our first look at the double bridge that was causing so much trouble. It was a mess.

The Iraqis had blown the supports of the fifty-foot center section of the big bridge and dropped it into the river some ninety feet below. That meant our heavy armor was stuck on this side. The narrow pedestrian bridge was left as the only option, and the Iraqis had blown a hole about ten feet long in the middle of that one, too.

Since the Abrams tanks couldn't provide protection up front, grunts would have to storm the damaged bridge. Tomorrow, the Marines of the Bull would attempt the first such dismounted river crossing since World War II, a dangerous daylight assault in which we would be funneled into an easy kill zone, have to patch a path across the gaping hole in the walkway, and all the while be surrounded by steel plates and girders that would send enemy bullets and shrapnel ricocheting all over the place. This would be a dangerous piece of work.

20

The Bridge

The Diyala Bridge was the crown jewel of this fight, for it was the only place anywhere along the entire Tigris River that offered any chance of a crossing. The Marines were on one side, and Baghdad was on the other. We had to get over there in a hurry.

Bullets were zinging from all around and the sky seemed to be burning as we hustled over to a small building that looked like an old guard shack only fifty meters to the southeast of our end. Gunfire ripped the steel bridge and everything around it, and that had to be brought under control if we were to have any hope of getting across tomorrow. The far end of the bridge seemed little more than piles of rubbish, an empty no-man's-land that led into clusters of buildings that were interspersed with the spiky tops of palm trees, but a steady beat of gunfire still came from over there. The battalion had already set about pulverizing the area.

Casey and I and our boys resumed hunting from the flat roof of the guard shack, because from there I could reach all the way over the river to the enemy's concealed positions. Two more of my snipers, Corporals Doug Carrington and Mike Harding, climbed up over the edge to join us, tripling our long-range firepower. I had assigned them to Kilo Company, and since I was now working on Kilo's dirt, we were able to team up. We laid down a hurricane of precision fire that scythed through any Iraqi troops we could see across the river.

Colonel McCoy was telling a newspaper reporter about then, "Coughlin's got seven or eight already, and he's still at it." Actually, I had brought down a witnessed and confirmed kill count of ten that day and possibly more. A kill must be confirmed for us to claim it, but when the action is fast and furious, the numbers become meaningless, because the overall mission is what is important. In such a case, as soon as we take a shot, we change our focus to a new threat and may never know what happened to the earlier target. We may think we have a kill, but the battle has moved on, so we aren't sure because we do not go searching to verify them. We can make an educated guess that it was a sure kill, or that the guy would probably bleed out, but there are too many variables in the equation. We don't have the time, inclination, or mission to check them all out. The shot itself would be recorded, but not a definite result.

The battle finally petered out late in the afternoon, and orders came down that nobody was going across the bridge tonight because of its damaged condition. Engineers would check out its structural integrity after dark.

Naturally, Officer Bob picked the lull in the battle to order Casey and me back to the Main headquarters. The Kilo Company commander protested that McCoy had given us to his command, and he needed snipers up front, where the action was hot. We had to control that bridge. After a lot of back-and-forth, a compromise was reached: I would stay at the bridge, but Casey would go back to hold Bob's hand and would send the Panda Bear and the turret gunners,

Marsh and Castillo, forward to relieve Tracy and Newbern. Griping every step of the way, knowing the Main was safe and under control without him, Casey returned to headquarters just as the sun was going down.

Darkness fell quickly, bringing an end to the hellish heat, but our day's work wasn't quite over. A Javelin missile team with advanced thermal optics joined us at the shack, and our little rooftop bristled with firepower. We were given the job of not allowing anyone to approach our positions or cause further damage to the bridge overnight, and we thought we could control it easily. Only a fool would try coming over the bridge to attack the hundreds of Marines who were gathering during the dark hours.

But about ten o'clock that night, somebody yelled a warning, and I went to full alert, jamming the gun into my shoulder. Everybody on the roof did the same and stared into the night. A crazy *hajji* was sneaking toward us after somehow evading everyone's notice. He had already crawled almost three-quarters of the way across the bridge before being spotted and was only seventy-five yards away when I locked my scope on his creeping shadow and saw that he was carrying something in his right hand. *Suicide bomber,* I thought, and instantly pulled the trigger. My bullet ripped a hole through the right side of his chest.

It was a sure kill, but then things went psycho. A roar of rifle fire thundered around us, machine guns joined in, and more and more bullets thunked into and around the corpse on the bridge as fire discipline broke down among the tired and edgy Marines, who had just endured a full day of intense combat. In about two seconds, at least twenty-five bullets peppered the poor bastard, and I heard a splash as whatever he had carried fell into the river.

That breakdown in discipline was not good, but I was too tired to worry about it. In fact, I was totally exhausted. There were plenty of people on the rooftop now to stand guard, so I wiped the man I had just killed from my mind, turned over on my back, laid my rifle on my chest, and went to sleep to a lullaby of artillery rounds that rumbled overhead and detonated dully along the far bank.

The horizon was already yellow with the first light of a rising sun on April 6, the eighteenth day of the war, when I awoke to a discordant devil's chorus of war noise. Individual Marines pumped rifle shots across the canal, a couple of tanks were booming with their 120 mm cannon, and artillery and mortars thumped out a steady harassment barrage. Enemy small-arms fire, RPGs, and mortars were still rattling back at us. Combat reveille for another day in the Corps.

I rubbed my overworked eyes, which still burned from all the sweat of yesterday, then bitched at the boys for letting me sleep so long, although I was privately grateful that they had done so. I felt rested, safe and cozy in my little corner of the world. The skeletal bridge across the canal remained empty but for the bullet-riddled body of the foolish Iraqi who had tried to sneak up on us last night. While I slept, someone had bestowed the macabre name of "Achdead" on the corpse on the bridge. Over in the forbidden zone, a car burned like a torch, and a curtain of thick dust and smoke swirled above the buildings.

Looking around, I realized that something was different. Overnight, permission had been given to change out of the filthy MOPP outfits that we had not taken off for three straight weeks, and everybody but the guys with me on the roof was walking around in brown-patterned desert camouflage battle dress. Good Lord, did they look comfortable. An attack by chemical or biological weapons was unlikely this close to

Baghdad, and a real problem had developed with heat exhaustion among the troops working in the heavy suits beneath the blazingly hot sun. Changing clothes had never sounded so good, so the Panda and I climbed down from the guard shack and headed over to where the Kilo Company headquarters track was parked in a broad courtyard, safely out of the line of direct fire from the Iraqis on the other side of the river.

The walk was only about twenty yards, but for the first time, I noticed the dreadful condition of the city through which we had fought. Yesterday, I had been much too busy to register any impressions, and the fight had unfolded in a sameness of monochrome brown. Now it looked like some scene out of a Hollywood war epic, only this was for real. Garbage littered the street, the acrid taste of smoke and cordite hung in the air, and because food was rotting in the shops and nearby homes, the city smelled like a barnyard. The bodies of animals and enemy soldiers decomposing in the heat added to the awful odor. Bullets had carved crude holes and scars in the walls, and broken glass crunched beneath my boots.

I found Lieutenant Colonel McCoy standing beside his Humvee, where he had been having a frontline conference with the regimental boss, Colonel Steve Hummer, and Major General James N. Mattis, the commander of the 1st Marine Division. A single lucky Iraqi artillery shell could have decapitated our leadership, but the day's mission was of such importance that the big boys had come down to eyeball it.

When Mattis and Hummer went off to talk to some of the troops who would make the river crossing, McCoy gave me a quick information dump and said there would be no repeat of what happened the previous day, when at Officer Bob's direction I had missed the opening of the fight. No lollygagging behind the line today. He told

me to take my snipers across with the assault troops and set up shop
on the far side of the river. He looked at his watch and said we would
begin in twenty minutes. That gave me just enough time to get out
of the MOPP suit and back to the shack.

As we spoke, Casey had driven up with our trucks, which con-
tained our clothes, and parked only about fifty yards away. Panda
and I were soon peeling away the squishy MOPP suits that clung to
us like a crude fungus. The simple act of putting on clean desert
cammies gave us the feeling of being reborn, and I felt as though I
were donning an Armani suit.

We joked with Casey and some of the other guys as we changed,
and they assembled packs with enough ammunition and supplies to
keep us going for another full day. Meanwhile, the tempo of Marine
artillery and mortars firing in support of the coming mission increased, switching from sporadic harassment fire to a thorough
preparation barrage of the area that we were about to attack. Huge
shells tore through the sky with the sound of ripping linen and exploded among the buildings and the palm grove beyond the bridge.

The volleys of artillery suddenly drew return fire from some hidden Iraqi guns, a salvo that reportedly was triggered by an order from
an Iraqi general using a cell phone. Everything changed in an instant. The Iraqi artillery, which had been quiet all night, was shooting back. That made me finish changing my clothes boot-camp fast.
I was snapping on my flak jacket when three shells came down toward us and someone yelled, "Incoming!"

There was no time to react, other than to realize that this was going to be close. To this day, no one has been able to explain whether
the devastating artillery rounds came from enemy or friendly guns.

BOOM-BOOM-BOOM!!! In quick succession, three big shells
exploded around us. One hit on the riverbank about fifty yards away

with a horrendous roar and blew a great gout of dirt and debris into the air. The second hit to the left of the nearby Kilo command Amtrac, and the third slammed directly onto the vehicle.

A thunderous explosion created a powerful rush of air that darkened the area, shrapnel slashed and rang about, and the concussion hammered the surrounding buildings. Marines were knocked down like rows of dominoes as a column of fire flew out of the rear of the Amtrac, along with the ripped bodies of the two guys who had been inside, smashed radios, maps, packs, and debris colored by a spray of burning oil and hot blood. All of us who had felt safe within the high walls of the compound now felt like mice trapped in a box, with nowhere to hide.

A thick overhead power line snapped with whiplash force and cracked Casey on the arm and sent him sprawling, stunned, into the dirt. He shook it off, caught his breath in the swirling dark smoke, and, unsure of what had knocked him to the ground, slapped his hands across his body, searching for the gooey sensation of blood. There was none, and he got back on his feet and roared off in his Humvee to bring up an ambulance and emergency medical teams.

The Panda Bear and I had ducked away from the blast and, shielded by the tall sides of our armored Humvee, were unharmed other than being thoroughly rattled and disoriented. Screams of wounded men mixed with calls for "Corpsman up!" When I looked over at the smoking ruin of the Kilo command track, I thought Colonel McCoy was dead. We had been standing right beside it, talking, only a moment before.

Through the smoke, fire, and chaos, my pal Gunnery Sergeant Jean-Paul Courville, the Ragin' Cajun, came across the courtyard. He stands a shade under six feet tall, his blond hair is cut short, and his 175 pounds are nothing but solid, lean muscle. When we had first

met several months ago, Courville had just finished a stint as a basic
training drill instructor and looked like a Marine television commer-
cial. "Hello, Gunny," I had said. "It's 'Gunnery Sergeant,' " he corrected. "Fuck you," I replied. After that we got along fine.

After seeing the devastating explosion, Courville, in an astonishing display of calmness and courage amid mayhem and confusion,
already was getting things under control. He got corpsmen busy
treating the wounded, assigned priorities on who was to be evacuated, then personally ducked into the still-burning Amtrac and
hauled out live ammunition, rockets and bullets that were in danger
of exploding from the heat. My personal negative feelings about
everything French do not extend to Courville, who is without question a ripped stud of a gunnery sergeant. Anyway, he's from Louisiana,
not Paris.

Then I heard a shout—McCoy's voice! He had walked to the other
side of a wall just before the shell hit and had survived the explosion.
Two of his Marines were dead and three had been wounded, but the
colonel yelled, "This doesn't change anything!"

He pushed the incident from his mind, for it is an accepted fact of
war that men die, and a leader must focus on the mission. The best
way to help the wounded and remove the danger is to finish off the
enemy, and that meant taking that bridge.

The Panda Bear and I hustled down to the guardhouse, and Mc-
Coy followed a few minutes later. "Ten minutes," he told me.

Various media Jackals, who had heard about the plan for a river
crossing, had been drifting in since daylight and jostled for position
among the grunts. Many of the news types looked dazed after the
deadly artillery barrage that had made them eat dirt, too.

Infantry Marines and combat engineers had scavenged the town throughout the night and had gathered a witch's brew of wooden planks, strips of metal, part of a steel gate, and anything else that they might throw across the hole in the pedestrian bridge. They gathered now, looking like big pack rats carrying their treasure.

We lined up against the walls and waited through a countdown that seemed to take forever. I had a powerful team to take across the river, for our group had grown some more during the morning. I had the Panda and the two snipers who had come over from Kilo, Carrington and Harding. Then, out of nowhere, came still another sniper, Staff Sergeant Dino Moreno, who had been the partner of Mark Evnin. There were few flaws and no weaknesses in this bunch, and a lot of sniper rifles would be going across the river in the first wave. Once across, we would take up positions and let our long guns reach out to help control the captured bridgehead. We could cause a lot of trouble.

Time slowed down again, as if to let me think a bit before going out on a narrow bridge that we fully expected to be swept by enemy fire and the same sort of heavy opposition that we had encountered the day before. A daylight assault on a bridge was dangerous, and I wondered why, in the ultramodern twenty-first century, some bright tactician in a war college had not come up with a better way of doing this.

"Let's do it," McCoy said calmly, and Sergeant Major Dave Howell walked out into the middle of the road, yelling, "Go! Go! Go!" From my position beside the protective wall, I helpfully mentioned, "Dave, you're going to get your ass shot off out there!" He didn't even look at me, and his example banished any residual fear in the kids, who broke away from their hiding places with a shout of defiance and hit the bridge at a gallop.

The first guys out opened fire to cover Marines and engineers who ran out to fling their loads of sticks and steel across the gaping hole, then fell on their bellies and grabbed loose ends to hold the makeshift patch in place so that no one would fall through. The first assault squad immediately pounded out in single file, ran across the patch, and dashed across the narrow bridge. Other Marines shouted encouragement to spur them, while Dave Howell tried to get them to move more deliberately: "This is a marathon, not a sprint! Don't bunch up!"

McCoy stepped forward, but Howell wrapped a big hand around the colonel's arm and stopped him. "We can't afford to lose you," the sergeant major ordered his colonel. Then I started to move, but somebody grabbed my uniform and stopped me in my tracks, too. It was McCoy. If he couldn't go, I couldn't go. He held tight and growled, "You wait for me." Howell had hold of the colonel, who had hold of me. As I stood there holding my sniper rifle and feeling like an idiot, more Marines thundered past, and Dino Moreno gave me a puzzled *What the hell?* look. I nodded for him to take off, and the snipers headed across without me.

After the first platoon and the snipers were on the far shore, sprawled out and shooting, McCoy was allowed to join the assault. Bullets pinged about, but the colonel walked across that bridge like John Wayne coming into a saloon, owning the place. While everyone else was sprinting around him, including photographers who dashed madly around with their cameras, McCoy moved at an almost casual pace, and with his radio handset clasped in one paw, he pulled his radio operator along with him. With his strange idea of fun, McCoy was playing a game within the game, trying to outcool his sergeants, men such as Howell and Courville, and I had no choice but to play along. If he wanted to walk across the damned bridge, then I had to walk, too, when the natural inclination of anyone with a brain was to run like hell.

The colonel is a big man, and his radio operator was also a large dude, so I carefully took a place right behind the two of them and matched the big guys step for step all the way across the broad Diyala Canal, being particularly careful to let them step on that rickety patch covering the hole before I did. When we reached the far side, McCoy looked over and said, "OK. Go have fun."

I could get on with my war.

21

The Worst Thing

There is a dirty part of war that is seldom discussed. Little is written of it, and much less is said, for no one wants to talk about killing innocent people. By crossing that bridge, we stepped into one such troubled moment, a terrible situation that seemed preordained, with an outcome that was inevitable before it started. No matter how many times you try to turn back the clock, the ugly result remains unchanged. We did not intend to kill civilians, but we did, and we would just have to live with it. We did nothing wrong, but every Marine who was there would be scarred by what happened at the Diyala Canal.

The irregular fedayeen guerillas had taught us, over and over, that just because an Iraqi was not in uniform was no sign that he didn't want to kill you. Our entire battalion had driven past the smoking remains of an Abrams tank that had been blown apart by a suicide bomber. We had been in brutal combat all day yesterday and had lost Marines to an artillery barrage this morning. Faced with an incredibly tense situation in a zone of ultimate danger, it was almost impossible—even unwise—for the average grunt to hold fire on someone coming steadily closer. *Threat or no threat?* Guess wrong and you and your buddies are dead.

The bridgehead on the far side of the river looked empty and desolate, as cratered as the dark side of the moon, when we finally got over there. Our gunfire had churned the area into a lumpy field of nothing, overlaid with a frayed carpet of battle junk. Abandoned RPGs and AK-47s lay everywhere, amid torn clothing and lost pictures from destroyed homes, empty fighting holes, and deserted bunkers. Rows of houses, most about two stories tall, and a line of shops occupied the left side of the road. Grunts from Kilo Company charged straight into them, yelling, *"Clear!"* as they surged from room to room and house to house. India Company veered right and worked their way through a large grove of palm trees that had been a nest for Iraqi troops. Our artillery had wrecked the oasis, but rifle fire still snapped on the morning breeze. Resistance had been light this morning, but we could not take anything for granted, and we pumped rounds into anything that looked like a potential threat.

I gathered my sniper team and went looking for a good position. Only a block from the waterfront, we came across a house tall enough to provide a good view. A big padlock secured the steel gate to the courtyard, and Dino Moreno pulled out his pistol and fired into it five times, each round smacking the padlock with enormous force. It held. I muttered about his lousy aim and opened fire at point-blank range with my own pistol, slamming two more bullets against the stubborn device. It danced, it dented, and the ricocheting rounds sang away, but the lock remained secure. It was the second bulletproof padlock that I had encountered in the war, and I made a mental note to buy stock in the Iraqi padlock company.

Our shots were answered from inside the courtyard by the mournful *moooo* of a cow, so I climbed up on some debris and looked over into what seemed like a cross between a petting zoo and a butcher shop. Cattle and sheep and goats and chickens milled about in utter confusion, stepping clumsily in and around the blown-away carcasses of other cows and sheep and goats and chickens. The poor beasts had endured a nightlong fusillade, watching their companions explode right next to them; there was blood and gore everywhere, and they were all mad with fright. I took a pass on this building. After killing at least a dozen men yesterday, I had no sympathy to waste on cows, but damn, how can you fight a proper war in a slaughterhouse?

The Marines secured the front ranks of buildings and the palm grove, then pushed on to established defensive positions about five hundred yards from the end of the bridge. My boys found a good high spot that gave us an unobstructed view up the main road, and all four snipers—me, Moreno, Carrington, and Harding—locked in on it. Since we could see clearly for about a thousand yards, we established an invisible "trigger line" on a curve in the road about eight hundred and fifty yards from our position. Anyone approaching our positions would be watched but not considered a true threat until he reached that point. We quickly noticed that the curve in the road was at the top of a slight downward grade, so gravity and the physics of momentum would conspire to pull a vehicle toward us. It was another reason to be careful in choosing our targets.

Almost as soon as I had my rifle pointed down the street, a white Toyota truck appeared about nine hundred yards away, and through my scope I saw that the driver wore a green military tunic. A second uniformed man stood in the bed of the truck, with a pistol in his belt and an AK-47 in his hand. No doubt about these guys, and they looked as if they were scouting us. The truck came closer, and I told Doug Carrington to take out the guy in back while I tended to the driver. When the truck reached four hundred yards, we did a short count and our sniper rifles barked as one. The driver slumped dead over his steering wheel, and Carrington knocked the passenger out of the back. The truck lurched to a stop.

More Marines were pouring over the bridge, which meant more rifles were pointing down the roads and machine guns were set up. The buildup had the potential for big trouble, because Iraqi radio stations were off the air, traffic cops had vanished, and there was no way to spread the word to civilians to stay the hell away from our bridge. Surely they knew of the ferocious fighting of the previous day and had heard the continuous shelling. But traffic continued to flow around the distant suburban area, with unwary civilian drivers passing faraway intersections as if going to work or to the store. Others were obviously just trying to leave town.

Another vehicle appeared at the top of the rise, came toward us, and showed no sign of slowing down. At about eight hundred yards, I put a round into the engine block, but instead of stopping, the car actually sped up! Marines around me, thinking of suicide bombers, opened up with a tremendous volume of fire; the driver was killed, and his car was riddled with holes. The passenger door came open, and a man about fifty years old got out and staggered away, moving clumsily, until he was dropped a few feet from the car. He was later found to have a pistol in his belt, but the driver was clean.

I grew concerned with all of the shooting going on. The snap of our sniper rifles firing at specific targets seemed to be signaling a general barrage of gunfire from the grunts. They were shooting just because we were shooting, just as everyone had opened up on poor Ach-dead on the bridge last night. Fire discipline was breaking down in a confusing situation.

Our attack was by no means complete, for although we had taken the bridge and were not advancing any farther today, we had to hold what we had captured. We had pushed the enemy out of his prepared positions but were still clearing the area and knew that those soldiers had to have gone somewhere, for we had not found enough bodies to account for them all. Were we facing a massive counterattack? Were suicide bombers going to come at us in cars and trucks? What about an ambush? The factor of uncertainty in such a supercharged atmosphere rose higher than the hundred-degree temperature.

I had a bunch of trained snipers with big scopes on their rifles, ideal for this kind of work, so I found the Kilo executive officer, and he agreed to let us use our advanced optics beyond a new trigger line. We would eyeball whoever was coming down the road and stop their vehicles by putting bullets into engines and tires. Anything that came closer would be free game for the grunts. That might get us out of what could easily become a shootout, with the possibility of civilians being caught in the middle. But communications in a war zone are always chancy, and not everybody had a radio, so the word did not reach all of the Marines who were still crossing the bridge and enlarging the defensive perimeter.

Another car came over the crest of the road. Carrington and I watched until it reached six hundred yards, still on the sniper side of the line, and then we shot the engine block. The vehicle didn't slow down at all but seemed to accelerate. There were two Iraqis inside, both wearing dark clothing, and although we couldn't be certain, we had no choice, because the car kept coming. I took the driver and Carrington zeroed on the passenger, and once again we fired together and killed them both. The car chugged a few times, veered to the side of the road, and gave up, but once again a slashing outburst of Marine fire savaged the vehicle and the people inside. I watched through my scope as bullets punctured shiny holes in the painted doors, blew out the tires, shattered the windows into webs of glass, and made the already-dead bodies jump.

"Godammit!" I yelled. "Stop shooting! Stop it! Let us do this!" We had already done the job, and the thunder of infantry fire that sliced up the vehicle was totally unnecessary. I yelled for the grunts to cease fire, but even that took time, until the shooting finally eased with a ripple effect, like a wave in a stadium crowd. One guy would stop firing only when the guy next to him stopped. This was terrible.

I heard the Kilo XO shouting down the line, "Let the snipers deal with the civilian vehicles!"

But all of the Marines had to be suspicious about the cars and trucks coming toward them, some even accelerating after the snipers shot them. These kids had been carefully trained for months to add their power to the violent supremacy of an attack, and that's just what they were doing. No one was going to let a truck that might be packed with explosives and driven by a suicidal madman get through and blow up in the middle of our lines.

The death toll began to mount out there, and the strain was growing intolerable. It was the worst possible time for anyone to come down that road, and everybody who tried it during the first hour after we crossed the bridge was writing his own obituary.

A fat guy in a white shirt, all by himself, came flying toward us in a pickup, and we blew him away. There was an AK-47 on the seat beside him. Good kill.

Ten minutes later, it all changed in the blink of an eye, and in the swirling fog of war, the inevitable tragedy emerged in the form of a blue Kia minivan that came over the hump of the hill. I decided to engage it as far away as possible. Carrington, Moreno, and I all fired into the engine block, but once again the motor kept running and the built-up momentum pulled it along. *Who are you people?* I screamed in my head. *What are you doing? Who the hell drives toward people who are shooting at them? Don't you know there is a goddamn war going on?* It was impossible to comprehend, impossible to stop, and I watched the van roll forward.

I could see the people moving inside, both in the front seat and in the rear compartment. They didn't seem to be military, for the driver and the passenger were in street clothes, and I could see no weapons, although that did not mean no weapons were in there. Who knew what was packed in the big cargo space? The van kept coming, now accelerating down the grade, and although I prayed for the damned thing to just stop, it eventually reached the trigger line and entered the kill box.

The Marines legitimately opened up on it, and a typhoon of bullets pummeled the van. I couldn't remove my eye from the scope and watched these innocent people die as rifle fire flashed and flared all around me. A middle-aged man and woman in the back of the van somehow lived through that hell of gunfire and spent the night hiding among the dead members of their family before crawling out the next morning with their hands raised.

Suddenly, I was present, but I wasn't really there at all. I snapped from the emotional overload, something I had never before experienced and did not believe was possible. My body began to react automatically to its years of training, but my mind totally disengaged from the awful scenes unfolding in front of me as people kept coming. Innocents were dying, and I was stuck right in the front row with a huge spyglass, not only watching the butchery in magnified detail but also participating in it, up close and personal. I was still a sniper, but I just wasn't home.

I don't remember all of the cars and trucks that were dealt with that day. A mother and father driving a big Mercedes were shot to death, but their little girl, clutching a teddy bear in the backseat, survived. I have no recollection of that bloody moment, nor of much else after the incident with the van.

There was no way for us to go into that uncleared area to help without exposing ourselves to getting killed, for Iraqi soldiers up that road were still shooting at us. Neither was there any way to set up warning signs or barriers, so Iraqis continued to come to the bridge, and they continued to die.

It did not come to a stop, because it could not, until our defensive perimeter was set. There was no way to separate the sheep from the wolves.

I could not count, and did not want to know, how many people I had killed in the past two days. My logbook would just have to wait, and it would never be complete. I don't remember when, and I don't remember how, but once the perimeter was firmly in place, I picked up my big rifle and walked away, back across that damned bridge, as lifeless as a zombie, not knowing or caring where I would end up. I was consumed in the totally unfamiliar world of a waking nightmare, and my only thought was a faith-shaken prayer. *Oh, my God, what have we done?*

Such incidents always happen in war, and they weigh heavily upon the warrior, for although he has done nothing wrong, he will carry the guilt and replay those images in his head for the rest of his life. And the legacy of not being able to discuss such terrible things has been passed down through generations of fighting men and women in many wars. You can't write home to Mom about it; you would never intimately whisper such gory details to anyone you love, nor discuss it philosophically with your friends over a beer back in the civilian world. How can anyone who wasn't there possibly understand? So it sucks at your soul like some private leech.

I was in such a daze that I did not even realize that the Panda Bear had fallen in step alongside as we trudged away from the kill box of the roadblock, back across the bridge, past the little guard shack where we had spent the previous night, past the blown-away Amtrac in the courtyard, back down the road, and out of the city, walking around advancing vehicles and men, until we finally reached the Main. We walked more than four kilometers, and I don't remember a single step. The Panda steered me to our trucks, where I finally could rest, get some food and water, and begin to awaken, at least enough to realize that I was totally exhausted and covered in thick dirt.

Casey took a hard look at me, as if he were a doctor, realizing that something dreadful had happened up there. He would later tell me that he barely recognized me when I came stumbling into camp, but he remained silent, knowing I wasn't ready to talk. My psyche, not my body, had been wounded, and I only said, "Dude, that was the worst thing I have ever seen. I haven't been this mad in a long, long time."

He was surprised by the emotion, because almost the only reactions he had ever seen from me had been confidence in my job and satisfaction when a difficult shot had been particularly well placed. I had always been considered to be the coldhearted killer, but I had been doing a hell of a lot of killing.

It would take several days before I could tell even my closest buddy what had happened, but during that interval, the media discovered the incident at the bridge, and everybody around the world soon was properly aghast at the carnage. It had been terrible to participate in it, but the firestorm of publicity was almost as bad. Insulting speculation and wild guessing ruled the day. The Jackals and their cameramen saw only the aftermath, not the actual event. They interviewed other people who also weren't there, and a couple who were, and knitted together stories that made us look like ill-trained, uncaring, trigger-happy gunmen. They even talked about us slaughtering people on a bus, although there had been no bus.

As skilled as those writers might be, they weren't there when the shit was coming down! They really didn't know what they were talking about, but there is a grim old saying in the news business: "Never let facts stand in the way of a good story." Photographs of the destroyed vehicles and dead people brought on a shitstorm of criticism from officials who were even more distant from the battlefield, some of whom were just playing cover-your-ass politics. The controversy increased until there was even a threat that Colonel McCoy might have to stand trial for war crimes. What total bullshit.

It was all a distraction from the true focus of the mission, and the most important point seemed to have become lost in the drama. We had fought our way to the heavily defended Diyala Bridge, captured it, and crossed it, and that long, curving, bloody road on the far bank would lead us straight into the heart of Baghdad.

Wasn't that why we were here?

22

The Overpass

Moments of history are built on seemingly minor points, and it was fortunate for the Marine Corps, and for the United States of America, that Lieutenant Casey Kuhlman was sitting around the Main headquarters, doing nothing, on Tuesday, April 8. Everywhere else in Iraq, the war was blasting ahead with incredible momentum. It seemed to be leaving Casey behind, and he was big-league pissed off.

Far down south, the British 7th Armored Brigade finally entered Basra. United States Army troops had begun launching heavily armored probes called "thunder runs" out of the Baghdad airport and into the southwest section of the tangled metropolis and were met by intense enemy fire. American Marines were building more and more temporary bridges across the Tigris River and steadily putting more men and vehicles on the other side. The noose was closing on Baghdad, and the Iraqis no longer had any illusions about winning this war.

Our battalion had crossed the Tigris overnight on a pontoon bridge laid parallel to the blown Diyala span. The darkness was impenetrable; Baghdad was blacked out, and we could not turn on any vehicle lights because they would pinpoint our positions. Casey, wearing night vision glasses, led our headquarters unit over in that pitch blackness, and every other vehicle lined up behind his Humvee, without radio communication. If he had gone over the edge of that narrow bridge, we probably all would have followed. We had drilled this follow-the-leader routine for weeks, and now, when it required a dangerous river crossing, he made the job automatic and quick. By the time dawn broke on April 8, the entire 3rd Battalion, 4th Marines, was completely within the Baghdad city limits. The Bull had arrived.

I had spent the intervening hours pulling myself together, comfortable among my buddies in the Main, where no questions were asked. After cleaning up, getting some chow and some sleep, and gaining the alone time needed to sort out my feelings, my spirits steadily improved. The awful events at the bridgehead faded into memories and shuffled away to their proper places deep within my brain, going into one of those private rooms where I could close the door on them. It was getting crowded in there.

I knew that I had to get back on track in a hurry, because if I kept acting weird, a spotlight of suspicion would swing toward me. There was still a war on, and I was a shooter and a leader, so feeling sorry for myself or letting a series of terrible events beat me down simply was not an option. If I let on that my confidence was shaken, it would spread like a virus among those around me, and I would not let that happen. Impossible.

I had stripped down my sniper rifle and cleaned it carefully, becoming lost in the muscle-memory routine of the rag and gun oil, and slowly was able to pull myself back from the abyss, with the promise to never venture so near that edge again. All that the incident at the bridge really proved was that I was human, just like everybody else.

Once we were across the Tigris, the Main headquarters was set up in the prickly palm grove, which put me almost right back where I had started the previous day. I felt no guilt now, no doubt—nothing but a renewed determination to get on with the job. What was done was done. That other stuff was yesterday.

I hunted up Colonel McCoy to iron out the situation with Officer Bob.

"So what's on your mind?" the colonel asked.

"I just wanted to find out what's going to happen next so we don't have a breakdown in communication like in the last attack when you had to scream into the radio to find me." I took a deep, frustrated breath. "Bob told me today that from now on I'm strictly staying with the Main. I just want to see if that's what you want." By going over the staff officer's head to talk directly with McCoy, I was close to insubordination, but this issue had to be settled.

McCoy had bigger things to worry about than this shit, and I knew it, but he growled, "I'll take care of it. You just get your stuff ready. We're going to check out what we think is a chemical factory. You follow me, and if we make contact, get to work. Be ready to go in twenty minutes." The boss gave me a slap on the back, and I walked off to prepare for the patrol.

The colonel was as good as his word, but it was a devil's bargain. I was going back into the fight, but Casey had to stay behind again, which meant that I was losing my security blanket. As much as I disliked that decision, it was neither illogical nor unexpected, for Casey had proven invaluable. His experience level had soared since the start of the war, and he was always busy, whether searching an Iraqi armory with enough weapons to equip a battalion or using his engineering training to help lay down those important new bridges. Such things win wars, and the battalion honchos expressed confidence in him.

Casey was blind to that; he just wanted to get back to the fighting. "I'm sick of being pissed off," he wrote in his journal. "I am just depressed . . . a monkey could do this job. I'm a glorified taxi driver. I would be the happiest man alive if I had a rifle platoon right now." Having had a taste of fire, he wanted more, and he considered anything less than a shooting battle to be a bullshit mission.

By splitting us up, Officer Bob had checkmated the development of my sniper team. We had already proven to other combat leaders how effective we were working together, but it had made no difference to Bob. He wanted both of us left behind but settled for Casey. When I broke the news that he was being quarantined, Casey just shook his head and said nothing at all, but it was easy enough to read the anger and disappointment in his thoughts. I left with the main body for the attack a few minutes later while Casey told his boys to stand down and pulled his truck out of the assault position.

That same day, with the Main and Tac HQs established and guiding the battle that was developing up the road, a couple of large Iraqi BM-21 rockets came howling into the area and exploded nearby. As usual, Officer Bob went bananas, got on his radio, and started yelling gibberish at the senior officers in the Tac, who were only a few yards away and knew as well as he what had just happened. Bob said that everybody had to pack up and move, although no one had been hurt and our counterbattery radar had already pinpointed the launch site and was guiding planes to attack and shut it down. Bob was ignored, but the incident spurred Casey to get out of the man's presence and find something useful to do.

One of the Secret Squirrels, an intelligence officer, told him that an abandoned antiaircraft missile launch site had been found nearby, and he wanted to check it out. Instead of assigning a grunt to provide an armed escort, Casey grabbed his rifle and went along to do the job himself. They came upon a carefully built position containing another of those huge French-built Roland antiair missile launchers, a state-of-the-art piece of defensive equipment, but useless because its operators had abandoned it. While the Squirrel rummaged through the trashed position, Casey found a discarded Iraqi flag: three broad stripes—red, white, and black—with three big green stars in the middle of the white one. It was not a new flag, and the colors had been dulled by time and exposure to the hot sun.

To most Americans, the Iraqi flag was just a flag, but this one was a relic from another era. Its design had been the banner of Iraq since 1963, but just before the Gulf War in 1991, Saddam Hussein added the *takbir* of "Allah Akbar" (God is great) in green Arabic script, between the stars, in an effort to portray himself as a leader of all Muslims. Unknowingly, Casey had picked up a flag that was considered a pre-Saddam symbol, a fact that was very important to Iraqis. Without much thought other than having a neat souvenir, he rolled it up, stuffed it into his backpack, and promptly forgot about it. That flag would be unfurled a few days later in a historic moment.

The morning's mission began with the Bravo tanks and Kilo infantry heading for a suspected chemical factory while the India grunts set up in a blocking position and cleared neighborhoods to the east. The military side of the operation was relatively routine, because our coordination was flawless and we all knew our jobs.

The problem was that we were no longer out in the desert or going through smaller towns. We were entering the congested suburbs of Baghdad itself, and Iraqis streamed out of the buildings and into the streets to watch us pass, most of them waving and smiling. Some even danced with joy. This was the kind of welcome that we had been told to expect, but after our previous experiences, it was unnerving. Our armored vehicles ground toward our objective without incident, and we kept studying the cheering crowd for signs of trouble. We wanted to join the celebration of freedom, but we didn't want to be ambushed or sniped at, or to kill any more civilians.

There was some talk later that the mission had been assigned mainly to give McCoy's battalion something to do, and there was no doubt that the Boss was impatient. He was drawn to danger spots as if by magnetism, and when he popped out of his Humvee to enter a large building that was taller than most of those surrounding it, Sergeant Major Dave Howell put his big arm around my shoulders and told me quietly, "If he keeps this up, he is going to get himself killed. Go watch out for him."

We followed McCoy inside what had obviously once been some sort of government building and found that looters had beaten us to the place and had stripped it bare, from the high ceilings to the floor, leaving behind only piles of junk and a musty emptiness. We ran up to the roof, and Baghdad spread out before us like a dusty checkerboard. Buildings lay out from our position at every angle, like spokes in a wheel, and parks and open spaces broke up the grids of streets. Automobiles were driving about, and people were outdoors in vast numbers. Were we going to have to fight through this?

I found a good vantage point in a rooftop corner, behind the ever-present tiara wall that every building in Iraq seemed to wear, and settled in. Other Marines spread out as I glassed the area and watched waves of civilians but saw no discernible soldier types. Maybe, I thought, we had broken their will to fight after all. I told the boys to stay sharp despite the whooping and hollering out there in the streets. As if to emphasize the danger, only a few minutes passed before we got into one of the strangest firefights of the war.

The colonel had gone back down into the building and called up to tell me it was time to drive over and check India Company, two miles away. I hurried down and linked up with him at the Humvees parked just outside the compound, and as we were saddling up, the sharp sounds of a short, vicious battle erupted inside the courtyard through which we had just passed. I had my rifle ready, but the high wall prevented me from supporting the Marines doing the firing, and by the time I popped around the corner, three Iraqi fighters lay sprawled dead about fifty meters away. Two had loaded rocket-propelled grenade launchers on their shoulders, and the third man carried a short AKM automatic rifle, the preferred weapon of Saddam's Special Forces.

Where the hell had they come from? This area was supposed to be secure.

An Amtrac sergeant needing to answer a call of nature had gone to the corner of the compound, which was covered by a layer of smelly garbage and sludge that indicated the Iraqis had also used it as a latrine. Luckily, with the combat rule of never letting anyone go anywhere unprotected, his gunner on the Amtrac was keeping an eye on him. When the Marine had his pants down, these three jokers crawled out of the slime and mire only four feet away, apparently thinking everyone had left the compound. Surprise was total, and the

Marine took off, yelling for his Amtrac mate to open fire, which he did with a 7.62 mm machine gun, and other Marine grunts quickly came up and joined the shooting. The Iraqis were killed before they could get off a shot. Sometimes it is better to be lucky than good, because those fedayeen nuts could definitely have done some damage.

McCoy came into the courtyard in a fury. To Darkside Six, the otherwise laughable incident meant that his battalion was getting sloppy, and he ordered Kilo to search the entire compound thoroughly again; then he dispatched the Bravo tankers to scour the surrounding area. The laughing, waving civilians parted quickly at the sound of gunfire and the sight of suddenly grim Marines who once again were wearing their war faces.

Sure enough, only ten minutes later, the tanks kicked over a hornets' nest, and the blasts of their big guns shook the streets as a duel opened with Iraqi troops protected in a strong bunker complex. An ambush point had been built right in the middle of an urban area. They obviously were not as concerned as we were about civilian casualties.

With Panda driving like mad, we were rushing toward the battle area in our Humvee until I once again realized the lack of wisdom in getting caught between Abrams tanks and whatever it was they were trying to kill. Instead, I spotted some Marines on a highway overpass and yelled for the Bear to get us the hell over there. He bounced the curb, churned into lower gear, regained speed, and power-slid the truck right up against the walkway to the overpass, as if he didn't want me to have to walk far. We ran to the crest of the bridge.

A Marine was shooting at distant targets in the same bunker complex the Bravo tanks were attacking. "Staff Sergeant," he said, "boy, am I glad you're here. I've killed three of them already, but they're too far out for me to hit with this piece of shit."

"How far?" I put my rifle against the metal railing and braced hard into it.

"About eight hundred yards." He was almost at the maximum range of his M16A4 rifle, a newer version of the standard infantry weapon. It had a low-power scope that increases accuracy but not distance.

"I'd say that piece of shit is doing you pretty good." The kid had done well. "Walk me onto where they are."

He pointed, then fired some rounds to kick up dirt in the target area. Through my scope, that was as good as a flashing neon sign. I glassed onto the bunkers made of concrete, logs, and sandbags and through a shifting haze of dust and debris saw a lot of enemy soldiers bobbing up and down, firing and dodging around. The Bravo tanks and the grunts were already putting the fear of Allah into them, and the poor souls had no idea that a sniper was joining the hunt. With no time to use the laser, I estimated the range, dialed in the dope, seven plus four and three minutes right, and settled down to work.

I centered up on the first target, about a half mile away, and squeezed the trigger, starting the familiar pattern of firing and re-loading with machinelike quickness, coming down on another tar-get as soon as I fired a shot. *Bang, hit. Bang, hit. Bang, miss. Bang, hit. Bang, miss. Bang, miss. Fuck. Bang, hit.* Four hits, three misses, one obscenity, and it was over.

Seven shots for four targets is a terrible ratio for a sniper, but of all the shooting I did in this war, I considered this the best. The fluid battlefield was cluttered, visibility was terrible, it was hard to read fir-ing lines, the targets were moving quickly and at crazy angles, and I had no trained observer to call the shots or targets. It was slapstick sniping at its best, and I loved it. I had literally shot away the linger-ing shadow of guilt from the bridge.

When the bunker complex was cleared, we set up a defensive perimeter a block and a half behind it, brought up the Main and the combat trains, and settled in for the evening.

Casey and I shared some MREs and tried to guess what might still be ahead. After the ambush today, we knew there were plenty of bad guys left out there who did not intend to let us go strolling through downtown Baghdad. Tomorrow morning, the entire city could be rising up against us, and we all again had visions of *Black Hawk Down* and of the dead Army Rangers being dragged through the streets of Mogadishu. We all knew the story and understood its significance.

But I had been in Somalia and knew there were huge differences between the two places. This was not Mogadishu, and we could handle this town. We had a veteran battalion supported by other aggressive Marine and Army units and all the air power we might need. "Not this time," I told Casey. "Not us. They fuck with the Bull and they get the horns." I slept well that night, with no visits from any acquaintances at all.

23

Sniper Team

The battalion staff had a dawn meeting in a real conference room inside a captured headquarters of the Republican Guard, and Colonel McCoy and his planners spread out maps of the built-up area we were about to enter. The entire 1st Marine Division was now across the Tigris, piling ever more stress upon the reeling Iraqi defenders.

Desertion was decimating the enemy forces, and there was little command and control over whatever remained of the Iraqi army. While the regulars might have packed it in and made a quick return to civilian life, the fedayeen and remnants of the Ba'ath Party militia were still around, and we anticipated that today's fighting could be as hard as anything we had yet faced.

Red circles on the staff's plastic map overlays marked important buildings in our zone, but reaching them would be a slow and deliberate process. We might have to clear every building, one by one, to get to our prime objectives, and while such a leapfrog tactic would be effective, it could take forever.

On top of that, disturbing news had come from the Jackals, who told us that they were concerned that their colleagues lodged in the hotels of downtown Baghdad might have been taken hostage by

the collapsing Iraqi military. They worried that some journalists
might be executed.

While the staff laid out the attack plan, those of us in the Main decided that the bright new morning would be a fine time to wash up
and do our laundry. This time we had an opportunity to do a really
good scrub instead of the hasty canteen showers and baby-wipe
baths that we had endured over the past weeks, and we got busy
cleaning our bodies, clothes, and weapons. We stuffed big plastic
trash bags into cardboard boxes, then poured laundry powder and
water into one and clear water into another and proceeded to scrub.
Cans of water were set aside for dousing ourselves in open showers.

That's how McCoy found us, and since he was as filthy as everyone else, he also deemed washing to be a good idea. We parted to
give the colonel some space, and Darkside Six stripped down without
hesitation, sloshed water over his head, and wrung out his clothes in
the buckets. Marines in the field don't stand much on ceremony. He
was standing buck naked in the middle of a parking lot, dripping wet,
when he gave me my next orders.

"From here on out it is going to be pure MOUT," he told me, referring to the specialized Mobile Operations in Urban Terrain for
which we had trained so hard during ProMet. We were going to be
knocking on, or down, a lot of Baghdad doors, and he said, "I want
you to integrate a Battalion Sniper Operation to support it. You can
use all the snipers that you need, but leave some at the company
level." Music to my ears. Sniper teams! I had been waiting the
whole war for this.

I expected some pretty nasty fighting downtown, and being able
to do some prior planning instead of having to react to the changing

battle could put my killers out where we could do the most good. I put on my wet and clammy uniform, which would dry in ten minutes, and took off for the conference room to find out exactly where we were going, how we wanted to get there, and what sort of resistance was expected.

There was nothing in established sniper doctrine to cover such an attack, so I had to wing it as the operations officer showed me the overall plan. Two major roads, separated by a distance that ranged from five hundred to a thousand meters, forked off from the starting point, then came back together, almost in a diamond shape. India and Kilo infantry companies would penetrate the area in their armored Amtracs and Humvees; then their grunts would start clearing the buildings while the Bravo tanks went up a middle road.

I leaned over the maps, calling on the hard-earned lessons of every combat situation I had ever been in, particularly the urban fights, such as in Somalia. I knew how to fight in cities. We could do this.

I first set up a picket fence of observation zones, using three sniper teams, and put other snipers with specific units for close-in support. Using their scout training, the teams would sneak into the planned zone of combat, get to some rooftops, and radio real-time intelligence to the company commander below, call in artillery fire on any strong resistance, and take down any targets of opportunity. Then the infantry companies would plunge through, and when the grunts passed the snipers, my boys would jump back into the lead position.

The goal was to keep at least one team in front of the advancing infantry and provide interlocking fire between the teams. With any luck, this could be a shooting gallery.

The problem was that my sniper teams would have to penetrate uncleared terrain during daylight hours. To overcome this, I would create a stronghold at the initial point of the attack, manned by all three teams, plus a borrowed team and two extra armored Humvees given to us just for this fight. Once the battle was under way, the teams would disperse and start jumping along the front.

As a final detail, I gave myself a bonus by making absolutely certain, through McCoy's direct orders to me, that Casey would be freed from the confines of the headquarters and at my side during the attack. Bob could not trump us this time. It was not just a gesture of friendship but an added margin of safety for me. Casey was totally familiar with the sniper drill by now, he didn't panic when under fire, and with his rank and command skills he could deal with other troops on the ground and other unit commanders by radio during a fight. Few people held all of those qualifications.

When I gave the word to my snipers, they smiled. There were targets to be harvested out there today, and they soaked up my confidence. I had a bunch of shooters on my hands, ready to go do their deadly work in this miserable war. By the time the armored vehicles came to life with grumbling engines and the loud clanking of treads began to crunch on pavement, it was all I could do to hold them in check. They all wanted to shoot somebody.

We took our four Humvees up to the line of departure, the same overpass from which I been shooting the previous day. From there we could see our target building, a tall structure about three hundred yards away, on the left-hand side of the road.

We took off like rabbits for it at the same time, threw a loose cordon of Marines around the building, cleared the stairwell, and got to the roof, where we posted a man at the door to prevent any surprise visitors. I took the northwest corner, Dino Moreno settled into the northeast section, and Sergeant Roger Lima and his spotter covered the blind spots between us. Casey set up the radios and at exactly 9:11 in the morning told the battalion we were in position. Sergeant Major Dave Howell came up to our roof to get an overview of the battlefield.

The grunts moved into the zone and hit the first row of multistory buildings with a bang, but they found little of interest and no resistance. The city was eerily quiet, but I would not allow myself to believe that the enemy had just run away, so I swept my scope across the rooftops and the roads and the windows of lines of apartment buildings.

After forty-five suspenseful minutes, Casey said that the battalion intel guys were reporting that a dark Mercedes carrying some Ba'ath Party officials was heading our way. Almost at the same moment, I saw the dark green Mercedes, containing three Iraqi men, move cautiously into my area, stopping and starting, almost as if the occupants were peeping around corners. Suspicious, yes, but a danger? The windows of the fine motorcar were rolled up, indicating these dudes were riding around in air-conditioned comfort. With the scope locked on, I could see that both passengers had AK-47s, and that was enough for me, so I adjusted for a high-angle shot. The Mercedes, although only 170 yards away, would be a tricky piece of work, since I was about eight stories above the target.

Shooting from such an angle makes a bullet hit below the point of aim, while shooting through glass will cause the bullet to rise. I had spent the idle time lasering ranges on various points in my zone and doing calculations in the gun book, and since snipers have formulas for everything, there was no real mystery to work out. I already had the dope figured and dialed it into the scope so the rifle would adjust the path of the bullet, which would change several times. This wasn't skeet shooting.

I lined up on the rear window of the moving target as it headed north, then fired. The bullet crashed through the glass to smoke-check the guy in the backseat right between the shoulder blades, only four inches above my aim point. Not bad for a high-angle, glass-stressed shot on a moving target in a combat zone. The Mercedes accelerated out of the area with the passenger in the backseat slumped over dead.

Downstairs, the grunts were charging hard and fast into the warren of apartment buildings, shops, and homes, under the watch of curious, not hostile, Iraqi civilians. A civilian car turned a corner and braked to a hasty stop when the driver found himself looking down the big barrel of an Abrams tank cannon and a Humvee's heavy machine gun. He shifted into reverse and sped away, and no one fired. We were pushing, but no one seemed to be pushing back, and the stillness of the battlefield bothered me. *Where are they?*

At 10:20 A.M., I spotted a guy on a distant roof and lased the distance at 1,025 meters, almost three-quarters of a mile away. Being up high, I had a clear sight line on him and the AK-47 he held. He was an amateur sniper hunting Marines from a rooftop, so he had to go. I did not think for a moment about him being another human being with a family, and in fact didn't really think about him as a person at all. He was a threat who had stepped into my world, and those would be the last steps he ever took. I calculated the wind to be about three minutes left, tweaked the scope, and brought the crosshairs to his belly, right about where his navel would be, so if my bullet drifted either up or down, there would still be plenty of target area. I fired and watched as the big bullet covered the distance in an instant and struck the soldier in his right chest with terrific force. The impact yanked him around in a pirouette; he dropped his weapon, fell over, and didn't get up.

Casey scanned his binos back to our north, the area in which I had shot the Mercedes, and saw one of the CAAT teams in a fight. They had taken some fire from a large field alongside the road and had called in mortars to suppress the enemy and opened up with their own chattering machine gun. They were justified in returning fire, but there was no way they could have seen exactly who they were shooting at, and vehicles of all sorts fled the area. "*Oh, my God!*" Casey shouted, and grabbed his microphone. One of the vehicles under fire was a van filled with a family. "CAAT Two, Hotel Five!" Casey barked, identifying himself to the CAAT commander. "Those are civilian vehicles you are engaging, and they have women and children in them. *Stand down!*"

The CAAT machine gun stopped immediately, and Casey watched with relief as women and children jumped from the van; then other civilians emerged from other cars, confused and scared, with their hands up. From his rooftop vantage point, from which he could see more than the guys on the ground, he had probably prevented a slaughter.

There were still threats in the area, and we had to be careful, not foolish. After another fifteen minutes of slow scope movement, I found a target, a uniformed soldier with an RPG launcher on his shoulder, in the third window from the left on the fourth floor of an apartment building. I checked my range card—exactly 427 yards northeast of our position. It was in Dino's zone, but he didn't have the angle, and I had a clean shot, so I killed the dude with a round dead center in his chest.

The battle was now advancing quickly through the streets, and it was time for us to move if we wanted to get out front. The India Company commander radioed that he could see a tall building a few miles away, which he believed to be a major hotel that towered over everything around it. "If we can get snipers up there, they should be able to see a long, long way," he said. From my rooftop perch, I could see that it was too far away for us to reach anytime soon, but we had to find another position.

We took off down the stairs and emerged from the dark interior into a battle that was still going on around us. Dave Howell took two snipers and went to link up with the moving tactical headquarters, while Casey, the Panda, and I headed for another tall structure, accompanied by four other Marines who had joined us.

We broke into a large industrial structure that had huge locker rooms on each floor and headed for the top. It was seven stories tall, but when the Panda and I got up to the roof, we found it was worthless as an overview site. While downstairs, there was no way to know that bigger buildings nearby blocked all of the sight lines on the roof. "Shit," I exclaimed. "We can't stay here."

Casey had lagged behind to establish rear security for us and was trying to make sense of a storm of radio traffic. The battalion was running into occasional hot spots, but there was no organized opposition truly worth the name. We met him about halfway up the stairs as we were running back down, and I yelled, "You took me to the wrong building, fucker!"

"What?" Casey replied incredulously. "This is the one we pointed to back at the other building. Jackass." Not exactly proper military courtesy, but the exchange of information was perfect.

"No, it isn't. This is the wrong one, so get me to the right one." I was hot. Time was wasting.

"What the fuck are you talking about? There isn't a better-looking place anywhere around here." It was a moot point, because we were already leaving, running down the stairs and arguing as we went. We burst through the door yelling, "Coming out!" and the harsh Iraqi sun, well into the morning sky by now, slammed our eyes.

Marines were everywhere, pushing through a confusing battle-field. Our plan was falling apart because of the lack of resistance, but why argue with success? We caught up with McCoy, who was receiving piecemeal fragments of official orders and adjusting to those frags as the battalion surged like the undertow pulling along a beach and sweeping everything before it. He called in the flanking companies to orient the battalion toward a technical university and the headquarters of the Iraqi air force.

I had his attention for only a moment and asked, "Sir, the battle's moving too fast, and our objectives are changing by the minute. Can you give me any idea of what's up next? Where you want us to go?"

"I know, I know," he replied, not even looking up as he studied his maps of downtown Baghdad and put his finger on one grid square. "We're going to take out this air force headquarters compound . . . right here. Find yourself somewhere to support that attack."

Casey marked the grids on his own map, and our Humvees raced through the tangled streets of the city, trying to get in front of our highballing mechanized battalion. Burning cars belched smoke, and the bodies of some dead dudes lay scattered about. To support the unfolding attack, we had to get into position before it was launched. That was the whole point of a mobile sniper team, but it meant driving headlong into the dangerous abyss of an urban environment.

The morning had been one of steady, small fights, and the intelligence officers thought the air force compound might be the first real stronghold of the day. Even as we whizzed through the streets, down canyons of uncleared Iraqi buildings with average citizens waving at us from windows, while we kept watch for the barrels of guns to appear from those same windows, Casey heard another call on the radio. The India Company commander wanted to know if his troops should proceed to a hotel that he had mentioned earlier. He was told to stand by, because that objective was not in our zone of operations.

We came up behind the air force compound, parked around a corner, and darted into an apartment building across the street. This was much too close for normal sniper work, but this was not a normal day, and there wasn't much choice. Casey, the Panda, and I ran through a short, narrow alley and, with fingers on triggers, burst through the doorway. Inside, we cleared the stairwell and approached the door that would lead to the roof, where I could set up shop for the attacking force that was already on the way.

But the door was locked, with another one of those damned Iraqi padlocks that are apparently made with some secret formula by people from Mars, because they are unearthly secure. I shook it, hit it, cursed it, and shot it three times, with one of the ricochet bullets nearly taking off my toe, then gave up. The roof wasn't going to happen. I really do want to buy stock in that company. Casey found a big window for me instead, and I got into it with the Panda protecting my ass while Casey tuned in the chattering radio to stay up with what was going on.

The orders had changed again. At twelve minutes past noon, Mc-Coy was told to forget about the air force headquarters and charge straight into the very heart of Baghdad. The big building that had been spotted by the India Company commander was the Palestine Hotel, where journalists and civilians might be held hostage, and it had suddenly been put into our zone of operations. The Bull was told to go and get it.

Overall, our battalion was to provide security for a number of key downtown buildings, including the embassies of Japan, Germany, the Vatican, Indonesia, and Poland, and the Palestine, Sheraton, and Baghdad hotels. The Army had gone through the area the previous day and, thinking they were taking fire from one of the hotels, had by mistake killed a photographer on a rooftop with a camera on his shoulder and shot up some rooms. But the Jackals who rode with us were urging us to hurry, worried that their colleagues might become targets of revenge by the fedayeen, looters, or enraged Iraqi militia types.

I knew nothing of the fresh developments. I had locked myself, physically and mentally, into a great position to support the attack that I expected to hit the air force compound. I calmly glassed the sprawl of empty buildings, looking for somebody to shoot, ready to fight a battle that had already been called off.

"Hey!" Casey yelled up the staircase. "Come on! We're leaving!"

I was aggravated. "But I have a good view from here!" I had survived a reckless drive through the city streets, run through the alley, gotten up the stairs, and met the padlock and was in a perfect shooting position. Now I had to go?

Casey brooked no argument, and the edge of his tone got through to me. "We have to go, man. Right now. I'll meet you at the truck."

"Where are we going?" I was already unfolding my arms and legs, shaking out the cramps, keeping a firm grip on the rifle and moving carefully to avoid smacking it against the walls.

"Downtown, dude. To some hotels," he called back over his shoulder. We ran for the trucks.

24

Our Iwo Jima Moment

It was April 9, Day 21 of the war, and Baghdad was falling.

Our Humvees roared through a traffic circle and blew past intersections, sailing on the belief that if we moved fast enough the bad guys would not have time to react. The plan to use our speed for security worked a little too well, because the good guys did not have time to react either. Casey looked into his side mirror and saw that the vehicles charging up the street right behind us were the Abrams tanks of Bravo Company. They were supposed to be in the lead, not us. Once again, we found ourselves amid the tanks in a combat zone, so we backed off and let two of the big guys rumble by before jumping back in line and tagging along behind them.

Baghdad passed in a blur, and with our view partially blocked by the bulk of the tanks, we were surprised when we broke into the clear and found ourselves in the center of a big plaza known as Firdos Square. Panda slid to a stop, and I dove to the grass, brought the scope to my eye, and started glassing for threats. Casey told our drivers to integrate into the Bravo defenses and then joined me on the long lawn.

It was a scene from another world. The ancient blue-tiled dome of the Shahid Mosque glittered behind us, and anchoring two cor-ners of the square were the modern Palestine and Sheraton hotels, both twenty stories tall and separated by a street. The Euphrates River was only about five hundred meters away, and a bronze statue of Saddam Hussein loomed thirty feet high, the right arm raised as if in reluctant welcome. A decorative fountain held little water. We were in full battle gear, lying in a park in the middle of a traffic cir-cle, and I was looking down the barrel of my sniper rifle for possible threats while civilians walked nearby and stood around watching us, like spectators at an odd sporting event.

The city was in turmoil, a ragged end to a smooth war. The air-port had been captured, thunder runs had subdued fierce resistance in the army sector, a Republican Guard barracks was on fire, Iraqi government buildings were now ours, the Bull had arrived, the Bravo tanks were parked in the center of the city, and a Marine sniper team—Casey and me—lay waiting and battle-alert in the grass, ready to smoke-check anyone who was a danger to our arriving Marines.

Once the foreign civilians in the hotels saw the American hel-mets and uniforms, they took to the streets in a human wave—pri-vate citizens, the foreign press, a horde of photographers, and even some antiwar protesters. Television cameramen zoomed in on our position.

Within moments, the streets began to fall into chaos, and the looting began, further complicating the job of trying to pick anyone who might be a threat out of the faces in this shifting crowd of hu-manity. This was like being on the field during a Super Bowl, trying to find a face in the stadium crowd, and I had to suppress every sense that I had to keep from being distracted, for nobody had blown a whistle and declared, "War over!" I submerged my emotions and depended on my experience and reflexes. As far as I was concerned, we were still fighting.

Up on the roof of the Palestine, I saw a man pacing back and forth and looking down over the square. The silhouette was dark against the bright cobalt sky, and I could not make out details, but based on our past experience with other roof-prowlers, I had to consider him a potential threat. *Sniper?* He sat down. He had something in his hands, and I steadied up on him in my scope and asked Casey, "See the guy on top of the roof?"

"Got him," Casey replied, focusing his binos.

"What's he up to?" A crowd surged around us, curious about the two Marines in the grass, one with a scoped rifle and the other working a big pair of binos.

"He has something in his hands."

"Yeah, I can see that." I took up a pound of pressure on the trigger. "But what is it?" Whoever he was up there was only two pounds of finger pressure from catching a bullet.

"Hard to tell. Tough angle."

As Casey spoke, the man turned. Luckily for his mother, the suspicious "weapon" was a laptop computer. I immediately swept my rifle away from the luckiest journalist in Baghdad, who apparently had gone to the roof to get better satellite reception.

The crowd thickened around us. Reporters and photographers ventured closer, curious about our warlike presence. I could hear the cameras clicking and actually had to wait for some of them to get the hell out of my line of fire. Some Jackals are born without brains.

There was no overt resistance, and in fact everyone seemed to be celebrating, but we nevertheless kept our war paint on. I had already killed three men that morning, and chances were good that I would have to do in some more before this day was done. I didn't want to smoke-check some dude in the middle of a block party, but if he looked like a threat, I would do so in a heartbeat.

Civilians were crowded into Firdos Square, whooping and hollering, but our tanks weren't parked out there as exhibits. Their cannons were loaded and ready to blow something apart, and none of McCoy's Marines were letting down our defenses. Bravo Company worked roughly to cordon off the area, and the India grunts hustled inside the hotels to clear the rooms. The situation, a by-the-book military operation going on in the middle of a carnival, had gone beyond bizarre and become the sort of experience American soldiers must have encountered in liberating European cities during World War II. It is difficult and dangerous to step instantly from the days of fighting into a warm sea of people who are ready to celebrate the end of combat that is not yet at an end.

We understood the sounds of victory. It was what we had longed for throughout the war, and the shouts rolled comfortably over us. Finally, we had come to the place where we were being welcomed as liberators.

"One minute the Marines are creeping along shot-up neighborhoods, looking to fight Iraqi militia or fedayeen guerrilla fighters," wrote John Koopman of the *San Francisco Chronicle*, our embedded reporter, who had become our friend, too. "The next minute they're in downtown Baghdad, being greeted as conquering heroes. What a difference an hour makes."

We repositioned the Humvees and moved to support the grunts from India who were prowling through the Palestine Hotel. We tried to stay focused as jubilant Iraqis surged around us, patting us on the back, hugging and kissing us and handing us small flowers, some of them thanking us in fractured English. Beyond the screen of welcoming Iraqis, more people were running around, looters who were hauling away furniture and everything else imaginable. If it wasn't nailed down, they stole it. There were no longer any police or law enforcement officers to be found in Baghdad, or anywhere else in Iraq, and that wasn't our job. We were still looking for the bad guys with guns and explosives.

Out of the crowd emerged a small group of people who appeared to be European, judging by their white skin, thick accents, and styles of clothing. They were shouting insults at us like "baby-killer" and "murderers" and "assassins." Venom spilled in a twisted wave of hatred from the so-called human shields, who had entered Iraq to place themselves between the mean American military and the glorious soldiers of Saddam Hussein.

A middle-aged woman thrust a calendar containing photographs of dead children into my face and screamed, "Look what you did! How could you kill all these innocent children?"

"And what kind of sick bastard makes a calendar out of them?" I snapped back. She will never know how close I was to punching her, because she triggered memories of the ugly scene back at the bridge. But I pointed out instead that those pictures could not have come from this war, because it had only started three weeks ago, hardly time enough to whip up a best-selling little antiwar calendar. Things started to get volatile.

Up came a surly group of Iraqi men, some of whom spoke good English, and they surrounded the protesters who were surrounding Casey and me. One man explained that they did not care for these rude people and that he and his friends had decided to beat them to death.

Now I had to protect the antiwar nutcases, so I tried to give the Iraqi mob a lesson in democracy. "In America, this sort of complaining is called free speech," I said. "They have a right to say whatever they want to say and should not be punished for expressing their beliefs."

"Yes," said the gang leader. "Yes, America. President Boosh. We will kill them."

I looked at him and said, "You don't understand. This is part of democracy, and you're going to have to live with it. You can't go around killing people just because you disagree with their political views. You get to say what you want, and they get to say what they want."

The men did not strike anyone, but the intimidated antiwar protesters decided to move along. The peace activists had been saved by a U.S. Marine, one of the very people they hated, from a brutal death at the hands of ordinary Iraqi citizens, whom they thought they were there to defend. Nobody ever said this had to make any sense. I realized that a rational discussion of democracy might be a long way off in Iraq.

The hotels were pronounced clear, and the fedayeen had not sprung an anticipated ambush, so things slowly came under control from a military point of view, and we relaxed a bit. Maybe I wouldn't have to kill anybody else today after all. The crowd in the square surged over to that big statue of Saddam Hussein, a monument to a man who no longer mattered. It had been erected only a year earlier to mark the sixty-fifth birthday of the tyrant, and Iraqi families had been prudent to pose for photographs before the statue. It was now the target of their revenge. They didn't have the man, but they had his likeness, bigger than life, arrogant even in cast bronze, and were no longer going to let it stand there to dominate their capital. Shoes were thrown at it, and then the clang of rocks hitting metal reverberated off the weathered bronze as the crowd moved closer, yelling and gesturing.

Reporters and cameramen followed the crowd, and live televised pictures of the action in the square were beamed up to satellites and down to viewers around the world—from the White House, where President Bush watched with Secretary of State Colin Powell, to the tea shops of the Arab world, where viewers sipped afternoon tea in small shops and tuned in the Al Jazeera network. The *Washington Post* would later observe that what happened next was "either splendid luck or brilliant planning on the part of the military."

Iraqi men shook the statue, beat on it with their fists, and even attacked the base with sledgehammers, but it would not budge. Saddam's right arm remained defiantly raised over the enraged crowd. Some pieces of metal were gouged out, but the thing remained firmly attached to the high pedestal. The Bravo tankers contributed a rope, and young men climbed up and looped it around the neck of the statue, and the cheering escalated. This was a bit unsettling, but we decided to let it ride and see what happened.

Suddenly a shot cracked out, and Casey and I dove through the crowd, forcing a path through the uncomprehending civilians, yelling for them to move aside. We were thinking, *Ambush!* and the idea of a firefight in the park with so many civilians caught between the warring sides was horrific. But the discharged round had been fired accidentally by a Marine, not a fedayeen. We took deep, relieved breaths and made our way back to our trucks, which were parked with the tactical command post.

While we were gone, an older British gentleman had come up to Jerry Marsh and the Panda, who were guarding our vehicles, and identified himself as a former member of the Special Air Services, an elite arm of the British military. He was in Baghdad working as a news reporter and explained that a few Iraqis had gotten a bit too aggressive with him earlier in the day. This fellow handed Marsh a small Walther pistol and sheepishly mentioned that he had shot the unruly buggers. The day kept getting crazier.

The damned statue was still there, missing a few chips and pieces but irritatingly insulting everyone by defying all efforts to pull it down. It was time for the Marines to get involved.

Captain Bryan Lewis, the CO of Bravo Tanks, came over to me, and we pounded each other on the back, spreading the giddiness of the moment. Three weeks ago, I had expressed some doubts about Lewis, but his combat actions and steady leadership had changed my mind so much that now I thought he could probably walk on water. He told me the statue was about to come down, not by muscle power but through the brawn of a massive M88 tank recovery vehicle called a "Hercules." The irony was enough to make us giggle: A strong machine named Hercules, for the son of Zeus, was going to rip down the statue of the deposed ruler in Baghdad, the home of another ancient civilization. History could be made of worse stuff than a duel of legends.

The seventy-ton M88 crunched its way to the statue and stretched out a long boom from which a braided steel cable could be attached. The crowd cheered even more, and the world watched.

Then, in a shocking and totally unexpected development that John Koopman of the *Chronicle* called a "less than diplomatic move," a young Marine scampered up the boom and wrapped a bright American flag around the face of Saddam Hussein. The cheers stopped instantly, and an ominous silence dropped over us, followed by a great moan of despair. It was as if buckets of cold water had been thrown onto the crowd.

Casey was in midgulp, drinking water from his canteen, when he heard the audible sigh of disappointment arise from the crowd, and he turned around and saw the red, white, and blue American flag up where it wasn't supposed to be. *There is always somebody who doesn't get the word*, he thought. Few things would paint us as "conquerors" faster than a Marine putting the Stars and Stripes on Saddam's head in the middle of Baghdad, under the gaze of an international television audience.

A pudgy Arab woman reporter wearing a flak vest and Kevlar helmet accosted Casey before he could wipe off his chin. "Take down that flag in the name of Allah and for the Iraqi people!" she shouted.

Casey paused for only a moment, then spun around, jumped into his truck, burrowed into his pack, and pulled out the rolled-up flag he had liberated as a souvenir a few days before. He leaped back out of the Humvee and was a blur in brown cammies moving fast into the crowd toward the statue, unfurling the Iraqi banner as he went. The colors seemed to glow in the afternoon sunshine.

Colonel McCoy was exasperated. He had a radio receiver at his ear and was listening to people yell at him about the American flag that had appeared out of nowhere, threatening to unravel the image that had been so carefully cultivated in the past three weeks. He was already under criticism for the episode at the bridge, and now he was staring helplessly at the sort of public relations debacle that could end a career.

But then some young Iraqi men saw what Casey was bringing forward, snatched the flag from his hands, and before you could blink, the American flag was removed from the statue, and the flag of Iraq took its place. The crowd resumed the cheers, particularly when they recognized the flag's pre–Gulf War vintage.

"Where the hell did that thing come from?" a bewildered McCoy asked me.

He didn't need to know the details, so I lied. "A local worker back in Kuwait gave it to us, boss. Saddam killed his family, and he asked us to fly it in Baghdad."

He looked at me, his brows scrunched. I looked back, my eyes filled with honesty and innocence, and walked away to congratulate Casey on saving the world.

A cable from the M88 was tied around the statue's hips, until a voice of reason pointed out that if the steel cable broke, it might snap back and kill a bunch of celebrating Iraqis on a television broadcast being seen around the globe. That would not be a good way to follow the flag fiasco, so a chain was rigged instead and looped like a noose around the neck.

It was clear that this would be the instant symbol of the end of this war and would carry the same momentous impact as the Berlin Wall being torn down. For Marines, the image had only one equal, the famous flag raising on Mount Suribachi during World War II, the moment that defines the Corps. This would be our Iwo Jima moment.

The M88 Hercules fired up its big engine and jerked forward. The statue came down. When it hit the ground, the Iraqi crowd went bananas; they spat on the prone figure and whacked it with their fists and sandals. Somehow they decapitated that huge metal statue with their bare hands and then used our chain to drag the bouncing head around the streets. The once invincible dictator, Saddam Hussein, had been toppled and now was just another Humpty Dumpty who had a great fall.

25

The Urban Hide

From the start, we had aimed to take Baghdad, and now we had it, but it was not turning out to be the complete victory for which we had hoped. We had lifted the tyrant's boot, but as the Americans moved in, civil authority disappeared and chaos filled the vacuum. The fall of the statue was the symbolic, not the actual, end of the war against Saddam Hussein. It also marked the beginning of surprisingly unstable conditions around Iraq that soon began to look like still another war.

Marines are trained to fight, and I had anticipated that we would be in Baghdad just long enough to hand it over to some sort of special Iraqi or Coalition occupation force. That would free us to move upcountry and knock heads with lingering organized Iraqi resistance in strongholds such as Tikrit and the Sunni Triangle. Instead, we collided with urgent, widespread, and sustained unrest within the capital city and, by default, became an occupation force.

Even as the statue was coming down, our battalion spread out to protect the hotels, the hospitals, several embassies, a bus station, the Red Cross center, and some government ministry buildings. Gangs of looters roamed everywhere, and thieves had stripped some of those places totally bare by the time we arrived.

Amid such increasing turmoil, the managers of the big hotels back in Firdos Square were happy to have the Marines around and eagerly gave permission for us to establish observation posts in rooms high in their buildings. We didn't really need permission, but it was polite to ask, and it was wise of them to comply, for we were the only real protection they had.

Casey and I stashed our Humvees in the valet parking area, closed off the street, posted guards, went up to the eighteenth floor of the Palestine Hotel, and entered the broad room that had been converted from a bar and lounge area into a ministudio. From here, Saddam's peculiar minister of information, Baghdad Bob, had regularly announced his fanciful hallucinations that the Americans were losing the war. Standing at the windows, I had a panoramic view of the traffic circle below and the ranks of apartment buildings that marched away to the north-northeast. We planted a pair of sniper teams squarely on what once had been the departed government spokesman's private turf.

To check out another room that was up even higher, a polite concierge ushered Casey and me aboard a cranky elevator, which was crowded with a bunch of reporters wearing Gucci-type military gear, flak vests, and helmets. I had spent my entire career as a sniper trying to be as invisible as possible, intentionally shunning the press and staying deep in the shadows, but in Iraq, it was impossible to keep a low profile. We said hello, but I felt peculiar about being in their midst. They had cameras and laptop computers. We had guns. They had deadlines to meet. We still had a war.

The journalists trooped out at the next floor, and we took the elevator on up to the top level of the Palestine, where the doors opened onto an inky black hallway. We flipped on our flashlights, got our guns ready, and checked the rooms but found them to be both empty and unsuitable for our tactical needs. So we rode the rickety elevator back down and went across the street to see if we could do better at the Sheraton Hotel.

The Sheraton's elevator was even worse than the one in the Palestine, but the manager took us to the sixteenth floor, where he presented us with a spacious corner room that had beige walls, a nice bed, a desk, two chairs, and a sliding glass door that opened onto a patio with excellent views to the south and west. From windows on the other side of the room, we could double-check the direction being watched by the boys over in the Palestine. We took it, and did not even have to use a credit card.

In a quick trip back downstairs, we grabbed more weapons, radios, and shower gear from the Humvees and got back up to the sixteenth floor as fast as possible to establish the flashiest urban sniper hide I had ever seen.

Usually, I am tucked into junk and dirt and trash, but this was a Sheraton hotel! In no time, we created observation posts and security points, made ourselves at home, and happily acknowledged orders to maintain our positions until further notice. I looked at the carpet, the clean walls, the tiled bathroom with running water, the cushy bed, and the patio with its exquisite view of Baghdad and knew there was a nice dining room downstairs. I felt supremely confident that we could handle this tough duty.

We radioed the teams across the street to coordinate our zones and made accurate range cards of the entire area, drawing diagrams and measuring distances with our lasers to exact points in the neighborhood and down the streets. If we had to shoot, the cards would quicken our reaction time. Then we started an observation log in which we would record what we saw below, since paper is better then memory. For instance, if the same car came by too frequently, we would know to keep an eye on it.

Casey and I finished the routine by going back over to the Palestine for a final check with the snipers there. We were joined by Bart Greene, our battalion air officer, who wanted to check out the Sheraton's dining room. That made the Palestine inspection go even faster, and we determined that the boys were set—an armed Marine guarding the door and snipers at the windows, sweeping the streets with sniper scopes and binos. With that routine piece of business done, we got back aboard the elevator and headed for the ground floor and the promise of a steaming buffet of food. We were tired of eating MREs.

The elevator, however, did not go all the way to the first floor. It stopped at the second, where a wide lobby area opened onto a broad outside veranda that gave clear views of the traffic circle, the big mosque, and the remains of the Saddam statue. We had stumbled into the press nest, where television reporters from around the world made their stand-up reports—*Live from Baghdad!!* The hot and brilliant beams of dozens of spotlights seared the surroundings, a combined artificial sun that could have lit up a Red Sox night game at Fenway Park.

The three of us walked out to the big porch where the Jackals were gathered, more than I had ever before seen in one place, and accepted some bottles of ice-cold water. Other than feeling slightly uncomfortable, there was no real problem being around the press types, for the embedded guys and girls plus the band of gypsy Jackals we had inherited early in the war had worked hard to gain our trust and break down the barriers that normally existed between reporters and warriors.

Richard Engel of the ABC television network, whom we had met earlier in the square, explained the various TV monitors to us, and we watched Marines, Army troops, and officers all over Iraq appearing on various television shows and interviewing with print reporters about the final dash into Baghdad. Engel said ABC was putting together a broadcast that would feature a spread of stars ranging from generals to politicians to pundits, and among them would be Lieutenant Colonel Bryan P. McCoy. The reporter asked if we could join the program, and we figured if it was good enough for Darkside Six, we might as well give it a go, too. It would be a fast way to let our families back home know that we were alive, safe, and in one piece.

Anchorman Peter Jennings in New York ran the show with the sure touch of a lion tamer, and Engel led off our portion by asking how we had ended up in the square. I told him, to his astonishment, that we had received information that the journalists might be held hostage, and we had come in to rescue them. "So the idea was that you were going to seize this hotel and help and get us out, is that correct?" he asked.

We all three had our helmets off but were still festooned with combat gear. We looked *good* on camera. Bart said, "Until a couple of minutes ago, I still thought there were shots coming out of here, and the Army had fired back a couple of days ago." Oops. The Army had *killed* journalists in that particular incident, but Engel let it slide.

The reporter said he saw us roll up into the square, and Casey confirmed we were in the first Humvees. Then Engel turned back to the hostage question, and I replied that things became dicey when the square was flooding with people.

"Yeah, we definitely thought there was something going on," I said. "There was a guy up on the roof with his laptop. And I had, you know, put him in my scope, looking to see what he was doing. I didn't know if it was an enemy or not without the use of my scope." Oops, again. I just admitted that I had almost plugged one of the Jackals. Engel had me confirm that I was a sniper.

"And so, if you thought he had something other than a laptop, that would have been it for him?"

Be nice, I told myself, wishing he would change the subject. "I would have been able to tell. I wouldn't have to think . . . you could see it. You can see pretty clearly out of that. So, yeah, I mean, if it was an enemy, we would have dealt with that." This TV stuff was harder than it looked.

Thankfully, Engel switched to Casey and asked what our job was now.

"The job for tonight will be to make this area secure," Casey replied. "We're not exactly sure what happens from here. I know that there are more people that we will have to deal with later, but for tonight, we'll just make sure that everybody's safe around here."

The reporter then asked if we felt safer now and whether we wanted backup support, and Bart sharply observed, "We feel as safe as we felt any other night."

Casey flipped the question back to Engel. "Do *you* feel safer now that we're here?" The reporter acknowledged, "I certainly do."

I pointed out that we always feel safe when we're together and that our security cordon was already in place, or else we wouldn't be standing here talking to him. I didn't mention we also had a thicket of sniper rifles pointed out of the windows directly upstairs. "Right now we're completely surrounded by friendlies. I mean, it may seem all nice and dandy up here when we're talking, but there's, you know, eight hundred or nine hundred other guys around here with whatever we take to the fight." Did we feel safe? Damn straight we did.

Jennings broke in to ask if the events of the afternoon meant that the war was over. That one kind of pissed me off. I didn't believe the war was over at all. "We're not done yet," I said. "We're in a safe environment right now, but we'll be prepared for whatever happens tomorrow. When the appropriate authority ever says the war is over, then that will be good news."

We chattered on for a bit more; then our few minutes of fame were over, and we went off to find the Sheraton dining room, where life was slower. The smell of good food was overwhelming, the plates were clean, silverware sparkled on white tablecloths, and the buffet seemed filled to bursting. *This is crazy*, I thought, three Marines in dirty cammies with helmets under their arms and wearing flak vests, checking out a buffet line. After being on the road for three weeks of combat, we would have been delirious with joy just to have a couple of cheeseburgers or a Philly steak-and-cheese sandwich. This otherwise rather ordinary hotel dining room seemed like a banquet at Versailles to us, and we thoroughly pigged out while the dull *whumph* of faraway explosions echoed from where engineers were blowing up captured enemy arms around the city.

The night passed quietly, and the only real shooting we heard was a brief duel between CAAT teams from different battalions who stumbled upon each other in the Baghdad darkness. No one was hurt.

Enrico Dagnino, the Italian photographer who had been with us during the ferocious Baghdad Two-Mile attack, came up to our room with a bottle of Johnny Walker Black Label, and that helped complete this slice of paradise. With others on watch, I sipped scotch whiskey and watched the small television set in the corner as the Al Jazeera network gave its tilted version of our triumph, complete with English script rolling across the bottom of the screen that kept referring to us as "invaders." Unreal.

I stripped down in the bathroom and took a long shower under a nice blend of hot and cold water, letting it gush in gallons onto my head, until I felt as clean and renewed as I ever had in my entire life. I washed out my cammies in the sink and took immense pleasure in not having to put the filthy things back on for a while. Wearing only my shorts, I climbed into the bed and just lay there, enjoying the feeling of being totally safe on the sixteenth floor of a luxury hotel. Although we had let our guard down somewhat, there was always a Marine with a rifle at the door. The only way the bad guys could get us was with a lucky shot of a rocket-propelled grenade, which was highly unlikely.

Our entire team rotated in and out of the room during the night, taking turns guarding the trucks, pulling observation duty, and resting or sleeping, but I didn't hear them. I stared at the ceiling for a while, and my mind raced with the mad events of a single day. I had been on a killing spree for a week and had started this morning by shooting three people. Then I participated in bringing down the statue of Saddam, was interviewed on a major television network, posted sniper hides in hotel rooms, and had telephoned home to California from the hotel but received no answer, and now lay snug and safe in a comfortable bed. Still, it was too early to rein in my sniper mentality and start the transition back into being a normal human being, because as I had told Peter Jennings, the war wasn't over yet. Finally, sleep pulled me down like an anchor.

For weeks I had been living in the rude conditions imposed by combat, sometimes catching a few winks sitting up but seldom being able to truly rest. Now I snored away the hours on clean sheets and dined in civilized surroundings. The press corps was over in the Palestine, which was a zoo, but the Sheraton, filled mostly with Iraqis who had left their homes for the safety of the hotel during the war, was as quiet as a library.

We spent four wonderful days in the hotel but knew that it couldn't last forever. The streets were awash in looting and disorder, there was heavy fighting still going on elsewhere in the county, and even in Baghdad, and our unit was bound to be given new orders soon. But after several days of being able to watch the news on television, I realized that despite the fighting elsewhere, the Iraqis no longer could mount anything that remotely resembled an organized force against us anywhere in this country. If there was any fight left in them, it was up to the fedayeen or the ousted thugs of the Ba'athist regime or the imported foreign fighters, because the regular army had been utterly destroyed.

On April 13, the battalion headquarters moved across town to an eight-story government building. It was no Sheraton, but it had electricity and was so spacious that each of us had a private room, giving us the first true privacy we had experienced since leaving the United States in January.

The new headquarters building was surrounded by a high wall, and just beyond that wall, Baghdad was disintegrating. Everywhere I scanned with my scope and rifle, looting and disorder rampaged on a scale comparable to the war itself. Inevitably, our battalion, an elite combat unit, had to be turned into policemen.

We were not law enforcement personnel. Instead of destroying a heavily armed force of trained enemy soldiers, we were dispatched to run around like rent-a-cops through utterly crazed city streets. Instead of smash-mouth fighting, we were suddenly thrust into opaque security and sustainment operations. The lean-and-mean American military force that had raced through Iraq did not have enough people to put a policeman on every corner in every city in Iraq. And the powers that be had not expected this swift and total disintegration of civil order, nor that it would last as long as it did.

The Iraqis were tearing up everything, constantly fucking with each other, settling old blood feuds and defending their homes and families. Most of the time, we could watch from afar, for it was impossible for us to intervene in all of the flashpoints of violence that were usually one-on-ones being fought by civilians who were going at each other for reasons we found incomprehensible.

They were shooting from passing cars and from buildings. I might see a confrontation through my scope but could not stop it. Had it been plain old South Los Angeles–style gang warfare, I could have busted caps on a few gangbangers to control the situation, but we were not the ones to sort out this ongoing mess, because we could not get the whole story of who was right and who was wrong.

A call would come in to headquarters, and off we would roar away to some crime scene, armed to the teeth and singing our version of the theme song from the *Cops* television show—"Bad boys, bad boys, whatcha gonna do? Whatcha gonna do when we come for you?" When we weren't off playing cops, our teams escorted staff officers to meetings elsewhere in the city, for it was still too dangerous to go out there alone or unarmed. The lovely and languid moments of liberation had not lasted very long, and now hardly a minute passed without the sound of a random gunshot.

The city's policemen began returning to work on April 14, but the streets remained wild. Casey and his boys were tagged to make one of the first joint patrols with Iraqi forces, and they set out in a strange convoy with a German television crew, a *New York Times* reporter, and an Iraqi police team led by a cunning officer who spoke marginal English and was named Mohammed. Two quick little Korean-made cars carried the cops, and eight Marines followed in two heavy Humvees.

At a bank that was being robbed, the brakes were slammed on and all four vehicles skidded to a stop in a cloud of smoke that billowed out of the doorway while yellow and orange flames danced inside. A man emerged, sputtering and choking, through the smoke, and Casey told his boys to keep some rifles on the potential thief, but he leaned back against the fender of his truck to let the Iraqi police handle it.

The cops grabbed the pudgy, middle-aged guy and began yelling in Arabic; then Mohammed threw him face first to the ground, where the screaming Iraqi police immediately began stomping the hell out of him. The yelling and action drew a crowd and left Casey with a problem: If he stopped the beating, it would be obvious to the cops, onlookers, and victim alike that the Americans were really the ones who were in charge. That wasn't the theme for this war, because we had ostensibly gone in there to free the Iraqis and return their government to its citizens and let them run it as they saw fit. But if Casey did nothing, the press was going to report that Coalition forces stood by idly and watched a man being murdered. It was the sort of ambiguous situation that was all too common around Baghdad every day.

Mohammed, tired after his exertions, stepped away from the thief to let his boys continue their brutal interrogation, and Casey motioned him over. While the cop made his way through the throng, Casey rested his hand on the pistol hanging in a holster on his right hip and lightly drummed his fingers on the butt of the weapon to draw Mohammed's attention. It was the only time during the war that Casey was happy that Iraqi people liked to stand very close to the person with whom they were speaking. Keeping a smile on his face, Casey spoke in a quiet, calm, and slow voice, so only Mohammed could hear. "If you or your boys beat someone else like that today, I'll put a bullet in the back of your head before you can throw the second kick." Mohammed looked hard at the big Marine, and Casey's eyes did not waver. The cop nodded in understanding, and they quickly hauled the guy away to the police station. It was another lesson in street democracy.

Meanwhile, I was assigned to a Force Recon platoon that went after high-value targets and large robberies, and with my background, I got up to speed in a hurry on their special tactics. The unit was officially called "Broadsword," but on the street it was known as "Baghdad SWAT." If the mission was special, they called for us.

On an early call, we headed into the ruined financial district of Baghdad, and while the troops moved in, I set up in a position of cover. A bunch of Iraqis came running from a building with their hands filled with Iraqi currency, and we stopped four of them, one of whom was a middle-aged man who stubbornly refused to take his hands from his pockets. He was only five feet from me, and I was well within my rights to shoot him dead, for he might have a weapon or grenade in the deep pockets of his baggy robe. I handed off my rifle and took out my pistol, and he pulled back, plunging his hands even deeper into his pockets, so I whipped the side of his head, forced him to the pavement, twisted his arms, and then yanked his hands out, arrest style. All the fool had in his pockets were some ten-thousand-dinar bills. He had risked his life rather than show other Iraqis that he was carrying a large wad of money that was becoming more worthless by the day.

On April 15, at four o'clock in the afternoon, Baghdad SWAT was sent to the Central Bank of Baghdad, which was being robbed once again and was ablaze when we arrived. A platoon from India Company cordoned off the area; then our assault force plunged through the smoke to clear the huge building. I climbed atop my Humvee, which had become my standard support position, and was searching window by window and door by door when I picked up some movement on the second story of a neighboring building, near a ladder. A guy with an AK-47 was creeping up on our guys in the swirling smoke that had made him almost invisible. "Almost" isn't good enough. I set up on him at only 168 yards through the rolling cloud and dropped him cold with two quick shots.

We recovered over ten million dinars and around a million U.S. dollars from the bank's vault that day, filling up Amtrac after Amtrac with money, which we hauled back to the Main headquarters compound. A million bucks, there for the taking. It had been a bank robbery, the bank was a catastrophe, and young Marines were actually sitting on piles of enough cash to make them rich, but we were all so focused on fighting and staying alive that I still believe not a one of us scoffed up so much as a dollar bill. The money ended up back at the American Embassy in Kuwait. We think.

Epilogue
Welcome Home

The nuttiness finally ended on April 19, when we handed off central Baghdad to the Army's 1st Armored Division and began our long trip south. Destination: Kuwait, then home. I had mixed feelings about leaving the combat zone, because the silence and lack of communication from my wife had become deafening, and the day that I would have to deal with the situation was drawing close. It had been hard enough to hold my focus when a mission was going on, but now that we were in a safe, isolated rear area, I had plenty of time for unwanted and unwelcome reflection about what was happening at home.

The battalion rolled back through towns where we had once spilled blood and lost friends killed and wounded. Our first stop was the awful Iraqi town of Ad Diwaniyah, the same shithole that we had so thoroughly messed up only a few short weeks before. The place was just as disgusting as we remembered, and we sat there for weeks, from April 24 until the end of May, waiting and rotting.

Our momentum was spent, and boredom, not the fedayeen, became the enemy. The jolt of coming to such a screeching, complete halt after combat left us with mental whiplash and morale contusions.

At least in Baghdad we had sodas and decent food, and we could look at the cool women and check out an empty palace now and again, but now even those minor pleasures were gone. In retrospect, cop duty with Baghdad SWAT was better than anything Ad Diwaniyah had to offer.

The Main headquarters was set up in what once had been some sort of Iraqi military boot camp, a spread of dusty one-story buildings that had motivational sayings painted on the walls in Arabic. Dirt covered everything, and our boots kicked through piles of spent cartridge shells as we cleared workspaces and dove into the usual blizzard of postcombat paperwork to account for all of our gear and caught up on the administrative details. Unfortunately, that did not take very long, and although we resumed training to keep the boys sharp, we could not run them twenty-four hours a day in broiling desert heat.

Our sanitary needs overwhelmed the available facilities, since our toilets were wooden benches with holes in them, perched above trenches dug by a backhoe. When the trench was filled with human waste, it was covered, and the stalls were shifted to a new trench. In the unbearable heat, the stink was awful, and the latrines attracted about a million flies that feasted on exposed flesh.

The tight cohesion that the battalion had forged in combat started to evaporate, and fights, arguments, and world-class bitching left many of us on edge. The auxiliary units that had been attached to us for the combat phase, such as the Bravo tanks, the engineers, and the Amtracs, were all sent back to their original units, so those bonds of brotherhood were broken, although not forgotten.

Most of the lieutenants hung out by Casey's truck, which became unofficially known as the "Bus Stop," for we were confident that sooner or later the Marine Corps would remember we were parked out here in the middle of hell and move us on over to Kuwait. The Bus Stop was an oasis for anyone who cared to stop by, and we sat around, hour after hour, day after day, swapping lies and rumors, betting on the date when we would leave, reading magazines and eating candy bars sent from home. We gave a lot of shit to Daniel Tracy, my communications guy, because he had not gotten killed in Baghdad as he had so often predicted. Instead, Daniel and the rest of the guys in our trucks came out of the war as tough combat veterans. The five pigeons that had gone along with the battalion as early warnings for chemical attacks had also all managed to survive the heat, wind, and bullets of the entire conflict. Their cages had been opened before we left Baghdad, and the birds flew away to a well-earned freedom.

Nobody wanted any more damned MREs. We would rather get sick from eating too many Snickers bars than rip open another MRE pouch. Care packages were gold, and time stood still. A virus swept the camp, causing vomiting and severe, stomach-cramping diarrhea that forced the Marines to use those damned toilets even more. Some guys caught it two or three times, but my own immune system proved to be tougher than the bugs, and I didn't get sick at all.

Every day was the same, and almost every hour somebody at the Bus Stop would stand out in the road, shield his eyes against the sun, and actually look for a bus, but then sit back down and say, "Nothing yet."

Our battalion—the Bull, the mighty 3/4—had endured a cauldron of combat. From the starting line of this war until the very finish, we were in it, and the eighteen- and nineteen-year-old boys who made up the heart of the battalion had grown even more than the veterans.

John Koopman of the *Chronicle* wrote, "These Marines saw a lot of combat. They fought as much as any unit in Iraq, and more than most."

We had battled in Basra, created the deadly efficient Afak Drill, fought hard in Al Budayr, Ad Diwaniyah, and Al Kut, charged across the bridge over the Diyala Canal, and gone straight into Baghdad itself, where we pulled down the statue. Our battalion had a piece of almost every major battle the Marines fought in Iraq. And, as Casey put it, "We cracked the skulls of anyone who tried to fuck with us." We had lost six good Marines dead, and we held a memorial service on Easter Sunday before a line of six helmets on six rifles that were bayoneted into the Iraqi dirt. More than twenty men were wounded.

Whether we would achieve military victory in Iraq had never been a question for me, and it had come much easier than I had anticipated. When I had factored in the possible use of weapons of mass destruction, I once guessed that our attacking Coalition force might sustain up to ten thousand casualties. Instead, although we were saddened by the loss of our comrades, the overall casualties for the war were extremely light, and the campaign was extraordinarily short.

We had accomplished what we had come to do, which was to liberate the people of Iraq.

Proof that the Iraqis were free from the yoke of Saddam Hussein was dramatically visible when we watched throngs of Shi'ite pilgrims heading to the Muslim holy sites, making their first religious pilgrimage, or hajj, in more than two decades. They were of a different faith, but we were proud to have removed the dictator who had forbidden them to make that sacred journey.

I am by nature an optimist. It was obvious from the chaos we found during our first day in Baghdad that the transition from war to peace would be neither quick nor smooth. It will take years, but I believe that at the end a strong and peaceful democracy will take root in that ancient land.

At the end of May, we transferred back to Kuwait. "Tomorrow," observed Casey, "we will be sleeping back in that sacred nation-state, which is just as dirty as this one."

There is an eternal question: What do you do with the warriors once the fighting is done? When the warrior returns to the rear, things change, and although I had been through this phenomenon many times, Casey had not. We had been together out where the killing was done and were suddenly back at a base where the administrative offices were air-conditioned to beat the desert heat, the troops had movies to alleviate the boredom, and there was more good food than you could possibly eat. These peculiar places are ruled by the REMFs, the universal derogatory military acronym for rear-echelon motherfuckers, and Casey had not been out of his truck for fifteen minutes before some pretentious senior officer curtly ordered him to straighten his uniform. He was taken aback by the order but dutifully adjusted his cammies, realizing he was walking on alien turf. He also wondered where that officer had been when the bullets were flying.

Then came the news about some of the awards that we expected to be distributed for the action in Iraq. Casey was more than satisfied to receive a Navy Achievement Medal with V for valor, and I was to receive another Bronze Star, also with the distinction of a V. But we were apoplectic to learn that Officer Bob, our ineffectual leader who couldn't find his way around the block, would receive not only a Navy Commendation Medal but also a bump-up promotion to command a rifle company. I was pissed off beyond belief, and at that moment, Casey stopped caring.

He knew he was on a fast track with the Corps, and in fact he was promoted, to the rank of captain, but I was not surprised when he said he would be getting out. After combat, it is hard to endure the peacetime bullshit, and he told me there were other things he wanted to do. Soon after his return to civilian life, he was accepted at a prestigious university's law school. I cannot imagine this guy, whom I had depended upon for my very survival and who had been my partner in battle, going to work in a coat and tie. After having been tested in combat, he returned to the civilian world viewing life differently and would no longer accept things at face value. The wide-eyed wonder and jumpy innocence I had first seen in him were gone, and today he is much quieter, calmer, and more thoughtful. There was no longer the burning need to prove himself, and Casey departed from the Corps cleanly, with memories but without longing.

I left Kuwait with a thirty-man advance party from the battalion, aboard an aircraft loaded with Marines from various units, and while they celebrated their flight back to the world, I dreaded what lay ahead. I smiled and kept my emotions to myself, all the way to California.

I had telephoned my wife from Kuwait and finally caught up with her when I managed to get the call patched through to her classroom. Instead of excitement, the conversation was impersonal and cold. *Oh, how you doin'? . . . The girls are good.*

By the time we boarded the plane, I was resigned to the inevitable. As I winged across the broad Atlantic Ocean, and then across the entire United States, her words from that brief conversation slammed my brain. *We need to talk.*

In thirty hours, we jumped from a desert in Kuwait to another in California and landed at March Air Force Base. Then seven buses took us on a two-hour ride over to 29 Palms, and the long odyssey finally delivered us to the Marine base. Highway 62 was ablaze with bright lights, yellow ribbons, and hundreds of signs. WELCOME HOME! WELCOME BACK!

We checked our weapons into the armory and then were bused to the official greeting ceremonies in the parking lot behind the base gymnasium. Spotlights turned the place to bright daylight, and several dozen tired, happy, and thankful men dashed from the buses into the waiting arms of families and friends, while a band crashed out the "Marine Hymn." There were hugs and kisses and enough tears to wash away the Kuwaiti dust that still clung to their uniforms.

I searched the crowd but did not see my wife, who was in the midst of the throng, almost as if she were hiding. Ashley was on her hip, but eight-year-old Cassie was nowhere in sight. Trying to hug Kim was like holding a stuffed animal, cushy but totally without feeling. "Hi," she said, but there was no joy in her voice. Then Ashley jumped into my arms, and her smiles and kisses lit me up. I had not seen my family since January, months ago. My wife said Cassie had chosen to sleep over at the home of a friend.

The drive from the base to our house, through the thickets of WELCOME BACK signs on street corners, took twenty minutes, and the conversation was almost solely between Ashley and me. I was tired and filthy from the trip and took a good shower, then put Ashley to bed and reluctantly went to the living room to talk with my wife.

The tension was thick enough to cut with a knife. I knew what was coming, and I would rather have been facing an armed enemy soldier.

She was in the living room, standing with her arms crossed, but not truly in a confrontational manner. She was just delivering a decision that had already been made, and as the clock chimed ten o'clock, she said with great finality, "I want a divorce. I've already seen a lawyer and filled out the papers." There were no tears. "Go by his office and sign them, so you don't get served at work," she added, and then she walked down the hall and went to bed. I sat down on the sofa in the living room, stunned but unsurprised. Welcome home.

I had spent hours—days—in Kuwait and Iraq reviewing what I might do if this happened, and during the slow, painful midnight hours, I had to make some important decisions that would guide the remainder of my life.

First, I wanted custody of my girls. Kim agreed easily enough, as long as she was allowed to be with them frequently. Again, no surprise there.

The other major decision flowed from that first one. I was coming up on twenty years in the Marines and had worn the uniform for my entire adult life. The decision to join, made as something of a lark while I was in college, had been the best thing I had ever done, and I would not change a thing about my career.

"Your job is over in the Corps," I told myself that night. "It's time to put in for retirement."

I announced my decision the next day, and it shocked everyone who knew me, but when I explained my reason, no one disagreed. A new breed of warriors, many of whom I had helped train, will continue the traditions and the fights to protect our country, but only

I can be the father to my kids. I am, and always will be, a Marine, but the title "Dad" comes first.

There was the inevitable feeling that something was unfinished.

I always considered myself to be foremost a sniper, even before considering myself a Marine. Being a sniper is a peculiar profession that can soak up your entire existence, and I was lucky to have been taught not only how to shoot but also how to deal with the stress of being a professional. I had learned not to let the job overwhelm the personal side of who I really was.

I take immense satisfaction in having demonstrated a new way for snipers to go about their business. We no longer have to just sit in a hole in the ground for days, hiding and waiting for a target to saunter by. Give us wheels and protection and we can become terribly efficient hunters who can alter the course of a battle with a few shots from the front edge of the fighting. Out front is where we belong.

But the war was done before I could finish proving the Mobile Sniper Strike Team concept. We had made a difference, and our work of employing precise fire in a mobile war eventually will force doctrinal changes. Future war tacticians will have a new, effective, and very deadly toy in their arsenal, and my boys created it. Hopefully, the new generation will pick up on what we did and improve it to a point where snipers cannot be ignored in battle planning. So was my point proven? Yes. One hundred percent.

I never took pleasure in killing people. Only a crazy person would. Instead, I was glad to have faced and survived many dangerous confrontations without ever showing an ounce of fear. Anyone who says he has no fear in a life-or-death fight is either nuts or lying or both. But my time to deal with the fear always came after the battle, when I would find some private place to maybe shake a little bit and sort it all out in my mind.

I maintained a stable mental plateau by being totally convinced that I had done the right thing and that I had saved a lot of people by killing the enemy. It is much better to think of lives saved than human beings killed.

The curious always ask, "How many people have you killed?" My answer is "I don't know, and it doesn't matter."

I spent a professional lifetime as a sniper, and the numbers can accumulate swiftly. Who in his right mind would insist on wanting credit for every single human life he had snuffed out? Yes, I have dozens and dozens of confirmed kills, and more that were never logged. A respected reporter once wrote that I might be the best sniper in the entire Marine Corps, but every sniper I've ever known can be the "best" at any given moment.

None of us would ever make such a claim on our own; to do so would be unseemly, and bragging is only for the bullshit artists, not for real snipers. Our job is not about singular glory, which is why we wear no special badges, but about the mission, and the body count is totally meaningless. Put a good sniper within a target-rich environment like a nest of untrained terrorists, and no "record" will stand for long. A sniper must have absolute confidence in his shooting ability and believe that no one is better, or he is going to screw up in a gunfight when people are depending on him. If you don't believe that you can walk on water, you have no business carrying a sniper rifle.

The "acquaintances" I saw drop in the scope of my rifle after I killed them will still come by to visit for a few moments in my dreams, but I hope not for much longer. Perhaps all of us can now find some peace and rest.

The realization of what my choice to leave the Corps meant only came to me fully when the battalion was double-tapped for another assignment back to Iraq in 2004 and drew the awful duty of fighting in hotbeds of terrorism such as around the city of Fallujah. They went to war without me, and as I read the names of more friends who were killed or wounded, I felt awful about not being there to cover them.

But for me, it is over. I have passed my rifle and scope to others who are also gifted in this arcane and secret craft, and there is no one left for me to shoot.

As I finished writing this book at the end of 2004, both of my kids were still asking if I was going back to the war. "No," I told them. "Daddy's wars are over." But I knew they would believe that only when my uniform came off for the last time, when I retired in early 2005.

I will never fight again.

INDEX